Chess Champion from China

The Life and Games of Xie Jun

Xie Jun

GAMBIT

First published in the UK by Gambit Publications Ltd 1998
Copyright © Xie Jun 1998

ISBN 1 901983 06 4

DISTRIBUTION:
Worldwide (except USA): Biblios Distribution Services, Star Rd, Partridge
Green, West Sussex, RH13 8LD, England.
USA: BHB International, Inc, 994 Riverview Drive, Totowa, New Jersey 07511,
USA.

For all other enquiries (including a full list of all Gambit Chess titles) please
contact the publishers, Gambit Publications Ltd, 69 Masbro Rd, Kensington,
London W14 0LS.
Fax +44 (0)171 371 1477. E-mail 100561.3121@compuserve.com.

Edited by Graham Burgess
Typeset by John Nunn
Printed in Great Britain by Redwood Books, Trowbridge, Wilts.

10 9 8 7 6 5 4 3 2 1

Gambit Publications Ltd
Managing Director: GM Murray Chandler
Chess Director: GM John Nunn
Editorial Director: FM Graham Burgess
Assistant Editor: GM John Emms
German Editor: WFM Petra Nunn

Contents

Introduction

The idea of writing this book originated from a series of coincidences, which occurred during my stay in London in 1997. When the possibility was first suggested, I had to think for quite a while before I believed it to be a good idea. I had always been quite hesitant about the idea of writing a chess book. The reason is obvious: my level of understanding of this game is fairly modest in comparison to the real top male players, even though I held the Women's World Championship title from 1991 to 1996. Few books would ever be written, however, if everyone reasoned like this. But there was yet another matter, as I was uncertain about my ability to express myself in the English language. Only when I was convinced that any language problems could be overcome did I accept the invitation from Gambit Publications Ltd to work on a book about my experiences as a chess player.

In some ways, the book seems special. It is a story about the chess world as perceived through the eyes of a female chess player from China, which makes it, of course, different from most other books. It features a realistic account of what happened to me, both on and off the chess board. When annotating the games, I made an attempt to give the reader an impression of the thinking process and the emotions that I experienced during the course of those games. I have intentionally chosen to select the forty games from 1985 to the end of 1997 that made the deepest impression on me, and which were significant for my chess career. Some of the games are very complex, whereas others are attractive due to their high entertainment value. In addition, I have added twelve positions which enable the reader to sharpen his or her tactical skills.

I would like to take this opportunity to express my gratitude to various people, who have been instrumental in my chess career. Firstly, I should of course mention my parents, to whom I dedicate this book. Their love and understanding have always been beacons for me. Many people have been involved in my chess education, even though only a few are mentioned in the book. I would never have been successful were it not for their patience and help. I would specifically like to mention Kees Nieuwelink for his contribution and advice with regard to the English language. Lastly, I would like to thank Ivo Timmermans, whose unflagging energy was crucial for the realization of this book.

I hope that the reader will enjoy this, my very first serious chess publication.

Xie Jun

Symbols

+   check
++   double check
x   capture
\#   checkmate
!!   brilliant move
!   good move
!?   interesting move
?!   dubious move
?   bad move
??   blunder
Ch   championship
1-0   the game ends in a win for White
½-½ the game ends in a draw
0-1   the game ends in a win for Black
(*n*)   *n*th match game
(D)   see next diagram
W (by diagram)   White to play
B (by diagram)   Black to play

1 My Childhood (1970-1985)

I was born on the 30th October 1970 in an army hospital in Baoding, about 120 kilometres from Beijing. At the time my father served in the army, which explains partly my parents' preference for the name Jun, which is best translated as 'soldier'. The name Jun is more often given to boys, but in my case it relates directly to the fact that the year of my birth was in the midst of the cultural revolution. During this turbulent period in modern Chinese history, it was common to minimize the differences between men and women, and this was also reflected in the names given to new-borns. In early childhood I lived together with my mother and grandmother in a room measuring ten square metres in the south-east part of Beijing, not far from the place where my mother worked. My father was away for most of the year. I cannot remember many events from those years, only that, for some reason, I did not go to kindergarten. Most of the time I spent playing with children from the neighbourhood, mostly boys. So, maybe my name is appropriate because I was quite boyish.

When I was six years old, my father returned from his service in the army and the family was complete at last. My parents sat together talking about how to educate their only child, in their eyes a naughty little girl. To stimulate me to sit down and concentrate, and hence be quieter, they chose *xiangqi*, a traditional game in China which is also inexpensive to play. My father taught me the basic rules of this game, which is sometimes considered the Chinese version of international chess. Soon thereafter my father became my first victim, but this only increased his interest in the game. He was very happy to take me to places where people would play, to find different opponents for me. Traditionally, xiangqi is a game played by men and as a little girl I got a lot of attention when I played. As a result of my father's efforts, my skill improved rapidly and I came to be regarded as a little genius in the area where I lived. I still remember those times during the summers, my father and I sitting on the street, both of us seated on one of my father's shoes as an improvised chair. Under the scant light of a street lamp my father used to sit behind me, waving with a fan in an attempt to give me fresh air and to drive away the mosquitoes, while I was trying my very best to beat my opponents, usually middle-aged or older men. Many spectators would stand or sit around the board, openly discussing the moves and giving suggestions, often interrupted by the question of who this little girl was. My father was always very pleased and proud to give the answer to that. Afterwards we would go home, me sitting on the back of his bicycle and my father talking while leaning backwards to give criticism about my mistakes during the games. By the time we arrived home, back to my mother and grandmother with news about my victories, they had just finished with the housework. I am not sure, even now, whether my father's prime motive was to enjoy watching me play, or to avoid doing the dishes himself. Probably both. The women in the house did not really understand xiangqi, but they were very happy for me and my father.

It soon became apparent that I had a talent for the game and I got stronger every year. My father told me later a story that he was once approached by people working for the television. They were making a programme about xiangqi and thought it funny to have this presented by an older man and a little girl – I was nine at the time. Unfortunately, shortly before the programme I broke my arm during sports lessons at school and the show went ahead without me. One year later I became Girls' Champion of Beijing.

It may be good to know that xiangqi has often been compared with chess because the two games have similar features such as attacking the enemy king and activating the pieces. However, there are also marked differences. The rules of xiangqi are more complex and the game is more open compared to chess: activity and attack have a higher priority and tactics play a more prominent role. Xiangqi is extremely popular in Asia and is one of the most popular games in China, where about 10% of the people play it actively. Games are usually played in the open air, which makes it a favourite summer sport.

When I became Girls' Champion, there was already a better woman player in Beijing, who was National Senior Champion. The authorities decided that one talent was enough for the city, so I was introduced to the trainer of international chess. And this is actually how I started to play chess. The rules were explained to me and as an exception I was admitted to the Beijing Team. This was a group of adult players who trained daily on the premises of the Beijing Sports Committee. A school was found nearby so I could get education in the morning. My first trainer was a national master, a very tall man in his forties. He was also the trainer of the National Team at the time. He might have been the trainer with the highest playing level in China, but it seemed he was not experienced in teaching children. But there were more reasons why this was a difficult period for me. I was ten years younger than the rest of the team and the other players had something better to do than to teach a girl how to play chess. Most of them would beat me from a queen down and did not feel very inclined to help me further. The Beijing Team was apparently too tough for me.

Therefore, I was transferred in October 1981 to the Children's Palace, where many children would stay during weekdays. These children were selected on the basis of having a special talent in one particular area and they were assisted by a group of trainers, who took care of the children for some hours in the afternoon after the normal lessons in the school. The word *manager* may be more appropriate than the word *trainer* because the level of training was not very high and the trainers' main tasks were to teach the children some basic theory about their game and to keep them busy with exercises. I was very lucky to meet my second trainer here, a patient man, not the strongest player himself but an excellent teacher for young children.

Sometime in 1982, I had to make a major decision when I was asked whether I would like to play chess more seriously. My parents were not very keen on my dedicating even more time to chess than I already did, because I was one of the best students at school and they felt it would be wiser to get a good education. My teachers had, of course, the same opinion. But I did not enjoy the educational system very much because the tempo of teaching was slow, with a lot of repetition, and I got bored very easily. So far, I had managed to get high grades, even if I missed out on some lessons due to chess activities. Luckily my parents gave the ultimate decision to me, only warning me to think carefully and to realize that there was no way back. But I simply decided to go ahead and I got what I wanted. I promised my parents that I would continue my studies and graduate one day from university and that they would not be let down. It is doubtful whether any twelve-year-old can truly understand the consequences of such a profound decision – I am still not sure how big a role chess should play in my life – but my chess career had started.

In the two years that followed, I managed to win some nice games, but it was clear that I could not yet make good results against senior players. Nevertheless, everybody considered me a promising newcomer. In 1984, I became National Girls' Champion (under 16) with the score of 9 out of 9 and qualified for the Women's Championship later that year. This was an excellent opportunity because all the nation's best players were present on that occasion. Chinese women's chess was getting stronger and stronger and the best player, Liu Shilan, had even qualified as a world championship candidate. I was pleased to come out sixth on my debut – that result made me the youngest national master in history. In 1985, I was even to improve upon that performance. I started by repeating the perfect score in the Girls' Championship, an event in which I had to take part to qualify once more for the Women's Championship. Now I finished third and came very close to winning the title. In the penultimate round I made only a draw from a winning position. Had I won this game – I won in the last round (against the same opponent!) – then I would have been first.

My first game stems from this very period. Qi Jingxuan is an International Master from Shanghai who was trainer of the National Team. He was the strongest Chinese player in the early 1980s and often represented our country at international tournaments. His visits abroad made him travel through Beijing quite often and he was a regular guest of the Beijing Team. I first got to know him in the period that I started playing chess. My trainer asked him to play a game against me with a queen down, and I will never forget his reaction. "How can I play a game a queen down?" he exclaimed in great surprise, but we played that game and he won.

Game 1 was played prior to the National Women's Championship. Qi Jingxuan played this game simultaneously with one other game.

Game 1

Xie Jun – Qi Jingxuan

Shanghai 1985
Sicilian, Taimanov

1	e4	c5
2	♘f3	e6
3	d4	cxd4
4	♘xd4	♘c6
5	♘c3	♕c7
6	f4	a6
7	♗e2	♘ge7 (D)

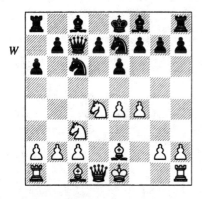

I have not been able to find this move in my database. In any case, at the age of 15 I knew practically nothing about the openings, so it did not make a big difference to me whether my opponents played established theory or not.

8	♘db5!	axb5
9	♘xb5	♕b6
10	♘d6+	♔d8
11	♘xf7+	♔e8
12	♘d6+	

I was thinking whether to repeat the moves or not. I was not so sure about my attack and, moreover, there was a top male player sitting on the other side of the board. But for some reason I decided to play on. Apart from the text-move, I considered also other interesting possibilities such as 12 ♘xh8 g6 13 c3 ♗g7 14 ♘xg6 ♘xg6 15 e5 with a big advantage for White, and 12 ♗h5?! ♖g8 13 ♘h6+ g6 14 ♘xg8 ♕b4+ 15 ♔f2 ♘xg8 16 ♗f3 with an unclear position.

12 ...	♔d8 (D)

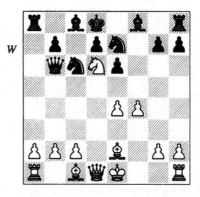

13 ♘c4!

The exclamation mark is not because of the move itself, but more for courage. It was simply a difficult decision.

13   ...   ♕d4

13...♕b4+ 14 c3 ♕a4 15 b3 gives White an easy win.

14   ♗d3   ♘g6

The alternative was 14...d5 but Black has a cramped position after 15 ♗e3 ♕f6 16 e5 ♕f7 17 ♘d6 ♕g8 18 ♗b6+ ♔d7 19 0-0 with a strong initiative.

15   ♗e3   ♕f6

Black cannot solve his problems with 15...♗b4+ 16 c3 ♗xc3+ 17 bxc3 ♕xc3+ 18 ♔f2 ♘b4 19 ♗e2, with a big plus for White.

16   e5 (D)

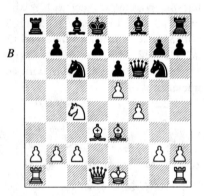

16   ...   ♕f7

Maybe 16...♕h4+ was to be preferred, but after 17 g3 ♕h3 18 ♕d2 (18 ♗b6+ ♔e8 19 ♗f1 ♕f5 20 ♗g2 ♘b4 21 ♘e3 ♕f7 22 0-0 ♖a6 leads to an unclear position, where Black can still fight) 18...♘b4 19 ♗e4 White is on top.

17   0-0   ♘h4?

Clearly not the best of Black's options but other moves give him a hard game as well: 17...♘b4 18 ♗e4 and

the pressure continues, or 17...♗e7 18 c3 ♔c7 19 ♘d6 ♕f8 20 ♗e4 and White is ready to play b2-b4.

18   g3   ♘f5

19   ♗b6+   ♔e8

20   g4   ♘h4

20...d5 is slightly better, but White should win after 21 exd6 ♘xd6 22 ♘e5 ♕f6 23 g5 ♕e7 24 ♗g6+.

21   ♕e1   ♗e7

I do not see how Black can save his position, for instance 21...g5 22 ♕g3 ♕g7 23 f5 and the pressure mounts. The text-move is a prelude to an attractive queen sacrifice.

22   f5   h5

23   f6   hxg4 (D)

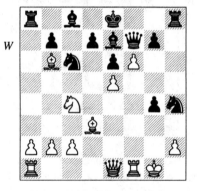

24   ♕xh4!!

A sweet revenge for his lessons a few years earlier. This time, the roles are reversed and it is my turn to play without the queen!

24   ...   ♖xh4

25   fxe7   ♕f3

It is curtains for Black: 25...♕g8 loses after 26 ♗c5 d6 27 ♖f8+ (27 exd6 is also good enough to win) 27...♕xf8 28 exf8♕+ ♔xf8 29 ♗xd6+ ♔g8 30 ♘b6 and 25...♕h5 is impossible due to the continuation 26 ♖f8+ ♔xe7 27 ♗c5+ d6 28 ♗xd6+ ♔d7 29 ♘b6#.

26 ♗e4!   ♘xe5

Or 26...♔xe7 27 ♗xf3 gxf3 28 ♗c5+ ♔d8 29 ♖xf3 ♖xc4 30 ♗d6 followed by mate.

27	♗d8!	♘f7
28	♗g6	♖a6
29	♘e5	♕e3+
30	♖f2	1-0

In the post-mortem he could not believe at first that the queen sacrifice was correct, possibly because it was me who played it! But he had to admit that it was not so bad after all, and this game probably changed his opinion about my talent for chess. In fact, afterwards Qi Jingxuan was quite happy to assist in my training. He became one of my long-time trainers and a member of my team of seconds during the first World Championship Match in 1991. We have always had a very good relationship and I am still grateful for all the effort and energy he put into my chess education. I do not believe that he would mind having this game presented as the first one in this book, because he always enjoyed seeing his student improve.

2 Arrival on the Chess Scene (1986-1988)

Since the early 1980s, Chinese women's chess had become stronger. The two Women's Grandmasters Liu Shilan and Wu Minqian had reached world championship candidate level, and they were followed by a group of young players including Peng Zhaoqin, who later became a candidate herself, and myself. Unfortunately, I was still too weak to be a member of the National Team. This team would come together occasionally to practise for major tournaments such as the Olympiads. A series of games were organized to select the members for the National Team, to represent China at the 1986 Chess Olympiad. I was still in the running after the first stage of qualification and the reward for this was a one-week chess trip to Moscow where we could play practice games against Soviet internationals. This was my first trip outside China and it made a great impression on me. I could speak only Chinese and neither Russian nor English, and did not know who was who in the chess world. So it happened that I played Women's Grandmasters such as Litinskaya and Levitina, without realizing that they were members of the Soviet Union's National Team and had qualified several times as candidates in the Women's World Championship cycle. Altogether, we played six games that week, four against the National Team and two against a team from Moscow. My score was 3 out of 6 but I had no reason to be satisfied. I remember very clearly my game against Levitina where my lack of experience became apparent. My position was advantageous and I tried to convert this into a win. After a while we reached an ending with opposite-coloured bishops in which I was two pawns up. Without truly understanding what was going on, I kept on playing for a long time but, surprisingly, I could not win! Nevertheless, it was a very memorable week. We played in the afternoons and in the mornings the Chinese group would visit various tourist attractions in the centre of Moscow. I had never seen so many foreigners in my life and all the buildings looked different from those in China. It must have been a very exciting week for me, because this was the only time ever that I did not suffer from the time difference when travelling abroad. But suddenly the week had gone past and I felt that it had been too short a trip.

Immediately after this week in Moscow, the second stage of the qualification took place. Only two more players could qualify for the National Team and I came third. In retrospect, this was not too bad. Another player who qualified joined the National Team in the Olympiad, but she only had a chance to play one game. The time had not yet come for the trainers to rely upon the newcomers. This changed by the end of 1986, when a group was formed around the core players of the National Team. Training sessions were held on a regular basis with more opportunities for younger players to meet the 'veterans' over the board. During that period, both Peng Zhaoqin and myself proved that we were the strongest players of the generation to come. It even happened that, after numerous games, I suddenly ended up being the top-ranked woman on the Chinese national rating list, much to my own surprise. Still, 1987 did not yield anything special for me and I spent most of the year studying chess. Chess was pure pleasure and winning or losing hardly mattered. The whole idea of ever playing for a World Championship never crossed my mind, and why should it? Maya Chiburdanidze had become World Champion at the age of seventeen and, at the same age, I did not even have an international FIDE rating.

When I recall the events of 1986 and 1987 my main memories are not of chess – my results were too modest. These were the years when I matured and began to think about other things in life. Over time, I changed from a light-hearted girl into a profound thinker and started to worry about the future. One of the main trigger factors was probably that, all around me, my old class-mates began to prepare seriously for examinations to qualify for the universities. This really required dedication, for not more than five or six percent of all students were admitted. How could I wait and not join them in their efforts, and feel pleased with only the results of some local Chinese chess tournaments? I started to have doubts about the direction of my career and in this reflective, almost melancholic, mood I entered the next year. But a few months later matters seemed to take a turn for the better.

My chess career got an unexpected boost in 1988, which started with the Beijing Team finding a sponsor. This made it possible for me to participate in the World Junior Championship later that year, and I realized that serious training and preparation was needed. One month prior to that championship the Beijing Open was held and this could hardly have come at a better time. It was the perfect opportunity for me to play against strong opponents and also the first international tournament in which I took part, although only five or six foreigners participated. In round one I played against the West German player Jörg Hickl in my first game ever against a player with an international FIDE rating – the games in Moscow were not counted. Moreover, it was my very first game against any foreign male player. At the time, the West German Hickl was an international master rated over 2400 – about the same strength as the top male players in China. There were still no grandmasters in China and IM was the top title. The feeling that I was about to play somebody really important, actually sitting face to face across the board, exercised my mind continuously and I felt very nervous. It all got worse when we sat at the board and I had a closer look. There he sat, a foreigner with a different colouring of the eyes and hair, with a high nose of a type I had rarely seen before. And who could tell, maybe I was the first Asian girl he had ever played. Would he have the same thoughts about me? It was hardly a surprise that I played the opening very timidly.

Game 2
Xie Jun – Jörg Hickl
Beijing Open 1988
Caro-Kann, Bronstein/Larsen

1	e4	c6	
2	d4	d5	
3	♘c3	dxe4	
4	♘xe4	♘f6	
5	♘xf6+	gxf6	
6	g3		

An interesting line. 6 c3 is more common, for instance 6...♗f5 7 ♘f3 e6 8 g3 ♕d5 9 ♗g2 ♕c4 10 ♘h4 ♗d3 11 ♕d2 ♗g6 12 ♘xg6 hxg6 13 b3 ♕b5 14 ♗b2 ♗d6 15 ♕c2 and White was slightly better in Kholmov-Bronstein, Moscow 1983.

6	...	♕d5
7	♘f3	♗f5 *(D)*

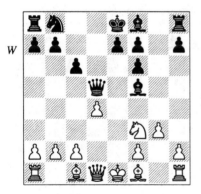

8 c4?!

Nowadays I would prefer the natural 8 c3 ♗e4 9 ♗g2.

8	...	♕e4+

9 ♕e2

Played in an attempt to simplify the position. There was nothing against 9 ♗e3 e5 10 ♗g2 ♗b4+ 11 ♔f1 ♕d3+ 12 ♕e2 ♘d7 13 ♖d1 ♕xe2+ 14 ♔xe2, with a complicated struggle ahead.

9	...	e6
10	♕xe4	

The development of the queen's bishop to c3 should be considered here, although Black has a flexible position after 10 ♗d2 ♘a6 11 a3 0-0-0 12 ♗c3 ♖g8 13 ♕xe4 ♗xe4 14 ♗e2 ♗g7.

10	...	♗xe4
11	♗e2	♘d7

A serious alternative is 11...♘a6 12 a3 0-0-0 13 ♗e3 ♗g7 14 h3 f5 15 0-0-0 ♖d7 with an unclear position. It is probably too early for 11...c5: after 12 0-0 ♘c6 13 ♗e3 ♘b4 14 ♘e1 White has a lead in development.

12	0-0	♗g7
13	♗e3 *(D)*	
13	...	0-0

Castling queenside was of course possible: 13...0-0-0 14 ♖ac1 ♖hg8 15 ♖fd1 ♘b6 16 ♘d2 ♗g6 17 ♗f3 f5 18 ♘b3 ♖d7 19 ♘c5 ♖dd8 20 ♔f1 ♘d7 leads to a complicated position. It is hard to judge who is better here, although the g6-bishop looks unhappy at the moment.

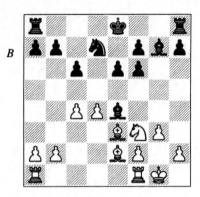

14	♖ac1	♖fd8
15	♖fd1	♘b6
16	h4	h6
17	♘h2!? (D)	

This is my own move, typical of the kind of uninhibited chess I played in those days. Now I feel that the knight has moved in the wrong direction and would suggest 17 ♘d2 as an improvement. Centralization makes more sense.

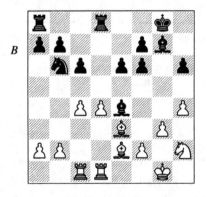

17	...	♖d7
18	♖d2	♖ad8
19	b3	♘c8

20 ♗f3!

At first sight, the preferred move is 20 h5?! to fix the h-pawns, but I soon realized that the pawn on h5 would be weaker than that on h6. After 20...c5 21 ♖cd1 cxd4 22 ♖xd4 ♖xd4 23 ♖xd4 ♖xd4 24 ♗xd4 f5 25 ♗xg7 ♔xg7 26 ♘f3 ♔f6, the pressure against h6 is gone and Black is already better.

20	...	♗xf3
21	♘xf3	h5
22	♔g2	

This move improves the position of the king, but the normal move would be 22 ♖cd1. I just wanted to see what Black had in mind.

| 22 | ... | ♘d6!? (D) |

With the idea of playing the knight to f5 and putting pressure on d4. It is not the only plan in the position. The alternatives 22...♔f8 and 22...e5 suggest themselves.

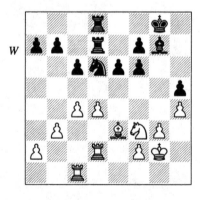

23 d5!?

A surprising move that sharpens the game. My opponent's face betrayed a look of disapproval.

23	...	♘f5
24	♗xa7	♗h6
25	♗b6	♗xd2

The only move. Inferior is 25...♖a8 26 dxc6 ♖xd2 27 ♘xd2 bxc6 (not 27...♗xd2 28 ♖d1 followed by c6-c7) 28 ♖c2 with excellent winning prospects for White.

26	♘xd2	♖a8

Black could also play 26...♖c8. The difference is that he would keep a pawn on the b-file instead of on the c-file, like in the game. Play could continue 27 ♘e4 ♔g7 28 dxc6 ♖xc6 29 ♗a5 ♖d4 30 ♖e1 ♘d6 and, again, it is difficult to assess who has the better chances. Now the a-pawn becomes a menace for Black.

27	♘e4	♔g7

Whenever he seemed to be in trouble, Hickl could not at all suppress his facial contortions, of course completely the opposite to Asian custom. On various occasions he held his head between his hands, his face expressing an awfully painful look.

28	dxc6	bxc6
29	a4 *(D)*	

By now, the game was gaining a lot of attention from the audience and many people gathered around us to see what happened. The feeling was in the air that something special was about to happen. And I realized that my position was not lost yet, as otherwise the spectators would lose their interest straight away.

29	...	♖d3
30	♖c3	♖xc3

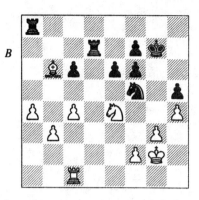

B

A difficult decision: should Black exchange rooks or not? Once more, the position after 30...♖d1 31 a5 ♔g6 32 b4 ♘d4 33 ♗c5 f5 34 ♘d6 is unclear.

31	♘xc3	♘d6?

Black overreaches in an attempt to complicate matters further. The position indeed becomes sharp, but White wins crucial tempi and is able to mobilize her pawns straight away. 31...e5 32 b4 ♘d6 33 c5 ♘c4 34 ♗c7 ♖c8 35 ♗b6 f5 36 ♔f1 e4 37 ♘e2 was better, when the game would probably peter out into a draw. It is difficult for either side to make progress. Even 31...♔f8, with the idea of bringing the king into the centre, was to be preferred.

32	c5	♘c8

Or 32...♘f5 33 b4 ♘d4 34 ♗c7 (it is too early for 34 b5 cxb5 35 axb5 due to 35...♖a3 36 c6 ♘xc6 and Black wins) 34...♔g6 35 f3 ♘c2 36 b5 ♘e1+ 37 ♔f1 ♘d3 38 ♗d6 cxb5 39 axb5 ♖a3 40 ♘e4 and White has the initiative.

33	b4 *(D)*	

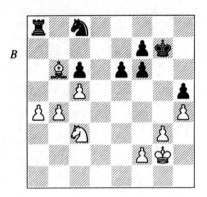

B

33   ...   ♘e7

After 33...f5 Black faces a difficult defence: 34 ♗c7 (White risks losing with 34 ♗d8 ♘d6 35 ♗e7 ♘e4 36 ♘xe4 fxe4 37 b5 ♖xa4 38 bxc6 ♖a6 39 c7 ♖c6 40 ♗d6 ♔f6 41 ♔f1 e5 42 ♔e2 ♔e6 43 ♔e3 f5 and suddenly it is Black who has all the winning chances) 34...♘e7 35 b5 cxb5 36 axb5 ♖a3 37 b6 ♖b3 38 ♘e2 ♘c6 39 ♘f4 e5 40 ♘d5 ♔g6 and, although I feel White is slightly better, the situation remains very tense.

34   b5   ♔f8

This appears to be an unfortunate choice some moves later. 34...♔g6!? is a better way to aim to improve the king's position.

35	**♗c7**	**cxb5**
36	**axb5**	**♖a3**
37	**♘e4**	**♖b3?** *(D)*

With the advance of the pawns, Black's defence has become more difficult. His best try is 37...♘d5 38 b6 ♖b3 39 c6 ♔g7 (not 39...♔e8 because of 40 ♘xf6+ ♘xf6 41 b7 ♔e7 42 b8♕ ♖xb8 43 ♗xb8 with a big advantage)

40 ♗d8 f5 (40...♘xb6 fails to the '*petite combinaison*' 41 ♗xb6 ♖xb6 42 c7 ♖c6 43 ♘d6, forking on e8) 41 ♘d6 (41 ♘c5 ♖xb6 42 ♗xb6 ♘xb6 43 c7 ♘c8 44 ♘d7 f6 is only equal) 41...f4 42 b7 fxg3 43 fxg3 though it looks like White is winning easily.

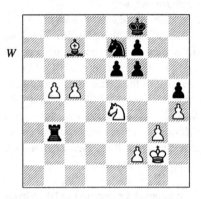

W

I knew that my advantage was substantial and that there had to be a win somewhere. On the other hand, it was almost impossible to ignore the fact that I was facing an International Master. The intoxication of imminent victory made me too confused to calculate the proper way forward.

38   b6?

A missed opportunity: 38 ♘xf6! was the move, as shown by Eric Lobron afterwards. The black king is boxed in after 38...♖xb5 (38...♔g7 39 ♘e8+ ♔f8 40 ♘d6 ♘d5 41 ♗d8 wins) 39 ♗d6. Now White prepares g4 to create another passed pawn. Black cannot stop this rather simple plan. In a way, the post-mortem turned out to be quite funny. Lobron clearly had a wonderful time and Hickl felt visibly uncomfortable. He tried desperately to find a reply to 38 ♘xf6 but there is none. From this moment onwards the draw is inevitable.

38 ...   ♘d5
39 ♘d6

39 ♗d8 would have been risky since Black takes over the initiative with 39...f5 40 ♘d6 f4 41 c6 (41 b7 fxg3 42 fxg3 ♘e7 43 ♗b6 ♘c6 might still be OK for White) 41...f3+ 42 ♔h3 ♖b1 43 g4 ♖g1. Suddenly, Black has created an attack from nowhere.

39 ...   ♔e7
40 ♗b8   ♔d7
41 ♘xf7   ♘c3
42 g4   hxg4

43	h5	♔e7
44	♘d6	♘a4
45	♘e4	♔f7
46	♗f4	♘xc5
47	♘xc5	♖xb6
48	♗e3	e5
49	h6	♖d6
50	♘e4	♖c6
51	♔g3	

51 ♘c5 f5 52 ♘d7 ♔e6 (certainly not 52...♖e6 53 ♘xe5+ ♖xe5 54 h7 ♖e8 55 ♗d4) 53 ♘f8+ ♔f7 54 h7 ♔g7 55 ♗g5 ♖a6 56 ♔f1 ♖a1+ 57 ♔g2 ♖a6 58 ♔h2 ♖b6 also leads to a draw.

51	...	♔g6
52	♔xg4	f5+
53	♔f3	fxe4+
54	♔xe4	½-½

This game drew a lot of attention and it created a stir in the media. It was unfortunately the only highlight of the tournament for me. For other reasons, too, it was a most memorable game. I felt for the first time that I was not so weak at chess any more. Besides, I realized that in order to communicate better with foreign players I would have to speak another language apart from Chinese. It was still possible to make myself understood in the post-mortem, by simply moving pieces and with the help of some facial expressions. But it was far from perfect and it dawned upon me that the time had come to invest some time in learning a new language. After this game I set myself the task of studying English with regularity and I have continued to do so ever since.

Back in 1988, I had little confidence in my own chess abilities and I am not sure how big my contribution was in the post-mortem analysis. An upbringing in the traditional Chinese way implies that you pay respect to your opponent and whatever he says should be held in regard. Therefore, I usually kept silent when variations were discussed and had thoughts of my own. Nowadays, I would not hesitate to mention any difference of opinion because an exchange of ideas may be valuable to both players. And if I am wrong I would simply like to hear this and understand the reason *why*. But in those days I was quite shy with my opponents.

The Beijing tournament was indeed a proper warm-up for the World Junior Championship in Adelaide. Yet the expectations were not high because my results had been going up and down in the preceding year. I just played natural chess without realizing that my understanding of many positions was insufficient. I won some games and I lost some, which seemed normal for any chess player. It would certainly be interesting to play other young girls in Adelaide who did have an international FIDE rating – I still had none – but I had no idea how strong the opposition would be.

I arrived in Australia with a child's eyes and, like two years before in Moscow, everything looked new again. It was astounding that I had landed in the midst of spring while I left China not more than ten hours earlier in cool autumn weather. Adelaide was a beautiful, quiet place and the people were very friendly. The tournament was held in a college. The students had gone home for their spring holiday, so the players and their coaches could be housed in the dormitories. Young players had gathered from all over the world, which created a great atmosphere. It was fun most of the time and it seemed that language did not matter. In any case, I enjoyed myself tremendously although it goes without saying that some additional lessons in English would have been welcome.

After a loss in the first round against an unknown player from Cuba, my performance started to improve and I began to score some full points. My confidence grew as I gradually moved into the upper half of the table. I managed to play a nice game against Ketevan Arakhamia. This achievement was special to me because Arakhamia was the top-seeded player and the World Junior Champion from the previous year.

Game 3
Xie Jun – Ketevan Arakhamia
World Junior Ch, Adelaide 1988
Sicilian, Sveshnikov

1	e4	c5
2	♘f3	♘c6
3	d4	cxd4
4	♘xd4	♘f6
5	♘c3	e5
6	♘db5	d6
7	♗g5	a6
8	♘a3	b5
9	♗xf6	gxf6
10	♘d5	f5
11	♗d3	♗e6
12	0-0 *(D)*	

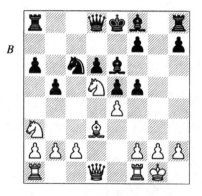

12 ...   ♗g7

Here there are several moves at Black's disposal. The latest word is 12...♗xd5 13 exd5 ♘e7 14 c3 ♗g7 15 ♕h5 e4 16 ♗c2 ♕c8 17 ♖ad1 ♕c5 18 ♗b1 b4 with counterplay, as in Z.Almasi-Krasenkow, European Team Ch, Pula 1997. An interesting try may also be 12...♘b8!? 13 c4 ♗xd5 14 cxd5 ♘d7 Seyb-F.Röder, Bavarian Ch 1986, with sharp play.

13	♕h5	f4
14	c4	b4?!

Even though some players still prefer this move nowadays, I cannot agree with them. After the queenside pawn structure becomes fixed, it is too easy for White to find a promising plan. The more dynamic continuation is 14...bxc4 15 ♗xc4 0-0 16 ♖ac1 and here the theoretical road branches into various paths. The main line runs 16...♖b8 (possibly better than 16...♘e7 17 ♖fd1 ♖c8 18 ♘xe7+ ♕xe7 19 ♖c3!, when White holds the initiative, Short-Sax, Candidates match (1), Saint John 1988) 17 b3 ♕d7 with complicated play, as in Sax-Kindermann, European Team Ch, Plovdiv 1983.

15	♘c2	♖b8

A recent attempt to rehabilitate this line was seen in de la Villa-Garcia Luque, San Roque 1996, but after 15...a5 16 ♖ad1 ♖b8 17 b3 h6 18 ♗e2 0-0 19 ♗g4 ♖b7 20 ♕h3 White had a lead in development.

16	b3	h6
17	a3	bxa3
18	♖xa3	a5

| 19 | h3 | 0-0 *(D)* |

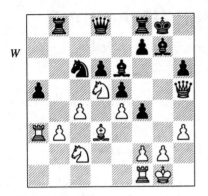

20 ♘c3

Played with the idea of putting the knight on b5, controlling the d4-square and looking at the pawn on d6.

20	...	♘b4
21	♖d1	♕c7
22	♕e2	♖fc8 *(D)*

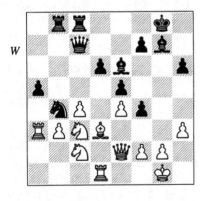

23 ♘e1

23 ♘d5 seems too direct as Black replies 23...♘xd5 (this is better than 23...♗xd5 24 exd5 ♘xd3 25 ♕xd3, and White dominates the light squares,

e.g. 25...♖b6 26 ♖b1 ♖cb8 27 ♘e1 ♖b4 28 ♕c2 a4 29 ♖xa4 ♖xa4 30 bxa4 ♖xb1 31 ♕xb1 ♕xc4 32 ♕b5 with a good ending) 24 exd5 ♗d7. Now, Black is ready to play ...f5, or even ...a4 to break up the queenside pawn chain.

| 23 | ... | ♕c5 |
| 24 | ♖da1 | ♘c6 |

24...♕b6 25 ♘b5 leaves White with a tangible advantage.

| 25 | ♘b5 | ♔h7 *(D)* |

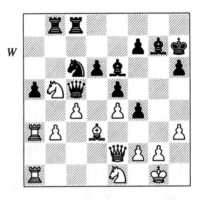

26 ♕h5!?

I did not expect that this queen sortie would lead to instant success. 26 ♗c2?? is an obvious blunder due to 26...♖xb5 27 cxb5 ♘d4, but 26 ♗b1! is more accurate; after 26...♖g8 27 ♕h5 ♗f8 28 ♘d3 ♕b6 29 ♗c2 White has the better of the game.

| 26 | ... | ♗f6 |
| 27 | ♗c2 | ♖xb5?? |

This attempt to seize the initiative backfires immediately. Black should have contented herself with a passive position after 27...♗e7 28 ♘d3 ♕b6.

| 28 | cxb5 | ♘d4 |

29	♗d1	♕c3	33	b4	♕xb4
30	♗g4	♗xg4	34	♘xf3	♘xf3+
31	♕xf7+	♗g7	35	♖xf3	♖f8
32	hxg4	f3	36	♕d7	♖xf3

To make matters worse, Arakhamia was by now in serious time-trouble. The game is decided.

37	gxf3	a4
38	♖c1	♕d2
39	♕f5+	1-0

The new champion Galliamova had taken off with seven successive wins and finished a full point ahead of the rest. My final score was 9½ out of 13 to share second to fourth place with Arakhamia and Zayats. It was a lucky circumstance that the Asian Junior Championship was incorporated in the World Junior Championship. This gave me the title and I received the Liu Shilan Cup, named after Asia's first Women's Grandmaster. It is worth noting that this World Junior Championship in Adelaide was one of the strongest in chess history. Many players became top grandmasters shortly thereafter, such as Ivanchuk, Gelfand, Lautier, Adams, Akopian, Serper and Piket. The same can be said about the girls group with Galliamova, Arakhamia and myself. During this tournament I first saw Zsuzsa Polgar in action, who was the only girl playing in the 'male' competition. She scored an impressive eight points, only one point short of winner Lautier, and did not lose a single game.

The Australian tour continued in Sydney, where an open tournament was held. The series of chess activities was part of Australia's bicentennial festivities, celebrating the fact that 200 years earlier the British Governor Arthur Phillip had founded a penal settlement at Botany Bay. The arrival of the First Fleet, soon thereafter, heralded the emergence of a new immigration policy. The open tournament started immediately after the World Junior Championship and many players prolonged their stay to play there. The contrast in scenery was thrilling. After the Adelaide countryside, quiet and with exotic flora, the sight of a huge modern city with skyscrapers all around was fascinating. It was great that we had ample time for sightseeing, in spite of the busy tournament schedule. The weather was hot and I felt relaxed throughout the week. A lovely country, Australia. I realized in Sydney that my nervousness for strange eyes and faces had disappeared. The uncomfortable feeling of facing foreigners at the chess board had gone and this was noticeable in my performance. The games were of good quality and I even managed to play for tournament victory in the last round. Unfortunately, I lost to Daniel King, who thus shared first place with Boris Gelfand. One of my better games was played in the penultimate round.

Game 4
Michael Adams – Xie Jun
Sydney Open 1988
Ruy Lopez, Anti-Marshall

1	e4	e5
2	♘f3	♘c6
3	♗b5	a6
4	♗a4	♘f6
5	0-0	♗e7
6	♖e1	b5
7	♗b3	0-0
8	a4	

Adams likes to play the Marshall, but apparently not with White.

8	...	♗b7
9	d3	d6
10	♘c3	♘a5
11	♗a2	b4
12	♘e2	c5
13	♘g3	♖b8 (D)

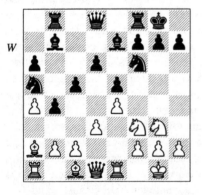

14 ♘d2?!

The wrong plan. 14 ♘f5 ♗c8 15 ♘3h4 (15 ♘e3 ♘c6 16 ♗c4 ♘d7 17

♗d5 ♗b7 18 b3 ♘b6 19 ♗xc6 ♗xc6 20 ♗b2 g6 leads to equality) would be more interesting. Black has several choices at this point: 15...♗e6 16 ♖e3 ♘e8 17 ♘xe7+ ♕xe7 18 ♘f5 ♗xf5 19 exf5 b3 was unclear in Kiik-G.Kuzmin, Tallinn 1985, whereas 15...b3 16 cxb3 ♗e6 17 b4 cxb4 18 d4 b3 19 ♗b1 ♘e8?! 20 ♘xe7+ ♕xe7 21 ♘f5 ♗xf5 22 exf5 ♘f6 occurred in Balashov-Razuvaev, Riga 1985. The players agreed a draw at move 29, but White did not play the strong 23 ♗d3. Lastly, 15...♘e8 is possible, with the follow-up 16 ♘xe7+ ♕xe7 17 ♘f5 ♕f6 18 ♕g4 ♔h8 in Sutovsky-German, Villa Martelli 1997. It is anybody's game.

14 ... ♗c8

15 h3

15 ♘c4 has been played before. In Tal-G.Kuzmin, Tallinn 1985, Black seized the initiative with 15...♘xc4 16 ♗xc4 ♘e8 17 f4!? exf4 18 ♗xf4 ♗f6 19 ♕c1 ♘c7 20 ♘f1 ♘e6 21 ♗g3 h5 22 ♘e3 h4 23 ♗f2 h3.

15 ... ♗e6

15...♘e8!? seems a solid alternative.

16 ♘c4

Black has an easy game after 16 ♗xe6 fxe6 17 b3 ♘c6 18 ♗b2 ♘d4.

16 ... ♘xc4

17 &xc4   a5
18 &d2
18 ♕f3 leads to an equal position after 18...♘e8 19 ♘f5 (or 19 &xe6 fxe6 20 ♕g4 ♕d7) 19...&g5.
18 ...   ♘e8 (D)

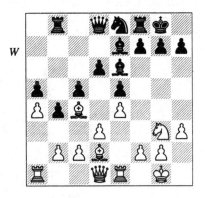

19 ♘f1?!
19 &xe6 fxe6 20 ♕g4 ♕d7 did not appeal to Adams, for understandable reasons, but it may have been his best option.
19 ...   ♘c7
20 ♘e3   &g5
21 &xe6   ♘xe6
22 ♘c4?!
After this move I consider the position to be slightly better for Black. The last chance to fight for an equal position was 22 ♕g4 ♘d4 23 ♖ac1 g6.
22 ...   &xd2
23 ♕xd2   f5
24 c3   ♖f6
25 ♔h2 (D)
25 ...   ♖b7!
Black mobilizes her remaining forces in an elegant way. The main

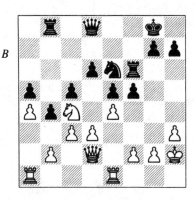

defect of the white position is clearly the absence of counterplay: Black has a grip on the d4-square and will launch a fierce kingside attack.
26 ♖f1
The opening of the f-file is not attractive for White, as his position is inferior after 26 exf5 ♖xf5 27 ♖ac1 ♖bf7 28 ♖e2 ♘f4 29 ♖e3 (29 ♖ee1 ♘xh3 loses instantly) 29...♕c7.
26 ...   f4 (D)

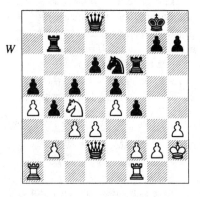

27 f3   ♖g6
This is the most efficient way to proceed. The attack has to be conducted

with pieces rather than pawns. It takes only a few more moves before Black is ready to deliver a knight sacrifice.

28 &fd1

This takes away the last piece from the kingside. 28 &ac1!? should be considered.

28	...	&g3
29	&f2 *(D)*	

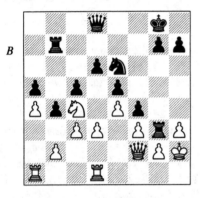

| 29 | ... | b3! |

This excellent move delays any counterplay on the queenside. Now Black gains the necessary time to give her attack enough impetus.

30 &d2

After 30 &e3 &h4 31 &f1 g6 32 &d5 &g5 nothing can stop the coming ...&xh3.

30	...	&f7
31	&g1	&f6
32	&f1	&fg6
33	&a3	

There is no alternative except to go for the b3-pawn. Other moves seem to fail, for instance 33 &e1 &g5 34 &f2 &d7 35 &b6 &e6 and Black has the

pleasant choice between ...&xf3 and ...&xh3.

33	...	&g5
34	&xb3	h6!

A last preparatory move.

35 &e2 *(D)*

The move-order 35 &b5 &xh3 36 gxh3 &h4 37 &b8+ &h7 38 &e3 &xh3+ comes to the same thing.

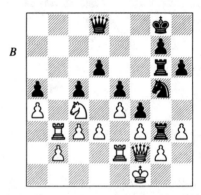

| 35 | ... | &xh3 |

This was just a matter of time. The rest requires no commentary.

36	gxh3	&h4
37	&e1	&xh3
38	&d2	&g1+
39	&f1	&6g2
40	&b8+	&h7
41	&a8	&xf2
42	&xf2	&g2
43	&e2	&xf2+
44	&xf2	&h4+
45	&g2	&e1
46	&h2	h5
47	&xa5	&g3+
48	&h1	h4

0-1

Adams's rueful remark in an English chess magazine revealed his sense of irony: "I thought she was quite cute until she beat me."

Shortly after the Australian tour I participated in my first Olympiad. This event was held in the birthplace of the ancient Olympic Games, Greece. It had been a long and tiring trip to Thessaloniki and the team captain decided upon arrival to give me a bye on day one. I could only regret that China was paired against Malta, a relatively weak opponent and the perfect sparring partner for a newcomer. As it happened, I had to wait one more round and spent the day looking around and getting used to the Olympiad atmosphere. Luckily I was allowed to play in all further matches after my debut in the second round. The following game is from our encounter with Yugoslavia.

Game 5

Gordana Marković – Xie Jun

Thessaloniki Olympiad 1988
Giuoco Piano

1	e4	e5
2	♘f3	♘c6
3	♗c4	♗c5
4	c3	♘f6
5	b4	♗b6
6	d3	d6
7	0-0	0-0
8	a4	

This line was quite popular in the late 1980s. Black has the choice between ...a6 and ...a5.

8	...	a5
9	b5	♘e7
10	♘bd2	♘g6
11	♗a2 *(D)*	

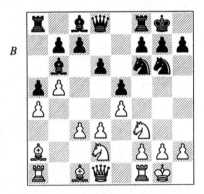

11	...	d5!?

I was trying to repeat what I had learned from other games – let's call it an attempt to follow theory – but I seem to have lost the thread in this position. Nowadays I would not choose this move because it increases the influence of the a2-bishop. Somewhat safer is 11...♗e6. Another good move is 11...c6 12 bxc6 bxc6 13 d4 ♖e8 14 dxe5 ♘xe5 15 ♘xe5 dxe5 with an approximately equal position, as in Psakhis-Schüssler, Lugano 1988.

12	exd5	♘xd5
13	♘e4	♗f5

Another try may be 13...h6, in which case White does best to avoid 14 ♗xd5 ♕xd5 15 ♗xh6?! f5!. But the normal 14 ♗a3 is good enough for a slight advantage.

14	♗a3	♖e8
15	♕b3	♗e6
16	♘fg5	

Here, 16 ♘eg5 was a better move. The idea of exchanging the e6-bishop is the same, e.g. 16...♘df4 17 ♘xe6 ♘xe6 18 ♖ad1 ♔h8. The difference is that Black does not get to play ...f7-f5 with tempo, while the remaining knight on f3 plays an important role in controlling the centre.

16	...	♘df4
17	♘xe6	♘xe6
18	♖ad1	♔h8! *(D)*

The start of activity on the kingside.

19	♕c2	f5

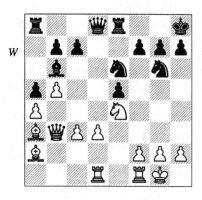

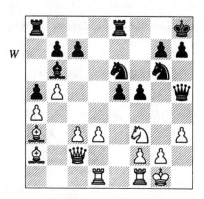

20 ♘d2?

I assume that White did not notice the impending danger, as otherwise she would have preferred 20 ♗xe6 ♖xe6 21 ♘c5 ♗xc5 22 ♗xc5 b6 23 ♗a3 ♕d7 24 ♖fe1 ♖d8 25 d4 exd4 26 cxd4 ♖de8 27 ♖xe6 ♕xe6 28 h3, when the outcome is wide open.

20 ... ♕g5
21 ♘f3 ♕g4

This provokes a serious weakening of the white kingside pawns. Black has two active knights ready to join the battle and it is difficult to find a proper defence for White, particularly because an exchange of the a2-bishop for the knight improves Black's position. In addition to the initiative on the kingside, Black would have full control of the centre.

22 h3 ♕h5 (D)
23 ♗d5?!

What about 23 ♔h1 ♘ef4 24 ♘g1? Flear analyses this in *New in Chess* magazine and he suggests 24...♕g5 25 g3 with an acceptable game for White. In fact, Black has a more promising

continuation in 24...♘h4! 25 g3 ♘xh3 26 gxh4 ♘xf2+ 27 ♖xf2 ♗xf2 28 ♕xf2 ♕xd1 29 ♕xf5 ♕xa4 leading to an easy win. Therefore, White's only choice is 23 ♗xe6 ♖xe6 24 ♗c1 (less attractive are the alternatives 24 d4 e4 25 ♖fe1 ♘f4 26 ♘e5 ♖xe5 27 dxe5 ♕g6, and 24 ♖fe1 ♖ae8 25 d4 e4 26 d5 ♖f6 27 c4 ♘f4 with a raging attack, the main threat being ...♘xg2; it seems in these lines that White is always one tempo short of trying to shut down the a7-g1 diagonal – it is impossible to neutralize the b6-bishop while also defending the kingside) 24...♘h4 (24...♖d6 25 ♗e3 ♗xe3 26 fxe3 ♖ad8 27 d4 e4 28 ♘d2 is not clear) 25 ♘xh4 ♕xh4 26 ♖fe1 ♖ae8 27 ♖e2 c6 and White should be able to defend this position. Black's attack has lost some of its force after the disappearance of the knights.

23 ... ♘ef4

The game has come to the part that many players enjoy best. One feels that Black should look for the right attacking motifs and decisive sacrifices.

Here I started to calculate mating moves, just like a computer would do.

24	♗xb7	♖ab8
25	♗c6	♖e6 (D)

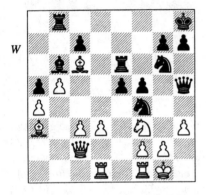

White is lost and the variations are not difficult to find. Both 26 ♔h2 ♘xg2 27 ♔xg2 ♖xc6 28 bxc6 ♘f4+ and 26 ♘e1 ♖xc6 27 bxc6 ♘h4 28 d4 ♘hxg2 29 ♘xg2 (29 ♘d3 e4 30 ♘xf4 ♘xf4 31 f3 ♘xh3+ 32 ♔g2 ♘f4+) 29...♘xh3+ 30 ♔h2 ♘g5+ will lead to a forced mate.

26	♘h2	♖xc6
27	bxc6	♕g5
28	g4	fxg4
29	hxg4	♘h4
30	♔h1	♘f3
31	♘xf3	♕xg4
32	♘e1	♘e2!
33	♔h2	♗xf2

0-1

For a long time, the Chinese team had high hopes of finishing in the top three. But in the end it was not to be: we missed out on the bronze medal by a single point. My personal score was 10 out of 13, with a rating performance of 2457, and I achieved my first Women's Grandmaster norm. Under normal circumstances this would have been good enough for an individual medal on any board, but this year was exceptional, for the true stars of the 1988 Olympiad were also seated on board two, where Judit Polgar scored a phenomenal 12½ out of 13 and Elena Akhmylovskaya 8½ out of 9. These were also the players who inflicted the only defeats upon me.

The finish of the Olympiad was strongly influenced by circumstances that had little to do with chess itself. On the rest day after round ten, Elena Akhmylovskaya married the American team captain John Donaldson in secrecy and the newly-weds left Greece in a great hurry. The Soviet team was informed of this happy event prior to round eleven, but the news must have come as a big shock. Even more so as Akhmylovskaya had been the best performer of the Soviet team up to then. It seemed that the remaining players were affected in their concentration. The Soviets squandered their lead and in the last round they were pipped at the post by an inspired Hungarian team. An extremely dramatic finish.

When you look back on an important event in your life, it is obvious that certain elements of that unique experience appear to have made a deeper impression than others. Special parts of the event will stay fresh in the mind, clear and accurate even after a long period, while other fragments will soon become blurred in the memory. This certainly goes for my own recollection of the 1988 Olympiad. For a long time I felt a strange mixture of emotions and had a remembrance of mostly irrelevant details, firmly imprinted on my mind. Naturally there was the initial feeling of pity, caused by the fact that both the team and I missed podium places by narrow margins – there is nothing worse than *two* fourth places. At the same time this feeling was overshadowed by one of good fortune – the euphoria of the newcomer who does not know yet the meaning of the word *sad*. Why feel bad? It had been a wonderful experience after all and our performance was fair.

Nevertheless, two details spring to mind when I remember Thessaloniki. The first is the Greek food in my hotel, which contained so many strange spices that I could simply not tolerate it. Nor could the other members of the Chinese team. Only the soup was tasty – nothing else. I started to develop a real phobia for Western food and wasted many hours trying to find something edible. It came as a relief when we found out that the local supermarket sold prawns. We boiled them with the cooking-apparatus that we had taken along from China and this partly solved the problem. However, it goes without saying that two weeks of prawns is hard to endure.

The second experience that left a profound impression occurred in the bus that took us every day from the hotel to the playing hall. At the time, I was still far from familiar with the chess world, although I had seen pictures of famous players. Then, all of a sudden and amid countless unknown players, I spotted the familiar likeness of Boris Spassky. *"What's this guy doing on our bus?"* flashed through my mind and I felt very upset. In my eyes, Spassky was the personification of an important era in chess history. How on earth was it possible that this man had to share a bus with mere mortals? I did not find the answer to that in 1988 and, even now, as I write these lines, that very feeling of extreme surprise is still vivid in my memory.

3 Clearing up some Knotty Points (1989-1990)

After the Olympiad, life in China proceeded as usual. Then, at the end of 1988, the National Team policy changed, possibly as a result of the young ladies' performance in Thessaloniki. It was decided that each of us would be coupled with one male player in a sort of teacher-student relationship. The underlying thought was that our understanding would improve more rapidly under personal guidance from a strong player. By good fortune I was connected to Ye Jiangchuan, who was the number one male player in China. The cooperation with Ye helped me tremendously and very soon I noticed how much I still had to learn. The immediate benefit of working as a tandem was that I played my games more seriously, knowing that they would be analysed in great depth afterwards. The other teacher-student combinations did not last for long, as far as I remember, but Ye and I worked very well and efficiently during the time we spent together.

On 1st of January 1989, I received my first international rating, which was 2310. I had no idea how this was calculated, but nevertheless I was quite happy. Some months later I also received confirmation that I had acquired the Women's International Master title. This did not come as a big surprise to me, nor did I feel very excited about it. I had already made one Women's Grandmaster norm and, on the whole, I had lost my fear of Women's Grandmasters. At least, I felt that the chances were even when I played most of them. But there was not much time to dwell on these issues, as more important events were about to take place.

In modern Chinese history, the year 1989 will always be associated with the incidents in Tiananmen Square, where thousands of people, mainly students, gathered for weeks to voice their protest. I had no real interest in what happened exactly – I was only eighteen – and it was difficult for me to understand the underlying political reasons for this massive demonstration. On the other hand, it was practically impossible to ignore what was happening outside. Indeed, the building of our chess club was situated less than 200 metres from Tiananmen Square and my daily trip to the chess centre led straight through the immense crowd. Initially, it felt quite special to be a witness to what seemed a historic event. Until the raid took place on the notorious 4th of June, and the city of Beijing was in total chaos. One day later, I had to go to Poland for a traditional woman's tournament. I could not at all focus on chess, overwhelmed by a feeling of sadness.

Under the circumstances, it was extremely hard to bring myself to take an interest in the tournament. The excitement of foreign travelling had gone for the moment, and all I could hope for was to achieve my second Grandmaster norm. It had been a long journey to Poland and the effect of the jet-lag was noticeable during the entire first game. Luckily I scored a full point. Alas, my physical state for the second game was even worse. When the clocks were already running, one of the organizers was kind enough to knock on my door to wake me up. I drew with difficulty and struggled throughout the rest of the week. After thirteen rounds, Matveeva had firmly taken first place, which was enough for her second grandmaster norm. I finished second with half a point less. After the tournament, I stayed for ten days at the Chinese Embassy in Warsaw, before the second part of the trip, which was to take me to Romania. All the time, I was accompanied by an elderly lady who spoke Russian, and who acted as my interpreter. She had been in Warsaw many times before and knew the place well. I noticed that, during my short stay, the value of the local currency fell fifty percent against the dollar. Things were changing in many countries.

The purpose of my stay in Romania was different. Here I had come to play practice games and to give one simultaneous exhibition. This fitted in with the cultural exchange programme between Romania and China and was part of an agreement between both governments. The duration of my visit in Romania was two full weeks, enough to get a good impression of the grim situation. Food was in short supply and vegetables were very hard to get. It was clear that the atmosphere was tense. Soldiers armed with guns could be seen on the street and one felt that people had a heavy burden on their minds. Later, I understood what was happening when I heard that a revolution had taken place which ended the regime of Ceaucescu. I will not forget the countless book shops, covered from top to bottom with pictures of him and his family. With the turn of Romanian history, this sight must have changed soon thereafter. I have not visited Romania since, and wonder sometimes how the situation is at the moment.

When I returned to China the situation in Beijing had quietened down. The city looked as it had before and people were back to work as if nothing had happened. But soon I was informed that while I was abroad the Beijing Sports Committee had issued some reforms, which had a major impact on our Beijing Chess Team. Sportsmen would get less security than they had before, especially because income would now be coupled to uncertain factors such as performance and the willing support of external sponsors. Since chess was not popular in China, we could only be very pessimistic about the future. The Beijing Chess Team had practically ceased to exist. Once more I felt like I was standing at a cross-roads, not knowing what to do next. Some of my friends had fled to

America. Others, still present, advised me to stop playing chess because they thought it a waste of time. They argued that it would be better for me to devote more time to serious pursuits such as a course of study. In fact, my own thoughts were going the same way. The mixture of the old system and the recent reforms seemed confusing. In order to give equal opportunities to everybody, a chess player would hardly get more than one visit abroad per year. It did not come as a surprise that I was not on the list of the National Women's Team, which was sent a few weeks later to Malaysia for the Asian Team Championship. I was replaced by another player, since I had already played in Poland and Romania. It did not seem to make any difference at all that I was, by now, the number one woman player in China on the rating list. To make matters worse, the absence of a sponsor meant that I could no longer go to the World Junior Championship in Puerto Rico. My dream of becoming World Junior Champion fell apart.

New rules were announced for the National Team stating that any woman chess player with an Elo rating over 2400 would get more freedom to decide upon her training methods and would qualify automatically for international events such as the Olympiad. But no woman player in China had ever reached that level. Besides, it was hard to imagine that anyone could ever attain it, playing mostly against opponents 200 rating points lower than that. So this rule did not make much sense to me. I felt sad and disappointed by what was in front of me and made up my mind: the National Women's Championship in September would be my last serious tournament, after which I would give up chess altogether. It was a simple and clear-cut plan, but this decision did not take into account the unavoidable which was about to happen: I became the Chinese Champion for the first and, so far, last time. I played well throughout the tournament and was able to secure overall victory by winning my game in the penultimate round. An additional win in the last round made me finish one point ahead of the rest. I had picked a bizarre moment to give up chess and I realized that an announcement with regard to my early retirement would not go down well at this point in time.

As a result, there was little choice for me but to participate in the National Junior Championship, which took place less than one month later. For the first time ever the tournament was held as a mixed group. And if it was not yet possible for me to play training games against top male seniors, I certainly looked forward to a trial of strength against the best male juniors. It would be a difficult tournament, I reckoned. In the first three rounds, even when I did not play very well, I scored three full points with some luck and took the lead. In subsequent games, the level of my play improved and I continued in a relaxed way. Maybe this had to do with my approach during the tournament. Every morning I started with physical exercise, after which I looked at a few games from Anatoly Karpov's games collection. After the game, in the evening, I studied English language until I went to sleep. I like to mention this because the games of Karpov were a source of inspiration to me. In particular, I like to focus attention on the game Karpov-Hort, which left a deep impression.

Anatoly Karpov – Vlastimil Hort
Moscow 1971
Sicilian, Keres Attack

1 e4 c5 2 ②f3 d6 3 d4 cxd4 4 ②xd4
②f6 5 ②c3 e6 6 g4 ②c6 7 g5 ②d7 8
≜e3 a6 9 f4 ≜e7 10 ≌g1 ②xd4 11
♕xd4 e5 12 ♕d2 exf4 13 ≜xf4 ②e5
14 ≜e2 ≜e6 15 ②d5 ≜xd5 16 exd5
②g6 17 ≜e3 h6 18 gxh6 ≜h4+ 19
♔d1 gxh6 20 ≜xh6 ≜f6 21 c3 ≜e5
(D)

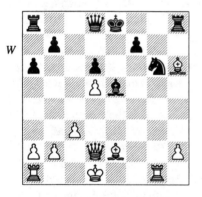

In this position, Karpov starts an amazing rook manoeuvre.

22 ≌g4!   ♕f6
23 h4   ♕f5

Now both 23...②xh4 and 23...0-0-0 lose material to 24 ≜g5.

24 ≌b4!
White attacks the b-pawn and makes queenside castling impossible due to 24...0-0-0 25 ≜g4.

24 ...   ≜f6
25 h5   ②e7

Black is forced to retreat; the bishop would be lost after 25...②e5 26 ≌f4.

26 ≌f4   ♕e5
27 ≌f3   ②xd5
28 ≌d3   ≌xh6

This capture loses by force, but Black's position seems hopeless in any case, for example 28...②e7 29 ≜f4.

29 ≌xd5
Maybe Black was hoping for 29 ♕xh6 ≜g5 30 ♕h7 ②e3+, when he has adequate counterplay. The text-move decides the game.

29 ...   ♕e4
30 ≌d3!   ♕h1+
31 ♔c2   ♕xa1
32 ♕xh6   ≜e5
33 ♕g5   1-0

I looked at this fascinating game in the morning before my own game against Peng Xiaomin, which was played in the middle of the tournament. Let us see what happened.

Xie Jun – Peng Xiaomin

National Junior Ch, Beijing 1989
Sicilian, Kan

1	e4	c5
2	♘f3	e6
3	d4	cxd4
4	♘xd4	a6
5	♗d3	d6
6	c4	♘d7

This move is not seen very often, but later the game transposes to familiar positions, which normally occur via different move-orders.

7	♘c3	♘gf6
8	♗e3	g6
9	0-0	♗g7 *(D)*

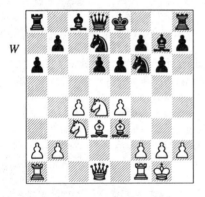

10 a4

An interesting attempt to play on the queenside. The alternative is 10 ♖c1 0-0 11 ♕c2 d5 12 ♘b3 dxe4 13 ♘xe4 ♕c7, with a complex position.

10 ... b6!?

With his last move, Black has given White the chance to push her a-pawn and increase the pressure on the queenside. Castling was certainly an option. After 10...0-0, White has several plans, each involving a different piece set-up. Not all the plans are equally effective, though. For example, Black seems to have adequate play after 11 b3 b6 12 a5 bxa5 13 ♘c6 ♕c7 14 ♘xa5 ♘g4 15 ♗d2 ♘ge5 16 ♗e2 ♘c5. Even more so, 11 a5 ♘e5 gives Black complete equality after 12 b3 (12 b4 ♕c7 13 ♕e2 ♘fg4 is equal, as well as 12 ♗e2 d5 13 exd5 exd5 14 cxd5 ♘xd5 15 ♘xd5 ♕xd5) 12...d5. So it seems that White's best is 11 ♖c1 b6 12 ♘c6 ♕c7 13 ♘e7+ ♔h8 14 ♘xc8 ♖axc8 15 f4, with a slight plus.

11	a5	bxa5
12	♘c6	♕c7
13	♘xa5	0-0

On 13...♖b8 White should play 14 ♕c2, although this obstructs the coming rook manoeuvre via f2. Still, I believe that White is better in that case. Let us look at some variations: 14...♘e5 15 ♗e2 d5 16 exd5 exd5 17 ♗f4 gives White a big advantage and, in this line, I do not believe in Black's compensation after 16...♘eg4 17 ♗xg4 ♘xg4 18 g3 ♘xe3 19 fxe3 0-0. A reasonable

move seems to be 14...♘g4, but White gets the upper hand after 15 ♗f4 f5 16 ♖fe1 pressuring the e-file. Lastly, 14...0-0 15 f3 ♘e5 16 ♗e2 is playable, if only Black refrains from the premature 16...d5? 17 exd5 exd5 18 c5! which would yield White excellent winning chances.

| 14 | f3 | ♖b8 *(D)* |

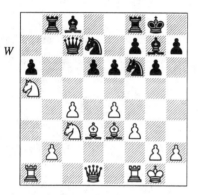

15 ♖f2!

Here, the influence of the Karpov-Hort game first becomes noticeable. That game undoubtedly helped me to make the right decision at this point.

15	...	♖e8
16	♖c2	♘c5
17	♗f1	♖b4?

This pseudo-active move is too risky because White gains an important tempo on the rook two moves later. The exchange of minor pieces with 17...♘b3 18 ♘xb3 ♖xb3 19 ♖d2 ♕b8 20 ♖xd6 ♖xb2 21 ♘a4 favours White slightly. However, more precise was 17...♖d8 18 ♖d2 ♗d7 19 ♗d4 and the position is unclear. Here, it would

be a mistake to take on d6. Black has the better game after 19 ♖xd6? ♖xb2 (not 19...♗a4 20 ♖xd8+ ♖xd8 21 ♕b1 and White has a large advantage, being ready to meet 21...♕xa5 with 22 b4) 20 ♘c6?! (20 ♖d2? ♘g4!) 20...♗f8! 21 ♘xd8 ♗xd6.

18 ♖a3! *(D)*

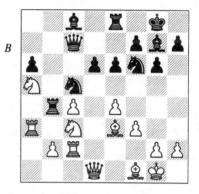

Another nice, multi-purpose rook move.

| 18 | ... | ♘fd7 |
| 19 | ♕d2 | |

Now the white knight threatens to go to b5, or even d5, and Black has no choice but to retreat his nicely placed rook. My queenside pawns will now come into action.

| 19 | ... | ♖b8 |
| 20 | b4 | |

The continuation of my original plan. It should be noted that taking on b4 gives Black a lost position. After 20...♖xb4 21 ♘b5 axb5 22 ♕xb4 bxc4 23 ♘xc4 White has won material and the win would be easier compared to the game.

20 ...   ♘b7 (D)

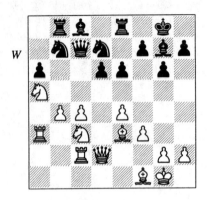

21 ♘d5!

Since all White's pieces are well placed, it is time for action.

21 ...   exd5

22 cxd5   ♘bc5

The best move under the circumstances. Black is even worse off after 22...♕d8 23 ♘c6 ♕h4 24 ♗g5.

23 ♘c6   ♖b6

24 ♗f4!

Played with the aim of putting Black under even more pressure. There was nothing against 24 bxc5!? ♘xc5 either, as long as White then plays 25 ♘b4!. Here, White should be on her guard. It is easy to overlook 25 ♗xc5?! dxc5 26 ♖xc5? ♗f8! – oops! A diabolical move backwards.

24 ...   ♘e5

It is not easy to recommend a better defensive move for Black. My opponent probably looked at the continuation 24...♘xe4 25 fxe4 ♘f6, after which I planned the logical 26 e5 (with the idea 26...dxe5 27 ♗xe5 and

Black cannot take twice on e5 since the c8-bishop will be *en prise*). The material balance is not disturbed in that case, but White has the initiative and can contemplate doubling rooks on the f-file. The attack will then be directed towards the black king.

25 bxc5   dxc5

26 ♖ac3   ♖b1

27 ♖xc5 (D)

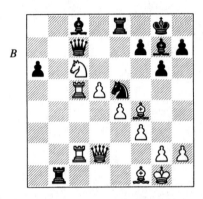

White is a healthy pawn up, and the position must be considered a technical win. The rest is relatively simple.

27 ...	♕b6
28 ♗xe5	♗xe5
29 ♘xe5	♖xe5
30 ♕f2	♗d7
31 ♖c7	♕d6
32 ♕d4	♖e8
33 ♖c1	♖xc1
34 ♖xc1	a5
35 ♕c5	

35 ♖b1, to prepare ♖b7, is a neater way to win the game.

35 ...	♕f4
36 ♖b1	a4

37	♖b7	♖c8		45	♖a8+	♔g7
38	♕d4	♖d8		46	♖xa2	♕xd7
39	♕b6	♕g5		47	h3	♕b7
40	f4	♕e7		48	♔h2	h5
41	♗b5	♖c8		49	♕d3	♕b4
42	♕e3	a3		50	♖b2	♕a4
43	♗xd7	a2		51	d6	♔h6
44	♖a7	♖c4		52	d7	1-0

It is an indescribable joy to win a game by using ideas that you discovered on the very same morning. For a moment, I had the feeling that I had found a 'key to the door of chess'. Of course, it is not possible to compare the level of the two games above. Nevertheless, I got a lot of pleasure from the fact that in my game, too, some nice rook manoeuvres played the decisive role. The Karpov-Hort game must have brought the right ideas into my mind.

For the girls, this mixed tournament was a very memorable one. The primary playing hall was not big enough for all the participants and therefore the games were played in two separate rooms. The top tables were situated in the primary hall and the rest in an adjacent room. From the start, the intention of the boys was perfectly clear: to kick the girls out of the primary hall. Unfortunately for them, I sat on board one after a few rounds and stayed there throughout the championship. But more girls were playing well and the boys got nowhere near their target. The last round was most enjoyable. I played on board one against another girl, Qin Kaiying, who ended in 6th place overall. Now it was time for us to tease the boys and they had to endure many a humiliating remark. The senior players who returned from the World Team Championship in Lucerne could hardly believe what happened and were very discontented with the boys' performance. A sweet victory!

Once more this was an important moment in my chess career. Only two months earlier I was thinking in all seriousness of giving up chess, but now things looked completely different again. As a result of the last two tournaments, my national Elo rating rocketed from 2300+ to more than 2400. Finally, I could escape from the seemingly endless and boring qualification games.

4 Entering the World Championship Cycle (1990-1991)

The advantage of having a national Elo rating over 2400 was that I qualified automatically for the zonal tournament in Malaysia in 1990. The Chinese Chess Federation could delegate two participants, and Peng Zhaoqin qualified later as the second player. There was not much opposition in Malaysia and we tied for first place, both of us with a score of 9½ out of 10. The next step for us was the interzonal tournament, which was, at the time, divided into two groups of eighteen players. Peng Zhaoqin played in the Russian city Azov, whereas the location of my group was, again, Malaysia. Therefore, in the summer of 1990, I returned hoping to qualify for the Candidates tournament. This time the tournament took place in a quiet mountain resort called Genting Highland. Many tourists visited this place and the main attraction was without any doubt the local casino. Gambling is usually not allowed in Malaysia but in this place, miles from anywhere, it seemed OK.

I experienced anew the difficulty of travelling abroad without a fair command of the English language. It was hardly possible to communicate with others and, therefore, I had little alternative but to stay in my room for most of the time. Every other player, except for the Danish girl, was escorted by at least one other person. The Soviet delegation was the largest one, consisting of several seconds, a team captain and even a medical doctor. Unfortunately it was impossible for me to have a second at my disposal due to the financial constraints. It was horribly lonely on the mountain and I spent the mornings and evenings waiting for phone calls from China. Apart from the chess games, there was just nothing to do. The high frequency of rest days, after every third round, was particularly disheartening. What to do when you have the whole day to yourself, but there is nowhere to go? I still remember that one day, when the room had to be cleaned, it was necessary for me to wait outside until the job was finished and I felt very uneasy with it. Also, during the tournament, the hotel was continuously filled with noise caused by construction work. A lot of players moved into another hotel after a while, but I wanted to stay. The noise made me feel less lonely.

Yet, for all the hardship, the chess went well and I managed to finish second with 12½ out of 17, one point behind Nona Gaprindashvili, who gave a very solid performance. My own achievement was good enough for another Women's GM norm and some of the games were really nice, such as the game I played in round two against Anna Akhsharumova, who now represented the USA. I knew that she was a tough player to beat. She had won the Soviet Union Championship before I started to play chess, and I feared that her husband, Boris Gulko, would have helped with her preparation.

Game 7

Anna Akhsharumova – Xie Jun

Interzonal tournament, Malaysia 1990
King's Indian, Sämisch

1	d4	♘f6
2	c4	g6
3	♘c3	♗g7
4	e4	0-0
5	f3	d6
6	♘ge2	

A less popular line than 6 ♗e3 and 6 ♗g5, and of course it was new to me.

6 ... c5

Black has a lot of choices here, such as 6...e5, 6...a6 and 6...♘bd7.

7	d5	e6
8	♘g3	exd5
9	cxd5	a6
10	a4	♘bd7
11	♗e2	h5 *(D)*

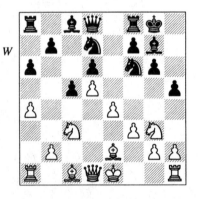

About five years later I faced the same position against Brunner (see Game 25). One noticeable difference

is that, here, I played the ideas that came to my mind. Against Brunner I followed 'my' theory a few more moves.

12 ♗g5

Brunner played 12 0-0.

12 ... ♕c7

Black has tried several queen moves at this point; 12...♕b6 and 12...♕a5 are possible as well. In Ivanchuk-Kramnik, Las Palmas 1996, play continued 12...♕e8 13 ♕d2 ♘h7 14 ♗h6 ♕e5 15 ♗xg7 ♔xg7 16 ♘f1 f5 17 exf5 gxf5 18 ♘e3 ♔h8 19 ♘c4 ♕f6 20 0-0 ♖b8 21 ♖fe1 b5 22 axb5 axb5 23 ♘a5 and White had the initiative.

13 ♕d2 ♘h7

In Christiansen-Fedorowicz, San Francisco 1991, the players agreed to a draw after 13...c4 14 0-0 ♖b8 15 ♗h6 h4 16 ♘h1 b5 17 axb5 axb5 18 ♘f2 b4 19 ♗xg7 ♔xg7 20 ♘a4 ♘c5 21 ♘xc5 ♕xc5. I found a comment by Dolmatov, who was of the opinion that 13...♖e8 would be a reasonable choice. He gave the variation 14 0-0 (if 14 ♗h6 then 14...♗h8) 14...c4 15 ♖ab1 ♖b8 16 ♖fc1 b5 17 axb5 axb5 18 b4 with an unclear position. My move, 13...♘h7, contains a different idea, as I plan to push the f-pawn.

14 ♗h6 ♕d8?!

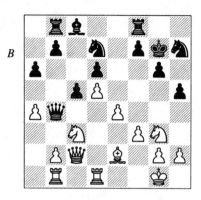

I was quite confused during the game, when I was searching for the most balanced way to complete my piece development. For some reason, I was not completely convinced about my chances on the kingside. It is not obvious where all the black pieces belong. Therefore, I decided to wait a little bit. 14...♖b8 would have been more logical.

15	♗xg7	♔xg7
16	0-0	♖b8
17	♖ab1!	♕a5

I disliked moving my queen for the third time within six moves, but there was no choice. If White is allowed the strong positional move 18 b4, Black cannot do anything on the queenside, even with the support of the queen.

18 ♖fd1

So far, White has played easily and logically. If I had now played 18...b5, she would have replied 19 axb5 axb5 20 ♖a1 ♕b4 21 ♖a7 with a comfortable game. I thought it was time to take some risks in order to get a more complicated position.

18	...	♕b4
19	♕c2? *(D)*	

A careless move. White should have stopped Black's plan with 19 b3 b5 20 axb5 axb5 21 ♘f1 f5 22 exf5 gxf5 23 ♘e3, when White's pieces are well placed.

19	...	c4
20	♘a2	♕c5+
21	♔f1?!	

Maybe Anna was getting ready for the endgame, but it is too early for

that. It was safer to put the king on h1, even though Black can then act in the same way as in the game. The position after 21 ♔h1 b5 22 axb5 axb5 23 b3 h4 24 ♘f1 h3 25 bxc4 hxg2+ 26 ♔xg2 ♘e5 is almost identical to the game, yet with one big difference: the white knight would be placed on f1, not on h1. This would give White better chances to defend. It is possible that after 21 ♔h1 Anna feared 21...h4 22 ♘f1 h3, but I would have preferred 21...b5 which gives the initiative on both wings.

21	...	b5
22	axb5	axb5
23	b3	h4
24	♘h1	h3
25	bxc4	hxg2+
26	♔xg2	♘e5 *(D)*
27	♕c3?!	

In view of what happens after this, it seems better to play 27 ♖b2, which leaves the c3-square for the knight. Maybe White missed my unexpected 28th move.

| 27 | ... | ♘g5 |

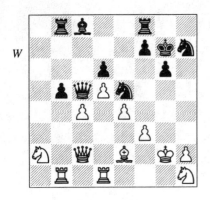

28 cxb5

28 ♖xb5 was not better. Again, Black gains a tempo by 28...♕a7 29 ♘b4 and continues 29...♗h3+ 30 ♔g3 f5 with a raging attack. If 28 ♘f2 then 28...♖h8 with the threat ...♖xh2+.

28	...	♕a7
29	♘b4	♗h3+
30	♔g3	f5
31	♕d4	♕e7
32	exf5 (D)	

After 32 ♘c6, Black has a luxurious choice between 32...f4+ 33 ♔f2 ♘xe4+ followed by 34...♕h4+, or 32...♘xe4+ straightaway.

32	...	♘gxf3!!
33	♗xf3	♕g5+
34	♗g4	

The white king has no shelter. 34 ♔f2 ♖xf5 35 ♔e2 (35 ♖b3 ♕g2+ wins outright) 35...♖xf3 36 ♘f2 ♖bf8 is no fun.

34	...	♗xg4
35	h4	♕f6!? (D)

Black should not play 35...♕xf5, because this would allow White to set up a defence with 36 ♖f1. But why not move the queen to h5? It was quickly established in the analysis that 35...♕h5! is the most powerful move; the variations are quite convincing: 36 ♖d2 fails to 36...♖xf5 (36...♖h8 is also strong) 37 ♕a7+ ♖f7 38 ♕d4 (38 ♕xb8 ♗h3! with a mating threat on g4) 38...g5, and 36 ♘c6 is simply met by 36...♗xd1. Both of us were already running short of time, so that partly explains the inaccuracy. For the rest, I can only add that, at first glance, the text-move looked more threatening to me than 35...♕h5!.

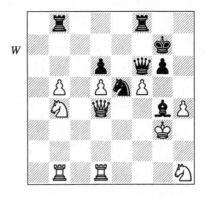

36	Rd2	gxf5
37	♘d3	Rh8
38	Rh2	♘xd3
39	♕xd3 (D)	

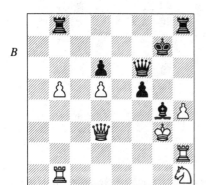

One pair of minor pieces has disappeared and it seems that White has successfully defended her king. However, she was in for a shock.

39 ...   Rbe8!

The second wave of the attack has been initiated. Black not only threatens 40...Re2, but even more 40...f4+, when if 41 ♔xg4, then 41...Re3. White finds the only defence.

40	Rb4	♕g6
41	♕d4+	♔f7
42	Ra2? (D)	

42 Rbb2 would have put up more resistance, but White cannot defend in the long run, e.g. 42...♗e2+ 43 ♔f2 Rhg8 and now 44 Rb1 ♗xb5! or 44 ♔e1 ♗xb5+ 45 ♔d2 ♕h6+ with a decisive attack in either case.

42 ...   Rxh4!!

I became ecstatic when I discovered the text-move and started to

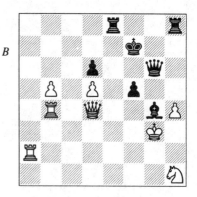

check the variations. My first hunch had been 42...♗d1+ but I could not find a mating combination. That forced me to look for an alternative move. And what a move it is! It seems as if the black pieces are dancing on the board.

43 Ra7+

The rook could not be taken, because White is mated after 43 ♔xh4 ♕h6+ 44 ♔g3 ♕h3+ 45 ♔f4 (alternatively 45 ♔f2 ♕f3+ 46 ♔g1 Re1+ 47 ♔h2 Rxh1#) 45...♕f3+ 46 ♔g5 Rg8+.

43	...	♔f8
44	♘f2	♗e2+
45	♔xh4	Re4+!
46	♕xe4	

46 ♔h3 allows mate in two, starting with 46...♗f1+.

46 ...   fxe4 (D)

Black has a won position. White's pieces are scattered and do not cooperate. It is time for the final assault.

47 Ra3

47 b6 ♕f6+ 48 ♔g3 ♕f3+ wins the house.

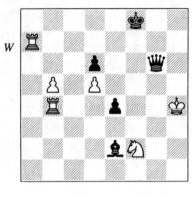

49 **Rbb3**
49 b6 leads to a quick mate after
49...♕h2+ 50 ♖h3 (50 ♔g5 ♕xg3+)
50...♕f4#.

49	...	♕f4+
50	♔h3	♗f1+
51	♔h2	♕f2+
52	♔h1	♗e2
53	b6	♗f3+
54	♖bxf3+	exf3
55	b7	♕e1+
56	♔h2	♕d2+
57	♔h1	♕c1+

47	...	♕g2
48	♖g3	♕xf2

0-1

"Beautiful stuff", concluded Paul Motwani in the British magazine *Chess Monthly* and I tend to agree with him. The decision to include this 'stuff' in my game collection was obvious. It does not happen too often – except for junior games – that you can play fresh attacking games like this.

In retrospect, I must conclude that this tournament was a good experience in learning how to overcome difficulties. Of course, one month in total solitude would make anybody stronger, but for me in particular this experience proved very valuable later on. In Malaysia I met Cathy Forbes, who had a double role – player and writer for *Chess Monthly*. She asked for an interview, with the help of the Singaporian chief arbiter Liong, who spoke both English and Chinese. It was the first interview I ever gave to a Western chess magazine. Later, at the Manila Olympiad in 1992, I saw Cathy again when she came up to me. I thought that she had come to congratulate me for winning the World Championship, but, in fact, she had come to remind me of this interview. The reason for asking me at the time, she explained, was that she had a feeling that I would surprise people. Sharp eyes indeed.

No more than two months separated this tournament in Malaysia and the Candidates tournament in Borzhomi, Georgia. In that period I participated in the National Women's Championship and ended in second place. It was a reasonable result, since I did not prepare specifically for this event. For various reasons this has been, thus far, my last appearance in the Chinese Women's Championship.

Eight chess players had qualified for the Candidates tournament in Borzhomi, six of them through the interzonal tournaments, plus two who were pre-qualified from the previous candidates cycle. This time I was accompanied by my second

Ye Jiangchuan. After a long and tiring flight from Beijing to Moscow, a representative from the local sports committee picked up Ye Jiangchuan and myself and escorted us to the hotel. The next morning we left for the airport, where we had to check in three hours prior to the flight to Tbilisi, a flight which lasted only two hours itself. After our arrival and more hours of waiting at the Tbilisi airport, a driver finally took us to the building of the Tbilisi Chess Association. We stayed some time in this four-storey building, where lots of people were hanging around. Some of them played chess in an adjacent room, while others were just sitting and talking. I noticed that the walls were covered with pictures of great Georgian women chess players, a truly impressive sight. I had already heard that Georgia is famous 'for wine and women chess players' and this seemed a first confirmation of this saying. How popular my Georgian colleagues really were became clearer later on.

When everybody was ready, we continued our trip to Borzhomi, a small town in a mountainous area. It may seem superfluous to mention that this trip, now by bus, lasted another two hours. The whole trip from Beijing to Borzhomi took more than one full day in total and I felt very sleepy when we arrived at our final destination. I merely emphasize these travel privations to clarify what sort of problems Chinese players usually have when they go abroad. The issue of time difference and travel time is poorly understood. But it has happened countless times that I arrived in Europe to play chess and started to feel fit only when the tournament was already halfway through. Of course, the obvious solution is to arrive one week before the start of a tournament, but for an event which lasts only one week in itself, this does not seem very practical.

Due to my late arrival in Borzhomi the opening ceremony had to be delayed. The drawing of lots indicated that I would play with the white pieces against Alisa Galliamova in the first round. The organizers had chosen to make the Candidates tournament a single-round event, meaning that the tournament would be held over seven rounds. I remember vividly that I got an advantage in the first round, but then, by the time I would have gone to bed in China, I spoiled everything within a few moves. Before round two I discussed the situation with my second. I was to play one of the weaker opponents, at least on paper, against whom everybody else would play for a win. Nevertheless, we opted for safety and a Ruy Lopez, Marshall Attack ended in a move repetition within twenty moves. This draw was most beneficial. Firstly, I had the opportunity to catch up on some sleep and, more importantly, I was released of all nervousness. After all, by starting with one draw out of two games, what is there to expect? After game two I made up my mind. Previously, only two Chinese players, Liu Shilan and Wu Minqian, had ever reached the Candidates stages and both of them had ended in the lower half of the table. I felt that it was reasonable to make an effort to score 50%. Then, all of a sudden, things went my way: I won three games in a row. First I beat Alisa Marić, then Elena Akhmylovskaya, only to find out that I had to play Nona Gaprindashvili in the round thereafter. I was probably the only person who was surprised by this pairing because I had always assumed that Ketino Kakhiani would be my opponent in round five. My pre-game preparation had in fact been against the latter. The damage was limited, though. Luckily, Gaprindashvili and Kakhiani play some of the same lines as White and on the board I got a variation that was familiar to me.

Game 8
Nona Gaprindashvili – Xie Jun

Candidates tournament, Borzhomi 1990
King's Indian, Averbakh

I have always considered it a privilege to play against Nona Gaprindashvili. Playing her in Georgia, her home country, is a special experience. Prior to every game, some handsome young man would come up to her on the stage and give her a bouquet of flowers. Apparently, there is a statue of Nona in her native town and she drives in a car with the special number plate 5555 (or 555, I do not remember exactly) related to the fact that she was five times World Champion. This tournament was probably her last chance to get back to the top and she fought extremely hard to qualify.

1	d4	♘f6
2	c4	g6
3	♘c3	♗g7
4	e4	d6
5	♗e2	0-0
6	♗g5	♘a6
7	♕d2	e5
8	d5	c6 *(D)*
9	h4	

Back in 1990, this was the normal move-order in the Averbakh Variation. Nowadays, White more often chooses to start with 9 f3 to keep the option of g2-g4. I have had some experience with this line myself: 9 f3 cxd5 (another interesting move is 9...♕a5, e.g.

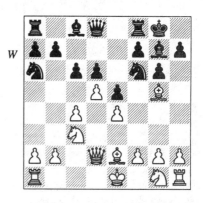

10 g4 h5 11 h3 cxd5 12 ♘xd5 ♕xd2+ 13 ♔xd2 ♘xd5 14 cxd5 f6 15 ♗e3 f5 16 g5 ♗d7, as happened in Yusupov-Smirin, Erevan Olympiad 1996) 10 cxd5 ♗d7 11 g4 (11 ♗b5 ♗xb5 12 ♘xb5 ♕b6 13 ♘c3 ♘c5 14 ♖b1 ♘h5 15 ♗e3 ♘f4 is the latest try, as in Yusupov-Gelfand, Dortmund 1997) 11...h6 12 ♗e3 (12 ♗xh6 ♘xe4 followed by ...♕h4+ is a well-known motif in the King's Indian) 12...h5 13 h3 ♘c5 14 0-0-0 ♕b8 15 ♔b1 ♖c8 16 ♖h2 b5. This was the continuation in Alterman-Xie Jun, Cap d'Agde 1994 (see Game 23). Later, my attack on the queenside proved decisive.

9	...	cxd5
10	cxd5	♕a5 *(D)*

To be honest, I had mixed up 10...♕a5 with the move 10...♗d7,

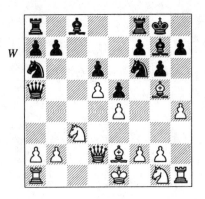

which was played by almost everybody up until then. I played my move quickly as if to indicate that I knew the position. I had no idea that move-order mattered here and was surprised when my opponent sank into deep thought. There was nothing else for me to do but start thinking myself and, rather slowly, I began to understand why Nona took her time over move 11. For instance, if White pretends that nothing is going on and plays 11 f3, then Black can continue 11...♘h5 threatening 12...♘g3. Moreover, Black's other option, 11...♘c5, is also interesting given the possibility 12...♘b3. I would like to add that, apart from 10...♕a5 and 10...♗d7, other moves have also been seen, such as 10...♕e8 11 f3 ♗d7 12 ♘h3 ♘c5 13 g4 h5 14 ♘f2 hxg4 15 fxg4 ♖c8 16 ♗e3 ♘h7 17 ♘d3 ♘xd3+, Ivanchuk-Topalov, Erevan Olympiad 1996.

11 ♖b1

11 ♖c1 leads to a complicated position after 11...♘c5 12 f3 ♗d7 13 ♘h3 ♖ac8, but I think that Black has

enough counterplay here. During the game, I was most afraid of 11 h5, which may be the strongest move. However, it seems to me that Black maintains a playable position after 11...♗d7 (11...♘c5 12 h6 ♗h8 13 ♖b1 ♕b4 14 f3 ♗d7 15 g4 ♖fc8 16 ♘h3 ♖c7 17 ♘f2 ♖ac8 18 0-0 leads to an unclear position as well) 12 h6 ♗h8 13 ♘h3 ♖fc8 14 f3 ♖c7 15 ♘f2 ♖ac8 16 0-0 ♘c5. Black has chosen a flexible set-up and it not easy to see how White can strengthen her position.

11 ... ♗d7 (D)

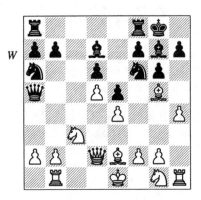

12 ♔f1?

This is possible, of course, but should White really resort to this kind of solution? Why not the more natural 12 h5? Maybe Nona disliked the continuation 12...b5!? 13 ♘xb5 ♕xa2 (even 13...♕xd2+ is possible, since Black has full compensation for the pawn after 14 ♗xd2 ♘xe4 15 ♘xd6 ♘xd2 16 ♔xd2 ♘c7 17 ♗f3 ♖ab8) 14 ♘c3 ♕a5 15 hxg6 fxg6 with an interesting position. I would probably have played 12...罝ac8, leading the game along quieter paths.

   12 ...   **罝ac8**

Now Black is well on top, having the more harmonious development.

   13 h5   **b5**
   14 a3

White is already in trouble. Alternatives are clearly worse and lead to positions that are very advantageous for Black, e.g. 14 ♗xf6 ♗xf6 15 罝c1 b4 or 14 hxg6 fxg6 15 a3 罝xc3! 16 ♕xc3 (16 ♗xf6 罝xa3!) 16...♕xc3 17 bxc3 ♘xe4.

   14 ...   **b4**
   15 axb4   **♘xb4**
   16 ♘h3 *(D)*

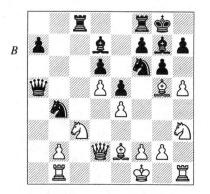

I now saw that the rook sacrifice on c3 would give Black a promising position. However, an important psychological factor came into play. As a matter of fact, I simply could not believe that Nona Gaprindashvili would give me such a chance. I was playing someone whose name I had read hundreds of times, in so many chess magazines, and I was convinced that this woman possessed some magical powers. There had to be a pitfall somewhere! The fact that I had lost to her only two months earlier, almost like a beginner, played a part in this as well. In the short post-mortem, Nona told me that she had known the type of position for the previous twenty years (i.e. from before I was born!). During the game I told myself to wait for a while and, if I could not find any better move than rook takes c3, I would go for it on the next move. This was silly, for I almost missed this opportunity to keep my advantage. I should have played 16...罝xc3!!, which leaves White basically with two options: 17 bxc3 ♘xe4 and White has nothing better than 18 ♕e1 (18 ♕e3 ♘xd5 19 ♕xe4 ♗f5 wins the white rook) 18...♘xd5 with a superior position for Black, or 17 ♕xc3 ♘xe4 18 ♕a3 ♕xa3 19 bxa3 ♘xd5 20 ♗f3 ♘dc3. Once again, Black is almost winning. White will be struggling to find useful squares for her pieces, whereas Black's position plays itself. Instead, I played the timid...

   16 ...   **罝c7?!**
   17 ♗e3   **罝xc3!**

Here, I failed to see any moves that I thought were better than the rook sacrifice and grabbed my second chance. Luckily it is not too late.

   18 ♕xc3   **♘xe4**
   19 ♕e1   **♗b5**

This eliminates the piece that eyes the light squares. From now on, the black knights will take up positions controlling the centre of the board.

20 ♘g5

After 20 ♗xa7, Black should not continue 20...♗xe2+ 21 ♕xe2 f5 22 ♗e3 ♘xd5 23 ♕c4 ♖f7 24 ♕c8+ ♖f8 25 ♕e6+ (25 ♕c4 leads to a move repetition) 25...♖f7 26 hxg6 ♘xe3+ 27 fxe3 hxg6 and the advantage has disappeared – although the position remains murky. But Black does not have to allow these complications. Much better is 20...♗h6 21 ♔g1 ♗xe2 22 ♕xe2 ♘d2 23 ♖d1 ♕xa7 24 ♖xd2 ♗xd2 25 ♕xd2 ♕b7, which gives White plenty to worry about. The pawns on d5 and b2 are weak and White still needs several moves to complete her piece development.

20	...	♘f6
21	hxg6	hxg6
22	♖d1	♗xe2+
23	♕xe2	♘bxd5 *(D)*

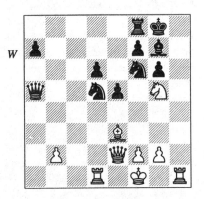

A sharp position has arisen. Black has ample compensation for the exchange and should now think how to mobilize her centre pawns. But how is White to proceed and finish her development? One idea is 24 g3, after which I intended 24...♘xe3+ 25 ♕xe3 ♕b5+ 26 ♔g2 ♕b7+ 27 ♘f3 ♖d8 28 b3 ♘d5 29 ♕d2 (29 ♕e4?? ♘f4+) 29...♘c7. Black is ready to play ...d6-d5. Some chess players would look at the immediate 24 ♖h4 but the prospects of this rook along the fourth rank, let's say after 24...♖c8, are not too bright for the moment. Nona decided on another move.

24	♗c1	♖c8
25	g3	

25 ♘e4 forces the exchange of one pair of knights, but Black is nonetheless better after 25...♘xe4 26 ♕xe4 ♕a6+ 27 ♔g1 ♘f6.

25	...	♘e7
26	♖h4	

Finally, White's h1-rook is activated.

26	...	♘f5
27	♖c4	♖f8 *(D)*

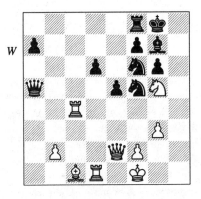

28 ♗d2?!

Nona by now had little time left, and she makes an inaccurate move. 28 ♔g1!, which controls the d5-square, would have been more precise. Black has several plans and they usually include the move ...d6-d5. It is extremely difficult to give an exact assessment of the many positions that can arise. The following variations illustrate some of the rich possibilities: 28...♕b5 29 ♖c2 (29 ♕d3?! d5 30 ♖c7 ♕b6 gives Black the initiative) 29...♕b6 is possible, but Black can also put the queen directly on b6 with 28...♕b6 29 ♕c2 ♘d4 (29...d5!? is interesting) 30 ♗e3. The situation is unbalanced.

| 28 | ... | ♕d5 |
| 29 | ♘f3?? | |

Now White's position is lost immediately. This was her last chance for 29 ♔g1, even though White can no longer prevent Black from controlling the a8-h1 diagonal with 29...♘d4 30 ♕f1 ♗h6 31 ♖a4 ♕b7.

29	...	♘d4
30	♖xd4	exd4
31	♗c3	♕c6
32	♗xd4	♖e8
33	♕d3	♘e4
34	♔g1	♗xd4
35	♘xd4	♕d5

| 36 | ♕b5 | ♖e5 |
| 37 | ♕d3 | ♘g5 |

I realized that the win would only be a matter of time.

38	♔h2	♖e4
39	♕b3	♕c5
40	♕b8+	♔g7

At last, White had passed the time control but her position is without any hope of survival. Nona took a long time before making her next move. In the meantime, I felt overcome by a feeling of sadness. It would be the end of Nona's chance to qualify, and maybe she would never get another chance to play for a world championship title.

41	b4	♕e5
42	♘c6	♕f5
43	♔g1	♕h3

At this moment, when Nona realized that she had no more chances and I was about to mate her, I could see the tears in her eyes. Every time when Georgian players won a game, the three to five hundred spectators applauded enthusiastically. But now there was a dead silence in the hall. It was evident that many people had come especially to watch her play. Then, after some thinking, she resigned.

0-1

I could not feel as happy as one would normally expect after winning such an important game. The whole situation had touched me and I felt too much sympathy for my opponent. Little was I to know that Nona would still get her chance in the last round of the tournament. Nona has always impressed me for her fighting chess and she was one of my great examples when I was a junior. In fact, I was delighted when I heard that one year later, in 1991, she took first place at the Interzonal tournament in Yugoslavia.

After five rounds Alisa Galliamova and I were leading with a 'plus two' score, followed by Nana Ioseliani with 'plus one'. My opponent in round six was Ketino Kakhiani – yes, this time I had checked the programme – who had not played well and was yet to win her first game. If I could win this game, with White, my chances to qualify would be excellent. A draw would not be bad either, because this would keep me in the running until the very end of the tournament. In the last round I had to play Ioseliani, albeit with the black pieces, but then everything was possible. However, the planned scenario proved too optimistic. In the early middlegame I produced some bad moves and Kakhiani took control. Little by little I saw my position deteriorate and I was not given a chance to get back into the game again. This was a horrible experience because any chances of qualifying seemed to disappear with it.

Ioseliani had won her game in round six but Galliamova had lost to Marić. This meant that there were now five players competing for the two tickets to the next round of the World Championship. Ioseliani was the sole leader with 4 points out of 6 games, followed by Marić, Galliamova, Gaprindashvili and myself, all with 3½ points. Anything was possible now. I was quite annoyed with my play in round six and it was a good thing that there were two rest days before the final round would take place. Now I had ample time to get over this bad experience and to prepare for my game against Ioseliani. My second and I did most of the preparation on the first rest day and left a little for the second day. The rest of that day we tried to relax. We walked around and suddenly found ourselves in a lovely market place, where I wanted to buy some fruit from a vendor. To my amazement he asked whether I was one of the chess players. Although he spoke only Russian, the question was perfectly clear. When he understood that I was indeed a chess player, he gave me the fruit for free and refused to accept any money – another striking example of how popular chess really is in Georgia. People there really adore chess players and they are proud of their champions.

In the morning before the last game, I sat for one hour on the balcony in the autumn sun. I felt comfortable and was day-dreaming a little. Then I told my second that I would make it to the final stage. He replied with nothing more than "OK, OK, you can win" because he, as he later confessed, did not want to make me feel sad. Still, I had a confident feeling and I can only recall having a similar reaction once more, during my match with Maya Chiburdanidze for the World Championship. On that occasion, I made a similar comment to my seconds, i.e. that I had a feeling I would win the match. However, on that occasion, having just lost two games in a row, the reaction of my seconds was different. They thought I had gone mad.

Game 9
Nana Ioseliani – Xie Jun

Candidates tournament, Borzhomi 1990
Ruy Lopez, Anti-Marshall

1	e4	e5
2	♘f3	♘c6
3	♗b5	a6
4	♗a4	♘f6
5	0-0	♗e7
6	♖e1	b5
7	♗b3	0-0

This very last game of the tournament was crucial, and any mistakes would be irrecoverable. As mentioned before, Nana was in the lead and I was one of four players who were half a point behind. If this game should end in a draw, then everything would depend on the results on the other boards.

8 h3

Nana chooses a solid line and does not want to see what I have in mind against 8 c3. I had played 8...d5 in round two.

8	...	♗b7
9	d3	d6
10	a3 *(D)*	

New to me at the time. Even my current database does not contain any older games with this particular position, so it may have been a novelty. Later the move 10 a3 gained some popularity, the leading exponents being Shirov and Adams. I even found a game played between Kasparov and Kamsky (Dos Hermanas 1996).

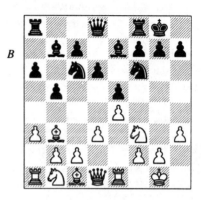

B

10	...	h6

For some reason 10...h6 has not found many followers. Most players opted for alternative moves at this point, such as:

a) 10...♘d4 11 ♘xd4 exd4 12 ♘d2 c5 13 ♘f3 ♘d7 14 a4 ♘e5 15 ♗f4 ♗f6 16 ♘h2 ♘g6 17 ♗d2 ♗g5 and White was slightly better in Lanka-Blatny, European Team Ch, Debrecen 1992.

b) 10...♘b8 11 ♘bd2 ♘bd7 12 ♘f1 h6 13 ♘g3 ♖e8 14 ♘f5 ♗f8 15 ♘h2 d5 16 ♘g4 c6 17 ♕f3 ♔h8 18 c3 ♖e6 with unclear play in Shirov-Topalov, Madrid 1996.

c) 10...♕d7 11 ♘c3 ♖ae8 12 ♗d2 ♘d8 13 ♘e2 ♘e6 14 ♘g3 c5 15 c3 ♗d8 16 ♗c2 ♗c7, as played in Shirov-Kamsky, Dos Hermanas 1996.

d) Lastly, I feel that the idea 10...♔h8 11 ♘c3 ♘g8 12 ♘d5 f5 is certainly worthy of attention.

11 ♘c3

I prefer the text-move to 11 c4?! which was introduced by Shabalov in his game against Sammalvuo during the Moscow Olympiad in 1994. After 11...♘a5 12 cxb5 axb5 13 ♗a2 c5 14 ♘c3 b4 15 axb4 cxb4 16 ♘e2 d5 17 ♘xe5 dxe4 it was not clear that White had achieved anything.

11 ...	**♖e8**
12 ♗a2	**♗f8**

Had I been more experienced I would have opted for the more flexible 12...♖b8 here. This would have prevented the knight manoeuvre to f5.

13 ♘h4	**b4**
14 axb4	**♘xb4**
15 ♗b3	**d5!?** *(D)*

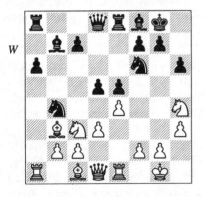

It is hard to criticize this move. Of course it is dangerous to open the centre, but what else should you do to disturb the balance, and increase the tension? I reckoned that the time had

come to take some risks. It was not likely that the opportunity would arise again later.

16 ♕f3?!

It is clear that Nana wanted to keep her options open. During the game she kept a close eye on the developments in the other games. A draw would probably be enough for her to qualify. In the meantime, I tried to focus on the position on the chess board, aware that I had to avoid losing at all costs. But, in chess terms, 16 exd5 seems more logical because it opens the centre, after which the b3-bishop becomes more valuable than its counterpart on b7. Then the game could have continued 16...♘bxd5 17 ♘xd5 ♘xd5 (White is also better after 17...♗xd5 18 ♗xd5 ♕xd5 19 ♘f5) 18 ♕g4 ♔h8 19 ♘f5, when Black faces a difficult defence.

16 ... g6

Now the f5-square is no longer available to White.

17 exd5	**♘bxd5**
18 ♘xd5	**♘xd5**
19 ♕e4	

This move came as a slight surprise, I had expected the more normal 19 ♕g3 or 19 ♕g4. Now I was not sure what to do next and switched to 'wait and see' tactics.

19 ...	**♗g7** *(D)*
20 ♗a4	

An interesting idea would have been to sacrifice the knight for three pawns, e.g. 20 ♘xg6 fxg6 21 ♕xg6 (not 21 c4?? ♘e7 22 ♕xb7 ♖b8) 21...♕f6 22 ♕xf6 ♗xf6 23 ♗xh6 ♔h7

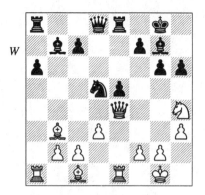

24 ♗d2 ♘f4 25 f3 ♖ad8, but Nana was apparently not in the state of mind to complicate matters that much.

20 ... c6
21 ♘f3 ♔h7
22 ♗b3

My opponent was clearly having great difficulty in finding the right plan. She spent a lot of time on her next move. The position is already too open to have complete control.

22 ... c5
23 ♕c4 ♖c8
24 ♕h4 f6 (D)

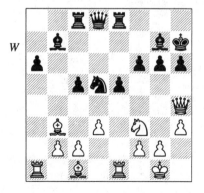

I was quite happy with my last few moves. Although Black has no reason for a celebration yet, at least I was strengthening my position with every move. And I could tell that Nana was still at a loss for a clear plan.

25 ♘h2 ♘e7
26 ♗d2 ♕d6
27 ♕g4 ♘d5

For no obvious reason, the knight returns to the centre. This cannot be the best move. I disliked 27...♖cd8 28 ♗a5, but 27...♖f8 seems OK. It stops the possibility of ♗f7 and the plan is to put the knight on f5. In addition, Black may have a reasonable alternative in 27...f5. I prefer Black's position after 28 ♕h4 ♕d4 29 ♕xd4 cxd4 30 ♗c4 ♘g8 but, for the moment, I wanted to keep queens on the board.

28 ♘f3 h5
29 ♕g3 ♘e7? (D)

I was determined to stick to my nice knight manoeuvre, but the knight moves have taken too much time. I simply missed that White could solve all her problems with a *'petite combinaison'*. Already, Black has to think about defending and, for this, the best move would have been 29...♖f8 30 ♘h4 ♘e7 31 ♗c3 g5 32 ♗xe5 fxe5 33 ♕xg5 ♖c6!? (not 33...♘c6 34 ♕xh5+ ♔h6 35 ♕xh6+ ♗xh6 36 ♗d5 ♗g7 37 ♗e4+ ♔g8 38 ♘f5, nor 33...♗h6 34 ♕xe5, in both cases with advantage to White).

30 h4??

White was in severe time-trouble, otherwise she would no doubt have

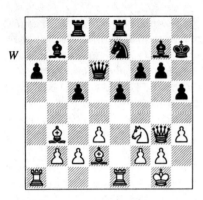

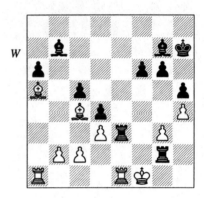

found 30 ⧄xe5! ♘f5 (30...fxe5 31 ♘g5+ loses immediately) 31 ⧄xf5 ♕xg3 32 fxg3 gxf5 33 ♔f1 ♗h6 34 ♗c3. It seems to me that the position is in White's favour, despite her being the exchange down.

| 30 | ... | ♘f5 |
| 31 | ♕h3 | ⧄c7! |

Now Black takes over the initiative and gets a big advantage. White cannot prevent the opening of the e-file.

32	♗c4	⧄ce7
33	♗c3	♕c6
34	♗b3	♕d6
35	♗c4	♘d4
36	♘xd4	exd4
37	♗d2	⧄e2
38	♗a5	♕f4
39	♕g3	

The ugly-looking move 39 f3 cannot save White's position either. After 39...⧄xe1+ 40 ♗xe1 ⧄e2 41 ♗b3 ♕e3+ 42 ♔f1 c4 43 dxc4 d3, the attack is unstoppable.

39	...	♕xg3
40	fxg3	⧄xg2+
41	♔f1	⧄e3 (D)

This move basically concludes the game.

42	♗xa6	♗a8
43	♗c7	♗h6
44	♗c4	⧄xe1+
45	⧄xe1	♗e3
46	♗f4	⧄g1+
47	♔e2	♗f3+
48	♔xf3	⧄xe1
49	♗d6	♗c1
50	♗xc5	♗xb2
51	♔f2	⧄e8
52	♔f3	♗c3
53	♗b3	g5
54	♗f7	⧄e3+
55	♔g2	gxh4
56	gxh4	♔g7
57	♗b3	⧄e2+
58	♔g3	f5
59	♗b6	♔g6
60	♗a4	♗e1+
61	♔h3	♗f2
62	♗d8	f4
63	♗c6	♗g1

It is mate on h2 and 64 ♗g2 fails to 64...⧄e3+, so White resigned.

0-1

It was unfortunate for Alisa Galliamova that she could not find the win in her game against Eliska Klimova-Richtrova, despite being an exchange up in the endgame. In the other important game, Alisa Marić, with the black pieces, beat Nona Gaprindashvili in a long game. This made the surprise complete. Alisa Marić and I would play the Candidates Final for the right to challenge World Champion Maya Chiburdanidze.

After the final result was known, the first thing my second tried to do in his excitement was to phone some Chinese news agencies. However, phoning home proved impossible because he had to pronounce the telephone numbers in the Russian language. Finally he got through to the Chinese International Broadcast Station in Moscow. I found out later that the news received extensive coverage in the media, something I was hardly aware of until my return. It was all the more surprising since the Western version of chess was not well known in China. However, Chinese really love 'brain games' and many people were happy with my result. As a symbolic gesture I was later elected one of the ten best Chinese sports(wo)men of the year, particularly due to this achievement in Borzhomi. This election is an honour for every sportsman, all the more because the voting is done by the readers of one of the larger newspapers in China.

Owing to the travel arrangements, Ye Jiangchuan and I could not go home. One month later, the Chess Olympiad would be held in Novi Sad, Yugoslavia, and the National Team would come by train in our direction. Hence, we travelled from Georgia to Moscow, and then further to Alma-Ata in Kazakhstan. The last part of our trip was a short flight to Xinjiang, just on the other side of the border. There we waited for the arrival of our colleagues who would join us ten days later. Xinjiang is a remote Chinese province, about 2500 kilometres from Beijing. Local people look different from the typical Chinese and speak their own language, which is difficult to understand. It was quite an experience for me to see such big differences. Luckily, my second knew some chess players and they did their best to make our stay an enjoyable one. Both of us felt very tired. For my second, this was a particularly difficult period. His wife was about to give birth to a baby and now he could not be at her side. It was a real pity that we could not fly back.

In all, we stayed two weeks in Xinjiang. It was a pleasant surprise that the head of the Beijing Chess Club came together with the rest of the team. He had indeed promised that, in the event of my qualification, he would come along to Xinjiang just to say hello. I had not expected him to stick to his promise, simply because it is a few days travelling from Beijing. Nevertheless, he came and he brought presents for my birthday from my parents and some of my friends. And there was delicious cake from the best bakery shop in Beijing.

Soon we had to take the flight back to Alma-Ata, where we planned to buy tickets for the train to Moscow, and from there on to Rome and Belgrade. This was easier said than done at a time when the Soviet Union was already on the verge of disintegrating. People were really crazy about money, especially hard currency, and simple things like buying tickets or renting ordinary hotel rooms proved possible only after tremendous efforts. Our stay in Alma-Ata lasted two days, enough to face numerous difficulties. Even people from the local chess authorities, who were extremely helpful, were powerless against the manifold attempts at swindling and corruption. We had Asian faces and none of us spoke Russian. In addition, we only had hard currency, which meant that people automatically charged us more.

One of the strange events that happened was when a local man offered his help to buy train tickets to Moscow. When he tried to get away too quickly, after handing over the tickets, my team leaders made him see us off at the railway station. It became painfully clear that the tickets were false and we were not admitted to the train. This time we did not let him escape until he had bought valid tickets for us. As a result we had to spend yet another day in Alma-Ata. Fortunately, things appeared OK the next day and we could continue our trip to Moscow. The plan had been to take a further train to Italy, where we had promised to play some friendly games against local players. In Moscow we discovered that it was, again, difficult to get the right train tickets. The problem was apparently that transport by train was very cheap and train tickets seemed very much in demand. By now, we started to run out of time and made the decision to fly to Austria, and continue from there by train to Rome. This went remarkably easily and our spirits rose rapidly when we finally sat on the train from Vienna to Rome.

The euphoria was short-lived, however, at least for me. At the railway station in Vienna I ate some fast food that was probably contaminated. I became very sick and the first thing we did upon arrival in Rome was to find a doctor. It was Saturday when we arrived, but soon a doctor was found who came to the hotel room to examine me. He gave a prescription for a Western medicine and left. Now there was only one more, unsolvable problem: where to locate a pharmacy, in the centre of Rome, that opens on Saturday morning? The same afternoon, when we were about to play our games, a pharmacy was still not found and I still felt miserable. My team leader decided to resort to some traditional Chinese medicine, with lots of raw garlic and thus an extremely strong smell. The odour of garlic was still surrounding me when we left two days later for Yugoslavia, but it appeared quite effective. Within days I made a complete recovery and the suffering was history once we arrived in Belgrade. The last part of our trip went according to plan. One of the charming things in Western and Central Europe is that you easily get the right train tickets, and for one standard price. Two days before the start of the Olympiad we arrived in Novi Sad and checked in at our hotel.

The Novi Sad Olympiad was well organized and very successful. It was abundantly clear that Yugoslavia has a rich tradition when it comes to the organization of chess events. It was also one of the best Olympiads for the Chinese squad, with a third place for the women and a sixth place for the men. It was the first time ever that a Chinese team reached a podium place. This was a brilliant performance, especially if you bear in mind that our players were quite inexperienced, back in 1990. The team consisted of four players of whom Peng Zhaoqin and I were the 'veterans'. The two youngsters, Qin Kaiying and Wang Lei, were at the time only sixteen and fifteen years old, respectively. For myself, I got the bronze medal for my performance on board one. I was allowed to play all fourteen games and I played well. I guess it was probably easier for me to play than it is nowadays. Everything was still fresh and I did not worry about the result in any of my games. I just tried to play good quality games and the result was secondary. In all honesty I should admit that the quality of my Novi Sad games was not particularly high. In order to write this book I have had to analyse several games from that period and I noticed many mistakes. Sometimes I truly played positions at 2500 Elo level, but other game parts were played at not more than 2200 Elo level. I found it puzzling that this never really seemed related to the *type* of position. The answer to the question *why* is not obvious, but I know that many chess players have similar experiences.

I had looked forward to playing Maya Chiburdanidze for the first time in my life. I had expected her to play against China, because we were following Hungary and the Soviet Union quite closely. Unfortunately, when the encounter took place in round six, she was not present and I played Gaprindashvili instead. Maya did play later in the match against Yugoslavia, where she beat Alisa Marić. An interesting meeting was also the game between myself and Marić in round eleven, which ended in a balanced draw after 39 moves. Yet, I did not think too much about the World Championship. I was still enjoying the result I made in Borzhomi and found it difficult to look far ahead. It seemed to me that there was still a respectable distance between myself and a top player such as Maya Chiburdanidze.

During the Olympiad it was actually decided where the Candidates Match between Alisa Marić and myself would take place. The Yugoslav Chess Federation expressed its desire to organize the match as a whole, but my own chess federation objected to this, arguing that this would give Marić the home advantage. After some discussion it was agreed that the match would be split between Yugoslavia and China, which was acceptable to all parties.

After the Olympiad we went back to China. The bus took us from Novi Sad to Belgrade and the next train stop was Budapest. There we landed in the middle of a big festival. December had arrived and the winter had set in. Three days later we got on the train to Moscow, the beginning of a long journey home which lasted two weeks in all. The train from Moscow to Beijing took us right through the heart of Siberia. The view was incredible and to some extent surreal. Nothing more than trees and fields covered with snow, and more trees, and more fields, day in, day out. Siberia was freezing cold and going to the dining-carriage was quite daring. It was so extremely cold in the passage between the carriages that everybody was even afraid to touch any metal with a bare hand, for fear that it would be stuck for the remainder of the trip. Trees, fields, snow, a view never to forget. Yet, no matter how beautiful the trip, it was also an assault on my health. All the hours on trains, buses and aeroplanes had clearly left their mark. My health was seriously affected and I felt in a poor physical state when I eventually returned to Beijing, having been away more than two months. Nevertheless, it had been the most special period of travelling in my life.

5 The Candidates Final (1991)

Two weeks after returning to China, just after the New Year, I had to leave for Yugoslavia again for the match against Alisa Marić. This time schedule was very tight and there was hardly time to rest between events. This time we travelled by aeroplane, more convenient in comparison to the Siberian Express train. It would have been the perfect flight, were it not for the fact that my luggage arrived some days later. Two seconds, Qi Jingxuan and Ye Jiangchuan, accompanied me and the three of us arrived in Belgrade one week before the start. People from the Chinese Embassy were helpful in getting temporary accommodation for us, where we stayed until two days prior to the start. Then we moved to the hotel rooms booked by the organizers. I even stayed one day in the house of the Chinese Ambassador, an honour because this is usually not allowed. Embassy staff had taken it upon themselves to show us round the town and we fully enjoyed this. At least, I tried to because I got a cold and the fever kept me confined to my bed for several days. This was most certainly a result of my weakened physical condition and the ever-changing weather. My body paid the toll for all the strain.

During our stay with people from the Embassy we followed our hosts to a local market. Surprisingly enough, a fisherman on the market knew who I was. In a way this reminded me of Borzhomi in Georgia, where chess was also extremely popular. The newspapers in Yugoslavia covered the match extensively. This was apparent because people seemed to recognize me at times while I was walking in the street. In the meantime, people from the Embassy had prepared a translation of an interview with Alisa Marić in a Yugoslav newspaper. She stated that in this year – 1991 had just begun – two periods would be important for her. The first period would cover our match while the second one would be in September. Knowing that the World Championship Match with Maya Chiburdanidze was scheduled for September, little imagination was needed to figure out what was meant. Naturally, she wanted to win this match desperately, but I think that such statements put more pressure on yourself than necessary. And playing at home is already more difficult than playing abroad.

I wanted to win, too, but I was less fixated on the result. I had just received the Women's Grandmaster title, and qualifying for the Candidates Final had exceeded my wildest expectations. I was a happy person. After such a series of good results, not to forget the third place at the Olympiad, and my current poor physical state to boot, I was happy just to be where I was. In fact, I did not even have enough energy to worry about the match. A loss would be a loss, so what? Somewhere, the success story had to end.

All in all, the quality of the match was not high. This could be expected, though, as both of us had had hardly any time for serious preparation. Some games were interesting, and even exciting, but too often the games were marred by inaccuracies. The seventh game (see Game 10, below), for example, played in the Beijing part of the match, is a striking example of the varying fortunes in this match. For myself, I think that I had only too recently approached the level needed to play this kind of match. Maybe I would have played more consistently if I had been in a better physical shape, who knows. Alisa, on the other hand, was able to put a tremendous amount of energy in every game. In total concentration, sometimes during the full six hours, she would sit down and not leave the chess-board. I left the stage once in a while to visit the ladies' room, to stretch my legs or simply to get something to drink. Alisa, in contrast, stayed motionless and never even got out of her chair. She just sat there, thinking. However, she suffered from an eternal fight with the clock. In almost every game she got into time-trouble and this influenced the outcome of some games in my favour. Alisa certainly played better than the outcome of the match (4½-2½ in my favour) suggests.

I was lucky in game one. A win from an almost lost position was more than I could have hoped for. After a draw in the second and a loss in the third game, I managed to win game four. Thereafter, the circus moved to Beijing where the second leg of four games would start two weeks later. Meanwhile, the Spring Festival took place in China, the traditional two-week family feast to celebrate the new year. Alisa had arrived on the first day of the Spring Festival, together with her parents, twin sister (also a strong player) and her second. For me, coming home with a lead of one single point was scarcely reassuring. Anything was still possible. Games five and six ended in two balanced draws and then came the extraordinary game seven.

Game 10
Alisa Marić – Xie Jun
Candidates Final, Match (7), Belgrade/Beijing 1991
King's Indian, Gligorić

This is not a game of the highest quality, yet it is one that stayed in my mind for a long time. As I mentioned before, luck was on my side during the Candidates Final. I survived a number of inferior positions that could easily have gone the other way. In all fairness, there is also another way of looking at this matter. It was characteristic of my uninhibited style of chess, around 1990, that I played with little knowledge and no fear. That explained why I often got complicated and original positions in which alertness proved to be the decisive factor. This game was the most dramatic one, with ups and downs for both players.

1	d4	♘f6
2	c4	g6
3	♘c3	♗g7
4	e4	d6
5	♘f3	0-0
6	♗e2	e5
7	♗e3	

This line was my opponent's main weapon during the match, and she obtained a real advantage in games one and three. This time we had both prepared well.

7 ... c6

This move became very popular once it was adopted by Kasparov in his 1990 match against Karpov. These games reached us just in time, and were very helpful in our preparation.

8 ♕d2 (D)

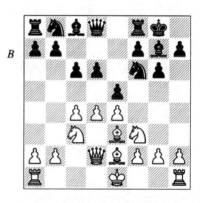

8 ... ♖e8

Still, that does not mean that I have to copy Kasparov's play! The text-move, 8...♖e8, went out of fashion for unclear reasons. To refresh the reader's memory, the exciting game Karpov-Kasparov, World Ch, New York/Lyons (11) 1990 proceeded with 8...exd4 9 ♘xd4 ♖e8 10 f3 d5 11 exd5 cxd5 12 0-0 ♘c6 13 c5 ♖xe3 (a fantastic exchange sacrifice!) 14 ♕xe3 ♕f8 15 ♘xc6 bxc6 and Black seemed to have enough compensation for the exchange. Gelfand-Kasparov, Linares 1992 followed the same path until Gelfand tried to improve with 15 ♘cb5 ♕xc5. Here, too, Black got ample compensation. This line can also occur via other move-orders, for instance 1 d4 ♘f6 2 c4 g6 3 ♘c3 ♗g7 4 e4 d6 5 ♘f3 (or 5 f3 0-0 6 ♗e3 e5 7 ♘ge2 exd4 8 ♘xd4 ♖e8 9 ♕d2 c6 10 ♗e2) 5...0-0 6 ♗e2 e5 7 ♗e3 exd4 8 ♘xd4 ♖e8 9 f3 c6 10 ♕d2.

Other replies that are seen frequently are 8...♘bd7 and 8...♕e7.

9	**d5**	**♘g4**
10	**♗g5**	**f6**
11	**♗h4**	**♘h6**

This may have been a new move in the given position. In fact, Black has many options at his disposal. Reshevsky and Stein were obviously in a peaceful mood (Los Angeles 1967) when they agreed a draw after 11...c5 12 h3 ♘h6 13 0-0 ♘d7 14 a3 ♘f7 15 b4 a5 16 bxa5 ♖xa5 17 ♘e1 ♘b6 18 ♘c2 ♘a4. More lively was the game Gligorić-Ristić, Yugoslav Ch 1995, which continued 11...♘a6 12 0-0 h5 13 h3 ♘h6 14 ♘e1 ♘f7 15 ♘d3 ♗h6 16 ♕c2 c5. Here, the players put up a real fight which lasted 63 moves and ended ... also in a draw.

12   0-0

12 ♖d1!? is an interesting idea, putting pressure on the d6-pawn. After 12...♘f7 13 a3, White can play an early b2-b4.

12	**...**	**♘f7**
13	**♕c2!?**	

Again, 13 a3 followed by b2-b4 is worth considering.

13	**...**	**♘a6**

14	**a3**	**c5**
15	**♖ab1**	**h5** *(D)*

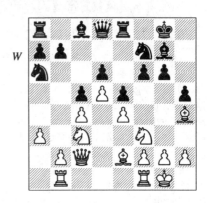

16   h3

It would certainly make sense to play 16 ♗g3 in order to wait and see what Black has in mind.

16	**...**	**♗d7!?**

Maybe the bishop move is not necessary for the moment. For, if Black plays ...f5 later on and plans to answer exf5 with ...♗xf5, one valuable tempo could be lost. So there is something to be said for the immediate 16...♖f8 17 b4 ♘h6 18 ♖b2 ♖f7 19 ♖fb1 b6. Still, this is a hypothetical point of view as the position is rather slow. The reader will notice that I play ...♖f8 one move later anyway, mainly due to the absence of a better plan.

17	**b4**	**♖f8**
18	**♘d2**	**♘h6**
19	**♖fe1**	

19 bxc5 releases the tension on the queenside, but is probably premature. In that case, I planned to slow down White's initiative on the queenside,

and generate counterplay on the other side, with 19...♞xc5 20 ♘b3 ♘xb3 21 ♖xb3 b6 22 ♗g3 (or 22 a4 g5 23 ♗g3 h4 24 ♗h2 f5) 22...f5 23 f3 ♕g5.

19 ... ♖f7

20 ♘b5

Marić could have gained a slight plus with 20 bxc5 ♘xc5 21 ♘b3 ♘xb3 22 ♖xb3 b6 23 ♕d3 ♖c8 24 a4.

20 ... ♗f8 (D)

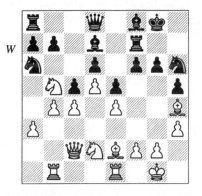

21 ♗d3?!

Both of us had played extremely carefully so far, focusing primarily on where to place the pieces. However, the time had come for White to play something active, such as 21 bxc5 ♘xc5 22 ♘b3 ♘xb3 23 ♖xb3 b6 24 ♕d2 ♕e7 25 ♖eb1. Again, White should be slightly better as the initiative on the queenside appears more threatening than Black's counterplay on the kingside.

21 ... ♖g7

I did not like to change the structure with 21...cxb4 22 axb4 ♗xb5 23 cxb5 ♘c7 24 ♖ec1 ♘e8 25 ♘c4 ♖c7.

White has the upper hand: though Black has a solid defensive position, there is little counterplay in this line. I looked for a while at 21...♗e7!? 22 ♘f1 g5 23 ♗g3 f5, which is more appealing. Then I suddenly decided on the text-move.

22 f3 g5?!

This pawn advance was tempting, but there was no need to reveal my plans this early. I would have done better to play 22...♗e7. Then White has more to think about, as ...f6-f5 is another interesting option.

23 ♗g3 ♗e7

24 ♘f1 (D)

Marić decides to use the knight to defend the kingside. The alternative, 24 bxc5 ♘xc5 25 ♘b3 ♘xb3 26 ♖xb3 g4 27 fxg4 hxg4, looks promising for Black.

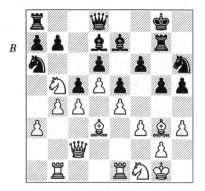

For a while I thought that 24...g4 was indicated, for instance 25 fxg4 hxg4 26 ♕d2 (better than 26 ♔h2 gxh3 27 gxh3 ♕c8) 26...♘f7 27 hxg4 ♗xg4 28 ♖b3 but I realized in time that

White would be slightly better. The main defect is that Black has played the breakthrough when her pieces are not yet ready to join in the battle.

24 ...   ♕f8!

I really like this move. Now, the bishop is transferred to a more active position (b6 of all squares!) and the queen improves its position as well.

25 ♘e3   ♗d8
26 ♘f5?!

Not the right way to stop my counterplay. White should have played 26 ♘c3! cxb4 27 axb4 ♗b6 28 ♕b3 ♘c7, with a dynamic struggle ahead.

26 ...   ♘xf5
27 exf5   ♗b6
28 ♔f1   ♗e8?

My time to make a grave mistake! Instead of this rather modest move, I could have obtained a clear advantage with 28...cxb4 29 axb4 ♗xb5 30 cxb5 ♘c7 31 ♕b3 ♕e8. The weakness of White's pawn structure should be fatal.

29 ♘c3!   ♖c8
30 ♘e4   ♖gc7

What else? 30...cxb4 31 axb4 h4 32 ♗f2 ♗xf2 33 ♕xf2 favours White.

31 ♕d2   h4
32 ♗f2   ♕e7?

The situation on the board has changed all of a sudden: my opponent and I both have to adjust our plans. I can readily admit that I realized too late that I had, by fixing the pawn structure on the kingside, given up my attacking chances on that side of the board. But the change must have surprised my opponent as well, who had to find the right attacking plan with little time left. 32...♖g7 was indicated, to defend my king.

Following my actual move, while Alisa was in deep thought I spotted the murderous 33 f4!. I feverishly tried to find a defence for Black but there seems nothing better than 33...cxb4 34 fxg5. Black's pawn-cover has disappeared in front of her king and White has too many attacking options. I will leave the possibilities to the readers, but in my view Black has little to hope for. I was greatly relieved when I saw White's next move.

33 ♗e3

Relieved, I made my reply quickly:

33 ...   ♔f8

By now, I was fully alert because I realized only too well the danger I was still facing. With the text-move I attempt to move the king away from the danger zone, but I felt strongly that a loss was imminent. In my mind I was already thinking about what variation I would play with White in game eight.

34 b5   ♘b8 (D)
35 ♗xg5!? (!!)

A brave decision but risky in view of Alisa's shortage of time. The text-move is good and guarantees White the advantage, but it requires accurate follow-up moves. Had White wished to opt for safety, then 35 ♗f2 suggests itself. White can still wait a few more moves and simply reach the time control. It is difficult to see what Black can do in the meantime.

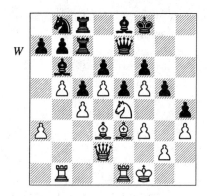

W

35	...	fxg5
36	f6	♕f7
37	♘xg5??	

White goes astray. She could have obtained a big advantage with 37 ♕xg5 ♕h5 (the only move because 37...♕g6 38 ♕d2! ♖d8 39 a4! ♖cd7 40 a5 ♗c7 41 b6 loses) 38 ♕xh5 (White's compensation is insufficient after 38 ♕d2 ♖d7) 38...♗xh5 39 ♘xd6 ♖d8 40 ♖xe5 ♖xd6 (40...♗xf3 41 ♗g6! wins instantly) 41 ♖xh5 ♘d7 42 ♖xh4 ♘xf6 43 f4. However, this was difficult to see with limited time.

| 37 | ... | ♕xf6 |
| 38 | ♘e6+ | |

38 ♘h7+ does not help either: 38...♖xh7 39 ♗xh7 ♘d7 40 ♗c2 ♔e7 41 ♖b3 ♗h5 42 ♖be3 ♖g8 is good for Black.

38	...	♔e7
39	♘xc7	♗xc7
40	♖e4	

40 ♖e3 might be better because after the text-move Black later gains a tempo with ...♗f5. But Black would also have the advantage in that case.

| 40 | ... | ♗d7 |
| 41 | ♖be1 | ♖g8 |

There is no need for Black to take risks with the seemingly attractive 41...♗xh3. It only leads to an unclear position if White plays the obvious 42 gxh3 ♕xf3+ 43 ♔g1 ♖g8+ 44 ♖g4 ♖xg4+ 45 hxg4 ♕xg4+ 46 ♕g2!.

| 42 | ♖1e2 (D) | |

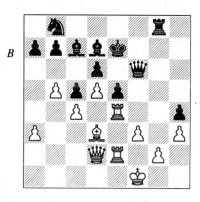

B

| 42 | ... | ♔d8 |

From now onwards I keep it simple. First the king goes into safety, then the dark-squared bishop and the knight will be activated.

43	♕e1	♖g3
44	♖f2	♔c8
45	♗b1	♗f5
46	♖ee2	♘d7
47	♗xf5	♕xf5
48	♖e4	♗d8
49	a4	♖g8

The position is lost for White. Her rooks have nowhere to go, as there are no open files. Black's minor pieces will decide the issue.

| 50 | ♖b2 | ♗g5 |

51	♕b1	♘f6	57	♕xf6	♖e8
52	♖e1	♕f4	58	♕f7	♔d8
53	♕d3	e4	59	♕f6+	♖e7
54	♕c3	♕h2	60	♕f8+	♔d7
55	♖f2	e3	61	♕f5+	♔c7
56	♖xe3	♗xe3			0-1

This game effectively ended the match (4½-2½) and now there would be no game eight after all. It is remarkable that I realized only after the match how lucky I had been in some games. Whenever I won, I always thought that I had played a reasonable game. It is possible that this is related to the suppression of negative thoughts during such a match. However, in retrospect, I feel that it would have been logical for Alisa to win the match if the middlegame positions that arose had taken their natural course.

One week later, the Beijing Open took place, which was to last for almost two weeks: eleven rounds plus two rest days. However, I was not able to participate. Immediately after the match with Alisa Marić I was sent to hospital, severely affected by a recurrent tonsillitis. The dry and hard March wind had broken down my last resistance. I developed a high fever and was put on an infusion with antibiotics straight away. I could not produce a sound for almost one week, and felt really sick. The only way by which I could still communicate was by nodding my head. Gradually my voice came back and I was very happy when I was discharged after a few days.

From my bed I had read the results of the Beijing Open in the newspapers, but consoled myself with the thought that I could, at least, participate in a closed tournament. This started some days later. It was the first international round-robin event in which I ever participated, about category nine or ten, and part of an Asian Grand Prix circuit. Most players came from the Philippines, Indonesia and China. However, I soon realized that I had not yet made a full recovery. It was not a surprise that my result was very modest. In fact, during most of 1991 I suffered from health problems and became a regular customer in hospital. I cannot say that I dealt with these problems in a sensible way. I never gave my body sufficient rest and, as soon as my body temperature had normalized, I rushed off to do everything as I had before.

6 My First World Championship Match (1991)

Two months prior to the World Championship Match I was invited to the Philippines to participate in an open tournament. It seemed an excellent idea to accept this invitation. A visit abroad was still a great experience for me, and now I also had the opportunity to get an impression of the country that would host the match with Maya. I got very excited during my first stay. The climate was wonderful and I noticed that the people were quite relaxed. Manila was full of Chinese restaurants, but it did not take long before I had discovered the seafood. For me, the daily trip to these seafood restaurants became one of the highlights of this visit. With regard to the chess tournament, the experience was less positive: it was one of my worst ever. I made a draw in round one but, thereafter, I continued to play badly. Only a handful of players had an international Elo rating and, as a result, I was paired every round against unrated players. The only reassuring thing about this was that I would not lose Elo points myself, but the final 'plus two' score was far from impressive.

After the tournament I went home to prepare for the World Championship Match. It was early days in the computer era and chess databases were not yet available to Chinese players. My seconds tried to find some games of Maya and this proved fairly easy. We set off and studied openings which occurred regularly in her games, but this did not prove to be an easy task. I was not even certain whether this would help me a great deal. Compared to Maya, my chess knowledge was minute and, even with thorough preparation, it would be impossible to rival her understanding of the modern openings. I would have to walk on thin ice if I wanted to surprise her. Here, I can only repeat what I have said several times before: lack of knowledge can be an advantage in practical play. Newcomers have no fear because they do not know what variations to be afraid of. In any case, it was clear that I was considered the underdog by many, for good reason. Altogether, I had played one serious match, against Marić, and not more than five international tournaments, the Olympiads excluded. But I, for one, believed in my chances. When two players play a match, I said naïvely to myself, they both have a 50% chance of winning. Maya would have to beat me first.

In the meantime, it was clear that chess was getting more popular in China. The media started to consider it a true sport and journalists became anxious to know how my preparation was going. I cannot say that I thought much of this attention at first, although I could not ignore the fact that so many people were following my steps. Unconsciously, I started to feel the pressure of the approaching World Championship Match. I realized this because, from time to time, I even got a bit nervous about it.

One month prior to the match, I received special permission to play in the 'male' National Championship. But fate struck once more. On holiday, outside Beijing with some officials and friends, I developed a high fever again. Instead of playing the National Championship I was sent to a resort to recover. I stayed there for about three weeks, not the ideal preparation for such an important match. However, it had one positive side: finally I could escape from intrusive journalists and from the pressure before the match. September was nearing and I got better again. There was a bit of panic when the fever returned just before the departure to Manila, but luckily it subsided just as quickly.

I got a feeling of familiarity when we entered Manila airport for the second time within two months. The Chinese delegation consisted of six members and included a team leader and his assistant, a medical doctor, two seconds and myself. Two journalists travelled with us to report back the latest news to the home front. The reception was heart-warming. At the airport, we were treated like real VIPs and we did not have to clear customs. The organizers had arranged limousines for our transport to the hotel, complete with an escort of policemen on motorbikes. It was a truly amazing sight, driving through the Manila night surrounded by flashing blue lights.

The World Championship Match was organized by the Philippine Sports Committee in collaboration with the City of Manila. It had been a long time since any non-Soviet player had challenged the World Champion and the Ladies' Match had almost never been played outside the Soviet Union. Therefore, this match was really important for Asian chess, especially with one participant from Asia itself. Nevertheless, the organizers and chess officials did their best to stay neutral and were anxious to assure identical conditions for both players. For instance, the hotel rooms were identical in size and positioned at two ends of the same floor. Believe it or not, even the allocated bodyguards looked alike.

The first game of the World Championship Match was also my very first game against Maya Chiburdanidze. It is difficult to voice my feelings at the start of this game. Prior to the match, I often told myself that my opponent was already World Champion at the age when I got my first international rating. It is easy to imagine that my mind was filled with mixed emotions. Maya was the better and also the more experienced player, while my primary weapon was my youthful enthusiasm. I got off to a good start in the match.

Game 11
Xie Jun – Maya Chiburdanidze
World Ch Match (1), Manila 1991
Ruy Lopez, Berlin

1	e4	e5
2	♘f3	♘c6
3	♗b5	♘f6
4	0-0	♘xe4
5	d4	♘d6
6	♗xc6	dxc6
7	dxe5	♘f5 (D)

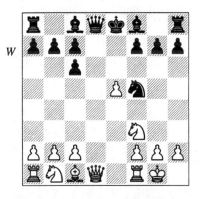

I had studied this line before and knew some of its theory, but had never played against it in a real game.

8	♕xd8+	♔xd8
9	b3	

Here, I wanted to play something safe. More often, White will choose between 9 ♖d1+ and 9 ♘c3, the latter as in the game Timman-Gelfand, Tilburg 1990. After 9 ♘c3 ♗e6 10 b3 ♗b4 11 ♗b2 ♗xc3 12 ♗xc3 ♗d5 13 ♖ad1 ♔e7 14 ♗b4+ ♔e8 15 ♘d4

♘xd4 16 ♖xd4 a5 the position was about equal.

9	...	♔e8

9...a5!? seems to be the natural reaction against White's last move.

10	♗b2	

Of course. It would be inappropriate to advance the c-pawn. Following 10 c4 a5 11 ♘c3 ♗b4 12 ♗b2, 12...h6 lets White keep a minimal advantage by 13 ♖fd1 ♗e6 14 ♘e4 a4 15 g4! (after 15 a3 ♗e7 Black is better) 15...♘e7 16 h3 ♘g6 17 ♘d4 a3 18 ♗c3 ♗xc3 19 ♘xc3 ♔e7 20 ♘ce2 c5 (and not 20...♘xe5? 21 f4) 21 ♘b5, but instead Black equalizes easily with 12...♗xc3! 13 ♗xc3 a4.

10	...	a5
11	♘c3	♗e6
12	♖fd1	♗e7
13	h3	

The pawn-push on the kingside has to be prepared carefully: 13 g4?! ♘h4 14 ♘xh4 ♗xh4 15 h3 h5 16 f3 hxg4 17 hxg4 ♗g5 gives Black the better game.

13	...	h5 (D)
14	a4?!	

A suspect plan. It was correct to transfer the knight to a more active square with 14 ♘e2. In that case, 14...c5?! is dubious on account of 15

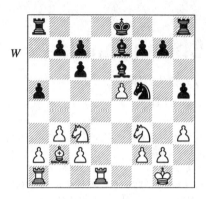

♘f4 ♖h6 16 c4. If Black continues with the standard plan 14...a4 15 ♘ed4 a3, then White has a choice between two promising possibilities: 16 ♘xe6!? fxe6 (16...axb2? 17 ♘xc7+ ♔f8 18 ♘xa8 wins) 17 ♗c1 ♖d8 18 ♗g5 ♗xg5 19 ♘xg5 ♔e7 20 c4, or 16 ♗c3 ♗d7 17 ♘xf5 ♗xf5 18 ♘d4 ♗d7 19 f4.

14 ...   f6!

Attacking the centre and complicating the position. Maya certainly knew how to make life difficult for her young rival. During the game I felt just like a pupil undergoing an examination. But I guess that, at this point in time, the things that bothered me came mostly from my inner self. I still had to adjust to the psychological strains of such a match. The text-move is more interesting and demanding than 14...♖d8 15 ♘e2 ♗c5 16 ♘fd4 ♘xd4 17 ♗xd4 ♗xd4 18 ♘xd4 ♔e7 19 f4 c5, when the position is simplified and it is hard to say who is better.

15 ♘e2   ♗d5
16 ♘e1!

Played with the right idea of moving the knight to better places. Also, the text-move opens the possibility, again, of pushing the g-pawn. In this first game, it was tempting to go for the simplifying line 16 ♘fd4 ♘xd4 17 ♗xd4 ♔f7 18 ♘f4 ♖ad8 19 exf6 ♗xf6 20 ♗xf6 ♔xf6 21 ♘xd5+, which leads to a likely draw. However, 16 ♘e1 is stronger.

16 ...   ♔f7
17 ♘f4   ♖ad8 (D)

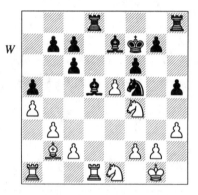

18 c4?!

But this is the wrong follow-up. Now, having studied a number of games in this variation, I realize that White should have been more patient here and waited for the right moment to make firm decisions. Therefore, 18 ♘ed3 is more accurate, giving Black an awkward choice. A satisfactory solution is not easy to find, because 18...g5 19 ♘xd5 cxd5 20 ♖e1 favours White.

18 ...   ♗e6
19 ♘f3   ♗c8!?

One of the reasons for me to return the knight to f3 was the line 19...罩xd1+ 20 罩xd1 g5? 21 exf6 兔xf6 22 ②xg5+! 兔xg5 23 ②xe6, winning, but of course Maya had spotted this too.

20 罩e1?!

It was much better to give up the d-file with 20 罩xd8 罩xd8 (20...兔xd8 21 罩e1 兔e7 22 e6+ forces Black back to the bottom rank) 21 兔c3 b6 22 ②xh5 罩d3 23 罩c1 and Black's compensation for the pawn is nebulous.

20	...	g5!
21	e6+	含e8
22	②g6	罩g8
23	②xe7	含xe7
24	g4	

The logical consequence. There was, however, little choice since the alternatives favour Black. Not much can be expected from 24 罩e2 g4 25 hxg4 罩xg4, but White also has serious problems to solve after 24 兔a3+ 含e8 25 罩a2 罩d3 26 ②d2 罩g6 (better than 26...b6 27 c5!) 27 罩b2 ②d4.

| 24 | ... | hxg4 |
| 25 | hxg4 | ②g7 |

25...罩d3? would be a serious mistake because of 26 ②e5! (and not 26 含g2 ②h4+ 27 ②xh4 gxh4, nor 26 gxf5 罩xf3 with a big advantage for Black) 26...罩xb3 27 gxf5 (Black dominates after 27 兔a3+? 罩xa3 28 罩xa3 ②d4) 27...罩xb2 28 ②g6+ 含e8 29 罩ad1 and Black cannot defend any more.

26 ②d4?

White should have gone for 26 兔a3+ 含e8 27 e7 罩d3 28 罩ad1 罩xd1

29 罩xd1 兔d7 30 兔b2 含xe7 31 兔xf6+ 含xf6 32 罩xd7 ②e6 with equality.

26	...	c5!
27	②f5+	②xf5
28	gxf5 (D)	

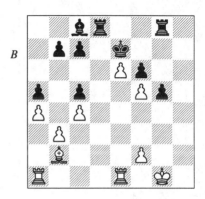

By now, I was quite satisfied with my pawn formation, which limits the activity of Black's bishop – and the e-pawn is not far from queening as well! It was not until Maya made her next move that, all of a sudden, I realized that I was in trouble. All my 'glorious' centre pawns are on light squares, which implies that I have great difficulty defending them.

| 28 | ... | 罩h8 |
| 29 | 含g2 | b6 |

White can defend after 29...罩d3?! 30 罩e3 罩xe3 31 fxe3 b6 32 含g3 罩h4 33 罩d1.

30	罩ad1	罩dg8!
31	含g3	罩h4
32	罩h1	罩gh8
33	罩xh4	gxh4+

A major decision, but what else can Black do? There is no way for her to

make progress after 33...♖xh4 (with the
idea of 34...♖f4) 34 ♖d3 ♖f4 (34...♖h1
35 ♔g4 ♖b1 36 ♗c3) 35 ♖f3.

    34 ♔h3   ♖h5 (D)

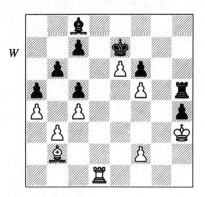

    35 ♖d5!
    The only defence; 35 ♔g4 is very
bad due to 35...♖g5+ 36 ♔f4 h3 37
♖h1 ♖g2.

    35 ...   c6
    36 ♗xf6+!
    This drawing combination is only
possible because the pawns are ad-
vanced enough.

    36 ...   ♔xf6
    37 ♖d8   ♖xf5
    Best. White avoids more tricky
variations such as 37...♗b7 38 ♖f8+
♔e7 39 ♖f7+ ♔e8 40 ♖xb7 ♖xf5 41
♖xb6 and 37...♗xe6 38 fxe6 ♔xe6 39
♖b8, which give some unnecessary
chances to White.

    38 ♖xc8   ♖f3+
    39 ♔xh4   ♖xb3
    40 ♖xc6   ♖b4
    41 ♔g3
    Here a draw was agreed in view of
the line 41...♖xc4 (or 41...♖xa4) 42 f4
♖e4!.

                          ½-½

    I could breathe again, and had passed the first examination. I have never asked
Maya what her feeling was when she played the first game against Nona Gaprindashvili. It may have been completely different. At last, the match had started.
After a bloodless draw in game two, the strange feeling of a special match had
gone and, for the first time, I could sit down and concentrate fully on chess. I was
the first one to strike a blow in game three.

Game 12

Xie Jun – Maya Chiburdanidze

World Ch Match (3), Manila 1991
Ruy Lopez, Chigorin

1	e4	e5
2	♘f3	♘c6
3	♗b5	a6
4	♗a4	♘f6

I was pleased to see a main-line Ruy Lopez, instead of an unfamiliar line, bearing in mind that my chess knowledge was still very limited. On the other hand, the opening play did not really bother me too much: if you do not know something, you often play without fear.

5	0-0	♗e7
6	♖e1	b5
7	♗b3	d6
8	c3	0-0
9	h3	♘a5
10	♗c2	c5
11	d4	♗b7
12	♘bd2	cxd4
13	cxd4	exd4
14	♘xd4	♖e8 *(D)*

Up to now, both players had made their moves almost without thinking as these moves had appeared numerous times in other games. I spent quite some time contemplating my next move. White has the choice between several candidate moves, for example 15 b3, 15 ♘f1 and 15 a4.

15 b4

Without any doubt the most critical

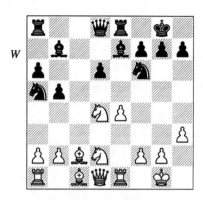

line. Pushing the pawn to b4 could bring problems to White later on, because it makes Black's counterplay on the queenside easier. But I judged that, in the meantime, White gains one important tempo and can dictate the course of the game during the next few moves.

15	...	♘c6
16	♘xc6	♗xc6
17	♗b2	♗f8?

It is hard to believe that this normal bishop move will bring Black quickly into a difficult position. One of the advocates of this particular line is Oleg Romanishin. See here how he solves Black's opening problems: 17...♖c8 18 a3 ♘d7 19 ♘f1 ♗f6 20 ♗xf6 ♕xf6 21 ♘e3 ♘e5, equalizing in Kotronias-Romanishin, Moscow 1989, and

17...♘d7 18 ♘b3 ♗f6 19 ♗xf6 ♕xf6 20 ♘d4 ♘e5 21 ♘xc6 ♘xc6 22 ♕d2 ♖ac8 23 ♗b3 ♘d4 and, again, Black had no difficulties in Popović-Roman-ishin, Novy Smokovec 1992. The latter game soon ended in a draw.

18 ♕f3!

An excellent position for the queen. White utilises the fact that Black has deprived herself of the freeing ma-noeuvre ...♘d7 and ...♗f6. The black position comes gradually under pres-sure.

18 ... ♖c8
19 ♗b3 (D)

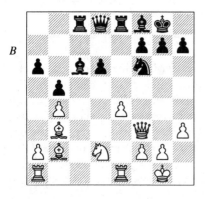

19 ... ♕e7?

This strikes me as too slow; 19...d5 is a better move. Still, it may not be the perfect moment for this pawn move as Black's pieces do not seem to cooper-ate very well. On the other hand, Black can hope for counterplay, or at least to defuse the attack. In a few moves' time this chance will be gone. Let us look at some variations: 20 ♗xf6 is the solid continuation, giving White a tangible endgame advantage after 20...♕xf6 21 ♕xf6 gxf6 22 exd5 ♖xe1+ 23 ♖xe1 ♗xb4 24 dxc6 ♗xd2 25 ♖e7 (or 25 ♖e2 ♗c3 26 ♗d5 with a slight advan-tage) 25...♖xc6 26 ♖xf7 ♔h8 27 ♔f1. White has the better pawn structure and the king will march to the centre – Black faces a difficult afternoon. It is even possible that more is to be gained from 20 e5 ♗xb4 21 exf6 ♖xe1+ 22 ♖xe1 ♗xd2 23 ♖d1 ♗h6 24 fxg7 ♕h4 25 ♕f5 with ongoing complications. After all these years, I am not sure any more which move I would have pre-ferred but a kingside attack has always appealed to me.

20 ♖ad1 ♗b7
21 ♕f5 d5?

Not the best timing, but Black is worse in any case. After 21...♘d7 22 ♘f3 g6 23 ♕f4 ♘b6 24 ♗f6, it is un-likely that Black's position can endure the pressure much longer. 21...♕d7 is another idea but 22 ♕f4 poses the same question: what are the right squares for the black pieces?

22 e5 ♘d7
23 ♘e4 (D)

The tension has reached its climax. It is easy to see how Black can go wrong, e.g. 23...dxe4? 24 ♖xd7 loses straight away and 23...♕xb4? 24 ♘g5 (24 ♕xd7 ♖e7 25 ♕d6 seems simple enough) 24...♘f6 25 ♖e3 h6 26 exf6 hxg5 27 fxg7 ♗xg7 28 ♕xg5 leaves no hope either. The only option was 23...♕e6 24 ♕f4 ♗xb4, when a com-plex situation has arisen. White can play for material equality with 25 ♘g5

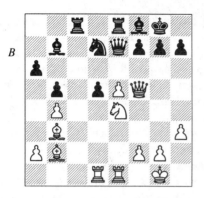

B

♕g6 26 ♕xb4 ♕xg5 27 ♗xd5, but it seems that Black can defend successfully. However, this line can be improved by the prosaic 25 ♖e3, with ideas of ♖g3 and ♘g5. White will

generate a massive attack, having invested only one little pawn.

23 ...   g6?

Now, any rescue attempt is in vain.

24 ♕xd7!   dxe4
25 e6!   fxe6

25...f5 fails to 26 ♕d4 (certainly not 26 ♕xb7? since 26...♕xb7 27 e7+ ♖c4! blocks the diagonal) 26...♗g7 27 ♕xg7+ ♕xg7 28 ♗xg7 ♔xg7 29 ♖d7+ losing a piece.

26 ♕d4   ♔f7
27 ♕h8   ♕h4
28 g3

Now, 28...♕xh3 29 ♕f6+ ♔g8 30 ♖d7 leads to mate, so Black resigned.

1-0

The sketchy idea that it would be an easy match lasted only until Maya levelled the score in the next game. In the beginning of this fourth game I missed a chance to obtain an advantage. As it happened, Maya played well in the complicated position that ensued but could not deliver the final punch. Even though she kept control, I managed to escape into a pawn-down rook and bishop ending, which was defensible, as I found out later. However, I could not save the game, possibly because I *thought* that the position was already lost. I had resigned in my mind and simply did not work any more to find a last line of defence. Lack of discipline or inexperience, whatever the cause, I felt very unhappy with my defensive performance.

Few people have ever heard that the World Championship Match almost came to a premature end on the rest day after round four. I was still not feeling all that happy and decided to unwind at the swimming pool. My doctor was present, and so were my second Ye and the head of our Chinese delegation. The three of them were standing at the opposite side of the pool, while I entered the water to relax. I could not swim at the time – nowadays I can – and stayed in the shallow part of the pool. The sun was burning and I heard the three men talking in the background. Then, I suddenly realized that the current in the pool was drawing my legs towards the deep end. I tried to resist but to little avail. Once my legs had crossed the edge, where the bottom takes a steep dive downwards, there was no support any more and I went deeper and deeper into the water. It all happened so quickly that I forgot to scream for help, busy as I was to keep my head out of the water. In fact, the last thing I heard before I went under was a far cry from my doctor, who saw me disappearing in the distance. Within moments, several people jumped into the water and dragged me out of the pool. Just in time... The story had a happy end, yet the head of our delegation no longer allowed me to go near the swimming pool without an escort. It would have made fantastic headlines in the newspapers, I suppose, but I had such a fright!

Back to the match. I knew that after my first loss the next game would be more difficult and, indeed, I lost the fifth game without putting up much resistance. After this round, my coaches decided to make use of the privilege of taking a rest day. I did not deem it necessary and was very eager to make up for the negative score. I wanted to forget these games as quickly as possible and get on with the job, rather than think about it for too long. But if you lose two games in a row, you need to recover. My trainers were right. So it came to game six, in which I played badly at some point but Maya did not take advantage and I managed to draw. This was an important game and I feel that Maya made a mistake by letting me off the hook. She still had a minute advantage when a draw was agreed after 24 moves and, therefore, she should have played on. A long game, with an unpleasant defensive task, would have put more pressure on me. Now I had time to recover.

The seventh game ended in a draw as well and Maya maintained her lead, with 4-3. She was quite happy and seemed in full control. Moreover, the FIDE rules stated that the reigning World Champion would retain her title in case of an 8-8 result. This meant that I needed at least two more wins – with no losses – to get in an advantageous situation. I decided that there was not much time left for action. White or Black, I would have to take my chances in every game.

Game 13

Maya Chiburdanidze – Xie Jun

World Ch Match (8), Manila 1991
Ruy Lopez, Anti-Marshall

1	e4	e5		8	...	d6
2	♘f3	♘c6		9	c3	♘a5
3	♗b5	a6		10	♗c2	c5
4	♗a4	♘f6		11	♘bd2	♘c6
5	0-0	♗e7		12	♘f1	♖e8
6	♖e1	b5		13	h3	♗b7
7	♗b3	0-0				
8	d3 *(D)*					

Maya was not interested in checking my preparation against 8 c3. Would I really have played 8...d5? I do not like to reveal the answer here, but it takes a brave player as White to take that risk and enter the complications of the Marshall. In the second match game, Maya avoided the Ruy Lopez altogether and played the Scotch instead. Towards the end of the match she switched to 1 d4.

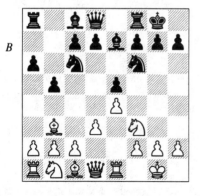

In game four of the match I had played 13...h6. I managed to get a good position but spoiled everything with one hideous blunder. In this game, I decided to change the move-order a little bit.

14	♘g3	♗f8
15	♘f5	

I doubt whether the pawn push to d4 leads to any advantage. A possible continuation could be 15 d4 cxd4 16 cxd4 exd4 17 ♘xd4 ♘xd4 18 ♕xd4 ♖c8 19 ♗b3 d5 20 e5 ♘e4 21 ♘xe4 dxe4 22 ♗e3 ♕xd4 (also possible is 22...♕c7 23 e6 fxe6 24 ♖ac1 ♕e7 25 ♕b6, as in Shamkovich-Lev, Holon 1986, when Black seems OK) 23 ♗xd4 ♗c5 24 ♖ad1 ♗xd4 25 ♖xd4 ♖cd8 26 ♖ed1 ♖xd4 27 ♖xd4 ♔f8 and the position is equal.

15	...	♘e7
16	♘xe7+	♗xe7 *(D)*

It is evident that the opening stage has been successful for Black, who has no problems whatsoever.

17 a4

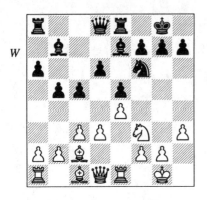

17 d4 exd4 18 cxd4 cxd4 19 ♕xd4 d5 20 e5 ♘e4 is unclear.

17 ...　　　　♗f8

The prophylactic 17...h6!? 18 axb5 axb5 19 ♖xa8 ♗xa8 20 ♗b3 ♗f8 21 ♗d2 seems to lead unavoidably to a draw. With the text-move I attempt to keep my options open.

18 ♗g5

This was to be expected. However, it seems more accurate to go for the exchange 18 axb5 axb5 19 ♖xa8 ♗xa8 20 ♗g5 h6 21 ♗h4 ♗e7 22 d4 cxd4 (Black should retain the centre pawns, as 22...exd4 23 cxd4 cxd4 24 ♕xd4 ♕c7 25 ♕d3 gives White a small edge) 23 cxd4 ♕c7 and the position becomes boring. It is conceivable that Maya tried to avoid simplifications as well, but it is no longer the position to do so.

18 ...　　　　h6
19 ♗h4!?　　　♗e7
20 d4

The last chance to simplify was 20 axb5 axb5 21 ♖xa8 ♗xa8 22 ♗b3 ♗b7 23 ♗a2 ♕d7, with a likely draw.

20 ...　　　　♕c7
21 dxe5　　　dxe5
22 ♕e2　　　c4!
23 ♖ed1　　　♕c5

If Maya had known that it was not to be her lucky day, she would now surely have opted for the line 24 ♗g3 ♗d6 25 ♗h4 ♘h5 (White has no reason to avoid a repetition of moves after 25...♗e7) 26 ♕d2 ♗c7 27 axb5 axb5 28 ♖xa8 ♖xa8 29 ♕d7 ♘f4 but Black is doing well here.

24 ♘h2?! (D)

24 axb5 would lead to a game which is easy to play for both sides.

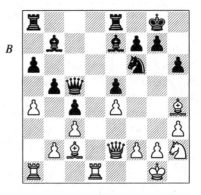

Now at last I had my chance to sharpen the game.

24 ...　　　　b4!

I was encouraged by the fact that the static equilibrium had disappeared for good.

25 cxb4　　　♕xb4
26 ♘f3

White plays the 'normal' move. However, during the game I felt that 26 ♖ab1! would be more astute. If

Black plays 26...♖ab8, White will gain some initiative after 27 ♘f3 ♘h5 28 ♗xe7 ♕xe7 29 b4 cxb3 30 ♗xb3 ♘f4 31 ♕e3. Of course, this variation is not forced and Black has many alternatives along the way.

26	...	♘h5
27	♗xe7	♕xe7!?
28	g3	

Was it possible for Maya to take the c4-pawn? Probably yes, I would say, although she has to play with care. Black soon takes the initiative because 28 ♕xc4 ♖ac8 (28...♖ec8 29 ♕e2 ♘f4 30 ♕d2 is less clear) 29 ♕b3 ♘f4 30 ♖d2 ♖c7 31 ♖ad1 ♖ec8 32 ♔h1 a5 33 ♗b1 ♗c6 gives ample compensation in return for the investment of a single pawn.

28	...	♕e6
29	♔h2	♘f6
30	♖a3	

I am not sure how to assess the position after 30 ♖ac1 a5 31 ♗b1 ♗a6 32 ♕d2 ♖ab8 though Black seems more active.

| 30 | ... | a5 |
| 31 | ♖e3 | ♗c8 |

With this move the balance starts to tip in Black's favour. The attack on h3 forces White to retreat.

| 32 | ♕f1 | |

Worse would be 32 ♘g1 ♗a6 33 ♖c3 ♖ab8 34 ♖b1 ♖b4 35 ♗d1 ♘d7 and Black has a firm grip on the position.

| 32 | ... | ♖b8 |
| 33 | ♖b1 | ♗a6 |

The alternative 33...♖b4 34 b3 ♗a6 35 bxc4 ♗xc4 36 ♕c1 ♖eb8 37 ♘d2

♗a6 gives Black the upper hand as well, but the advantage seems minimal.

34	♕e1	♖b4
35	b3	♖eb8
36	bxc4	♘d7! (D)

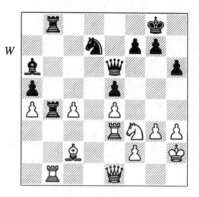

In return for the sacrificed pawn, Black has targets on a4, c4 and e4. In addition, every black piece is more active than its white counterpart. Black has acquired a huge advantage but the situation remains tense for a while.

| 37 | ♖eb3 | |

37 ♖xb4 axb4 38 ♘d2 ♘c5 39 ♕e2 ♖d8 40 a5 ♖d4 leaves White without a constructive plan and Black can reinforce her position at will.

| 37 | ... | ♕xc4 |

The appropriate way to maintain the pressure. Black would give everything away with 37...♖xb3? 38 ♖xb3 ♕xc4 39 ♖c3, when White equalizes.

| 38 | ♖xb4?! | |

Not convincing but White had an awkward choice. I do believe that Black should ultimately win the ending after 38 ♗d3 ♖xb3 39 ♗xc4 ♖xb1, but the technical task seems far from easy. 38 ♕d1 seems the most stubborn defence. Black stays in command with 38...♕c5 39 ♕d2 (39 ♖e3 ♖xb1 40 ♗xb1 ♖b2 41 ♔g1 ♘b6 makes life easier for Black) 39...♗c4 (interesting is 39...♖c8!? 40 ♖xb4 axb4 41 ♗d1 ♘f6 hoping for 42 ♖xb4 ♗e2!) 40 ♖xb4 ♖xb4 41 ♖xb4 axb4 42 ♔g2 ♘f6 43 ♕d1 ♗e6. Black can combine the threat of advancing the b-pawn with possible attacks on the king. I suspect that White's position will soon crack under the pressure.

38   ...   axb4

I made up my mind to keep rooks and trade queens instead. I am not quite sure whether this decision was correct. Black has a most promising position after 38...♖xb4 39 ♖xb4 axb4 40 ♕d1 ♕c3 41 ♔g2 ♘c5.

39   ♗b3   ♕d3!? (D)

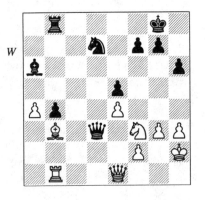

40   ♕d1?!

I had expected the logical 40 ♔g2 ♗b7 (White can play for a win after

40...♘c5?? 41 ♗xf7+ followed by 42 ♘xe5) 41 ♗d5 ♗xd5 42 exd5 e4 43 ♘h2 ♕xd5 44 ♖xb4 ♖xb4 45 ♕xb4 e3+ 46 ♘f3 ♕a2 47 ♕e1 exf2 48 ♕xf2 ♕xa4, when Black is a clear pawn up. Is it enough for a win? It goes without saying that I would have tried to reach the adjournment without changing the position too much. That would be a nice assignment for my seconds to spend the night with!

40	...	♕xd1
41	♖xd1	♘c5
42	♖b1	♗d3
43	♖b2	♗xe4
44	♘xe5	♘xb3

Necessary in order to remove blockade number one.

45	♖xb3	♗d5
46	♖b2	

46 ♖d3 b3 47 ♖xd5 b2 48 ♖d1 b1♕ 49 ♖xb1 ♖xb1 offers White no hope of survival.

46	...	b3
47	♘d3	

White's remaining forces concentrate on the blockade on the b2-square. It will not be easy to clear that second blockade, so I should have acted very swiftly here. The only winning plan consists of 47...♖a8 48 ♘c5 and now 48...f6 49 ♖b1 ♖b8, e.g. 50 ♘a6 ♖b6 51 ♘c5 ♗c4 52 f4 b2 53 a5 ♖b5 54 ♘a4 ♗b3! 55 ♘c3 ♗c2 and Black wins. This is a line which I should have been able to calculate, with some effort, but I did not realized that time was so dear. So I played the unforgivable...

47 ...   f6? *(D)*
...squandering a vital tempo.

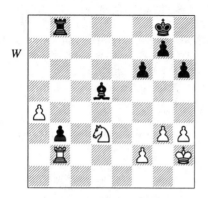

After the game I went up to my seconds, Ye Jiangchuan and Qi Jingxuan, and my mood was excellent. I was actually waiting for them to compliment me on a well-played game, but without hesitation they showed the following moves to me: 48 a5! ♗c4 49 ♘c1 ♖a8 50 ♖b1!!. I was shocked. It can be seen easily that Black has nothing better than to agree to an immediate draw with 50...♖xa5 51 ♘xb3 ♖b5 52 ♘d2.

48 g4??

Giving Black the chance to bail out with 48...♖a8! 49 ♘c5 ♖c8 50 ♘d3 ♗c4 51 ♘c1 ♗f7 52 ♘d3 ♖c3 53 ♖d2 ♖c4 54 ♘b2 ♖c2 55 ♖xc2 bxc2 56 ♘d3 ♗c4 57 ♘c1 (the ideal bishop versus knight position) 57...♔f7 58 ♔g3 ♔e6 59 h4 (or 59 ♔f4 g5+ 60 ♔e3 ♗f1 with good winning chances for Black) 59...♔e5 60 ♔f3 ♔d4. Black has a big advantage which seems enough for a win.

48 ...   ♗c4?? *(D)*

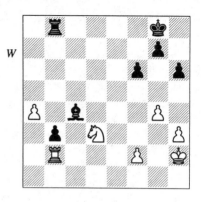

49 ♘c5??

49 ♘c1!!, with the very same idea, would save half a point again. White simply pushes the a-pawn, forcing Black to move the rook to the a-file. Then White continues ♖b1!! making ♘xb3 followed by ♘d2 possible. It is remarkable that both Maya and I missed this simple idea during the game.

49	...	♖c8
50	♘e4	♗d5
51	♘g3	♖a8

51...♖c2? 52 ♖xc2! bxc2 53 ♘e2 leads to the same lines as mentioned above (comments to White's 48th move) but the text is winning straight away.

52	♘e2	♖xa4

The game is over.

53	♘c3	♖a2!
54	♖b1	♖xf2+
55	♔g1	♖g2+
56	♔f1	♖h2

Finally, my opponent stopped her clock to resign.

0-1

The match score had been levelled at 4-4.

For the first time, I felt that I had played a good game. It is fair to say that this game definitely changed the character of the match. The general opinion was that I had a better chance now, also because my play seemed to have matured during the match. In all fairness, I had the feeling myself that Maya was not at her best throughout the match. The timing coincided with huge changes in the former Soviet Union, and many states were fighting for the right of independence. In Georgia, civil war had broken out and I cannot imagine that Maya ever had a peaceful mind. She was far away from home and only able to follow the latest developments in Georgia via CNN on the television in her room. Her situation was not enviable.

In the meantime, my team worked very well together and everybody was lending a helping hand. Almost all the team members stayed in the playing hall throughout the duration of the game, and the support made me feel really good. Maya had brought her mother, and Grandmasters Kuzmin and Tseshkovsky as her seconds. The latter two did not show up very often in the playing hall. This was not necessary, of course, because the game was televised live on one of the TV channels in the hotel. Maybe they wanted to follow the events in the Soviet Union as well, or preferred to work in quietude during the games. I could tell that Maya's team worked well together, though, because sometimes she changed her openings and surprised me with fresh ideas.

We made another two draws in the match and it got to 5-5. That was the moment when I knew that I could win this match. It is not easy to explain, but in such a match, there is at times a certain feeling between the players. Where I started to get filled with energy, I noticed that Maya began to get tired of the match. In any case, it did not come as a surprise to me that I won the next two games as White, and drew my game with the black pieces very comfortably.

I have made a deliberate choice to present game fourteen in this book. It is not a game of high quality, nor does it allow of extensive analysis, but it is by far the most dramatic game of the World Championship Match and also my most memorable one. The game shows two nervous players at work, with high stakes involved. I was in the lead with 7½-5½ and was determined not to lose. Nevertheless, I got a difficult position by move fifteen and a completely lost one five moves later. Then Maya stopped working and I again managed to escape with half a point. I am not sure whether a similar game has been seen in any previous World Championship Match, but I considered myself very lucky. Still, the special circumstances should not be underestimated. In the series of matches between Karpov and Kasparov, there were also numerous games that were marred by blunders. This simply happens when two players are under extreme pressure. In no way can such a game be compared with an ordinary tournament game. Yet, as the penultimate game of my first World Championship, I think that game fourteen deserves a place in this book, particularly in view of these 'special effects'. When you see this game you may wonder whether it was really played in a World Championship Match. The answer is: "Yes, and it was a decisive game!".

Game 14
Maya Chiburdanidze – Xie Jun
World Ch Match (14), Manila 1991
Fianchetto Grünfeld, ...c6

1	d4	♘f6
2	c4	g6
3	g3	

Maya chooses a quiet line this time. In game twelve she had played the Four Pawns Attack against my King's Indian set-up and that game ended in a draw. In all previous games she had tried 1 e4.

3	...	c6

If my memory is correct, this was the first time ever that I played a system with ...d5 rather than ...d6 – the answer of the die-hard King's Indian player.

4	♗g2	d5
5	♘f3	♗g7
6	0-0	0-0
7	♗f4 *(D)*	

A rare move and new to me. White usually chooses between 7 ♘c3 and 7 cxd5.

7	...	♘e4?!

Why did I not take the pawn on c4? Well, I would have loved to play 7...dxc4, which must be the best choice. But it was also clear that this had to be part of Maya's home preparation. Recently, I saw a number of interesting games with the position after 7 ♗f4, for instance 7...dxc4 8 ♕c1 b5 9 ♗h6 (that may have been the idea

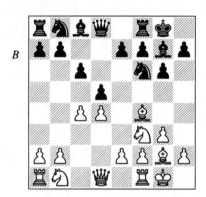

behind the pawn sacrifice) 9...♗b7 10 ♗xg7 ♔xg7 11 ♘c3 ♘bd7 12 e4 b4 13 e5 bxc3 14 exf6+ ♘xf6 15 ♕xc3 ♗a6 16 ♘e5 ♘d5 17 ♕a3, with an unclear position in Romanishin-Macieja, Koszalin 1997, which soon ended a draw. Another try is 7...♕b6 8 ♕c1 ♗f5 9 c5 ♕a6 10 ♘c3 b6 11 cxb6 axb6 12 ♗h6 ♘bd7 13 ♗xg7 ♔xg7 14 ♘h4 ♗e6 15 ♕d2 ♖fd8 16 h3 ♘e8, when Black had equalized in Romanishin-Gofshtein, Ischia 1996.

8	♘c3	♗f5
9	♕b3	

I had expected 9 cxd5 cxd5 10 ♘e5 but this may not be the ideal winning attempt for White.

9	...	♕b6!?

Here, I could not find any reasonable alternatives. The reason is that d5 is already under serious pressure. I rejected 9...♕d7 because of 10 ♖fc1 (the position after 10 ♘e5 ♗xe5 11 dxe5 dxc4 12 ♕xc4 ♘xc3 13 bxc3 ♖d8 is unclear) 10...dxc4 11 ♕xc4 ♘a6 12 ♘e5 with a big advantage to White.

10 cxd5 ♕xb3

10...♘xc3 11 bxc3 ♕xb3 12 axb3 cxd5 transposes to the game.

11 axb3 ♘xc3
12 bxc3 cxd5
13 ♘e5

The more cautious 13 ♘d2 ♖d8 14 ♗c7 ♖c8 15 ♗xb8 ♖axb8 gives Black enough counterplay.

13 ... ♖d8
14 ♖a5 (D)

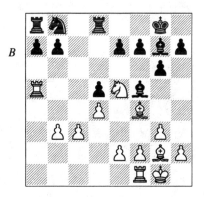

14 ... ♗e6

Now, 14...♗xe5 15 ♗xe5 ♘c6 16 ♖xd5 is impossible, but I should have gone for 14...e6. Of course, I saw this move, but, having completely overlooked White's move 14 ♖a5, I felt quite uncertain. Instead of taking my time to put my mind at ease, I lashed out with the text-move. 14...e6 also

leads to a slight plus for White, but Black keeps a solid position. Play could continue with 15 ♖b5 f6 16 ♘f3 ♖d7 17 ♘h4 (17...♗g4? is bad due to 18 f3 ♗h5 19 ♗h3 ♔f7 20 e4 dxe4 {20...g5? loses outright after 21 exd5 ♖xd5 22 ♗xe6+ ♔xe6 23 ♖e1+} 21 d5! and White is much better) 17...♘c6 18 ♘xf5 gxf5 19 ♖a1 ♖ad8. Black is not without counterplay and the position looks defensible.

15 ♖b5!

The rook moves are surprisingly strong. I counted on 15 c4 ♗xe5 16 dxe5 ♘c6 and Black retains a flexible position.

15 ... g5

I did not like the looks of 15...♗xe5 16 ♗xe5 ♖d7 17 c4 f6 18 ♗f4 and White has a large advantage. But the text-move also has its drawbacks.

16 ♗xg5

This is a good move, but 16 ♗e3 is even stronger. How is Black to cope with the numerous threats? I do not see a clear way out, for example 16...♘c6 (16...f6 17 ♘d3 b6 18 ♘b4 loses material, and so does 16...b6 17 c4) 17 ♖xb7 ♘xe5 18 dxe5 ♗xe5 19 ♖xe7 (better than 19 ♗xg5 ♖db8 20 ♖xb8+ ♖xb8). The endgame seems to offer no hope for Black.

16 ... f6
17 ♘f3 ♗d7

The only move: 17...fxg5 18 ♘xg5 ♗d7 19 ♗xd5+ e6 20 ♘xe6 would give White too much in return for her investment.

18 ♖xb7 fxg5

19 ♘xg5 (D)

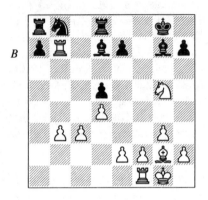

19 ... ♗c8

In such a position it is almost impossible to make a reasonable choice, especially when there are only bad, worse or worst moves. Such is the case here. The text-move is bad, but alternatives are no better either: 19...e6 20 ♗h3 ♖e8 21 ♖xd7 ♘xd7 22 ♗xe6+ ♖xe6 23 ♘xe6 and 19...♗c6 20 ♖c7 ♗f6 21 ♘e6, both with a large and almost winning advantage for White.

20 ♖b5?

Here, Maya simply missed 20 ♖xe7 ♗f6 21 ♘f7 ♖f8 (21...♗xe7 22 ♘xd8 ♗xd8 23 ♗xd5+ wins the rook on a8) 22 ♘h6+ ♔h8 23 ♖f7! (care is needed; White would lose her knight after 23 ♗xd5 ♗xe7 24 ♗xa8 ♔g7) 23...♘d7 24 ♗xd5 ♖b8 25 e4. Five pawns for a piece should guarantee the win.

20 ... e6
21 c4 ♗d7? (D)

Now, having had the opportunity to play ...e6, it is my turn to make a mistake again. Not a big surprise, since

the numerous liquidations inevitably take their toll on the ability to calculate. The first alternative was 21...♗f6, but this is inadequate due to 22 cxd5 a6 (22...♗a6 23 ♖a5 is very good for White) 23 ♖a5 ♖a7 24 ♘xe6 ♗xe6 25 dxe6 ♗xd4 26 ♖d5. In this line, White has four pawns for the piece, which would still yield some winning prospects. However, the saving move was 21...♗xd4, with the follow-up 22 cxd5 ♗a6 23 dxe6 ♗xb5 24 ♗xa8 ♗f6. White also has four pawns for the piece but there is an important difference compared to the previous line. In the latter case, both players have one more piece each and this favours Black. The knight is under siege, while Black has counterplay against e2. The situation is unclear.

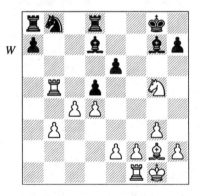

22 ♖b7

Very strong is 22 ♖xd5!! exd5 23 ♗xd5+ ♔f8 24 ♗xa8 ♗xd4 (24...h6 25 ♘f3 ♗g4 26 e3 ♘d7 27 ♗e4, followed by ♘d2, is good for White). At first I thought that Black was fine in this line, but White can take on h7 without problems: 25 ♘xh7+ ♚e7 26 ♗f3 ♗f5 27 ♘g5 ♘d7 28 e4 ♗g6 29 h4. The white pawns will soon come down like an avalanche.

22   ...   h6

I decided to drive the knight away from its dominant position. White still has an edge after 22...♗c8 23 ♖c7 ♘a6 24 ♖xc8!? ♖axc8 25 ♘xe6, yet 22...♘c6 looks worth considering.

23   ♘f3?

Maya misses the last chance for a real advantage. It was still possible to get a 'four-pawns-against-piece' position with 23 ♖xd7! ♘xd7 (23...♖xd7 24 ♘xe6 ♘c6 25 ♗xd5 ♖xd5 26 cxd5 ♘xd4 27 ♘xd4 ♗xd4 28 ♖d1 ♗b6 29 ♔g2 probably loses) 24 ♘xe6 dxc4 25 bxc4 ♖ac8 26 ♘xd8 ♖xd8 27 e3. The white pawns are difficult to block and Black is bound to lose the a-pawn as well.

23   ...   ♗c8

Now Black is OK again.

24   ♖b5   ♘c6

In view of the match situation – and the shaky course of this game – I should perhaps have repeated moves with 24...♗d7 25 ♖b7 ♗c8.

25   cxd5 (D)

Once more, I had to face too many choices. There are four serious candidate moves. One loses, one gives a big advantage to White, one equalizes and the last one gives a big advantage to Black. I chose the second best. Let us look at some lines. Variation one is 25...♘xd4? 26 ♘xd4 ♗xd4 27 d6 a6

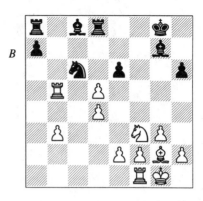

28 ♖b4 ♗c5 29 ♖g4+, winning, while 25...♖xd5 26 ♖xd5 exd5 27 ♘e5 ♘xd4 28 ♗xd5+ ♗e6 29 ♗xa8 ♖xe5 30 f4 leads to a large plus for White. Since the game leads to a fairly equal position, how then could Black have got an advantage? Well, the developing move 25...♗a6! would have been forceful. After 26 ♖c5 ♘xd4 27 ♘xd4 ♗xd4 28 ♖c6 ♗xe2 29 ♖e1 ♗b5 30 ♖cxe6 ♖f8, White can no longer defend the f2-pawn, and Black has good winning chances. Unfortunately, I missed this move and went instead for...

25   ...   exd5?
26   ♖a1   a6
27   e3

27 ♖c5 ♗b7 28 e3 ♖ac8 29 ♖ac1 ♘b4 30 ♖c7 ♗c6 should lead to a draw as well.

27   ...   axb5!
28   ♖xa8   ♗b7
29   ♖a1! (D)

At last, we have reached a roughly equal position. From now on, neither side made any serious errors.

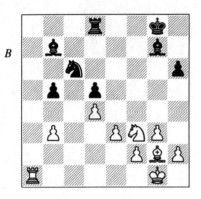

29	...	♗f8
30	♗f1	b4
31	♘d2	♔f7
32	♗d3	♔f6
33	♗b5	♖c8
34	♔f1	♘d8
35	♔e2	♗d6
36	♗d3	♖c3
37	♗b5	♔e7
38	♔d1	♗c8
39	♖a7+	♖c7
40	♖xc7+	♗xc7
41	♗e2	♘f7
42	h4	♘d6
43	♗d3	♗g4+

44	♔e1	♔f6
45	♔f1	♗h3+
46	♔g1	♗e6
47	♔g2	♔g7
48	♔f3	♗d8
49	♔g2	♘e4!
50	♘xe4	dxe4
51	♗c2	

It is important to keep the b3-pawn. White would be lost after 51 ♗xe4? ♗xb3.

51	...	♔f6
52	♗d1	♔e7
53	♔f1	♔d6
54	♔e1	♗h3
55	♗e2	♔e7
56	♔d2	♗c7
57	♔e1	♔f6
58	♗d1	♔f5
59	♗e2	♗g2
60	♗h5	♗f3
61	♗e8	

Here we agreed a draw.

½-½

I guess that the draw was justified. Neither player deserved more than half a point for her performance.

The next game was the fifteenth of the match. My lead of 8-6 meant that a draw would suffice to end the match and to replace the 'old queen'. The exact date was the 29th of October 1991, and the next day I would celebrate my 21st birthday. With this introduction, I need not explain any further how eager I was to do a good job on that particular day. I was ready for a complicated game but also ready to take a draw offer at any point in time. It would be fantastic to finish a nice job at the right moment, would it not?

Game 15

Xie Jun – Maya Chiburdanidze

World Ch Match (15), Manila 1991

Modern Defence, Classical

1 e4 g6

Again a clever choice from Maya. This kind of modern defence forces you to work on your own during the game. Besides, Black's position is flexible, with a lot of options. It was clear that Maya would fight for a win until the very end.

2 d4 ♗g7
3 ♘f3 d6
4 ♘c3 a6

The text-move introduces a line which is not seen very often.

5 a4

I decided to play safe. As I was in the lead, it would be my opponent who needed to seek winning chances, not me. Moreover, I was aware that the Pirc/Modern Defence used to be the main weapon of Georgian players. Therefore I wanted to avoid any risks and so prevented Black from playing ...b7-b5. The other line is 5 ♗e2, as in Khalifman-Popov, St Petersburg 1997. That game continued 5...b5 6 0-0 ♗b7 7 ♖e1 ♘d7 8 ♗g5 c5 9 a4 h6 10 ♗h4 cxd4 11 ♘xd4 ♕b6 12 ♘b3 ♗xc3 13 bxc3 ♘gf6 14 axb5 axb5 15 ♖xa8+ ♗xa8 16 ♘d4, with comfortable play for White.

5 ... b6
6 ♗c4 e6

7 0-0 ♘d7
8 h3 ♗b7
9 ♗e3

9 ♖e1 seems to be the normal continuation.

9 ... ♘e7
10 ♕d2 h6 *(D)*

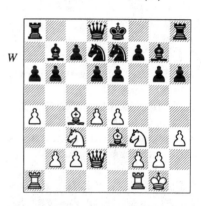

11 ♘h2

To be honest, I did not like this move so much. When I checked for similar games with my computer, I found, much to my surprise, a game Armas-Glek, Wijk aan Zee 1995, with exactly the same position but... with Black to move! That game had, of course, a different move-order: 1 e4 g6 2 d4 ♗g7 3 ♘c3 d6 4 ♘f3 ♘d7 5 ♗c4 e6 6 ♗g5 ♘e7 7 ♕d2 h6 8 ♗e3 a6 9 a4 b6 10 0-0 ♗b7 11 h3. From here onwards, it continued 11...c6 12 ♗b3 b5 13 d5 ♘c5 14 dxe6 ♘xe6 15 ♖ad1 ♘c8 16 ♗xe6 fxe6 17 ♗f4 b4 18 ♘e2 c5, with an unclear position. Black soon won the game.

11 ...   **♘f6**

12 ♗d3

Even this position has been played before, in Armas-Ivkov, French Team Ch 1991. White played 12 f3 h5 13 ♖ad1 c6! 14 ♕f2 b5 15 ♗b3 ♕c7 16 ♖fe1 ♘d7 17 axb5 axb5 18 ♘f1 0-0 19 g4 hxg4 20 hxg4 b4 21 ♘b1 c5, with a complex position.

12 ...   **♕d7**

After studying the above mentioned games, I almost believe that Black should play 12...c6 at this moment. Having thought about it for a bit longer, I guess that a good reply for White must then be 13 ♖a3!? b5 14 b4! ♖b8 15 axb5 axb5 16 ♖fa1. With the only open file under control, White should have the better chances.

13 ♖ad1

I could not decide upon an active plan, so I just put my pieces in the centre to await Black's intentions. Maybe it is better to play 13 ♘f3 instead, as it prevents any black pawn moves in the centre.

13 ...   **d5!** *(D)*

14 f3

I really like this move, which keeps the tension between the centre pawns. The alternative 14 e5 seems stronger, but after 14...♘e4 15 ♗xe4 dxe4 16 ♘g4 ♘f5 17 ♘f6+ ♗xf6 18 exf6 0-0-0 19 ♖fe1 e5! 20 dxe5 ♕e6 Black

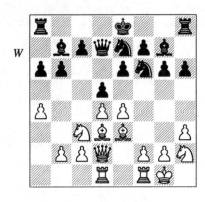

takes over the initiative and will dominate the centre.

14 ...   **♘h5**

15 ♕f2   **f5**

16 g4!

Born out of necessity, but it is in fact a strong reply. At first sight, it looks like 16 e5 is safer, but it turns out not to be so. It may lead to the variations 16...c5 17 f4 (17 dxc5 ♗xe5 18 ♗d4 ♗g3 seems unclear) 17...cxd4 18 ♗xd4 g5 19 fxg5 hxg5 20 ♘f3 ♘f4 21 ♘xg5 ♘eg6 and Black has adequate counterplay, or 16...0-0-0 17 f4 g5 18 fxg5 hxg5 19 ♗xg5 ♖dg8, with enough compensation for the pawn.

16 ...   **dxe4**

17 fxe4   **♘f6**

18 ♘f3!   **0-0-0**

The only move: 18...♘xe4 19 ♗xe4 ♗xe4 20 ♘xe4 fxe4 21 ♘e5 ♗xe5 22 ♕f7+ ♔d8 23 dxe5 is devastating.

19 ♘e5   **♕e8**

20 ♕e2   **♘xe4?!**

This gives White the opportunity to simplify. A better line for Black was 20...a5 21 exf5 gxf5. If White now tries to exchange the light-squared bishops, Black is first to grab the initiative: 22 ♗a6?! ♖g8 23 ♗xb7+ ♔xb7 24 ♔h2 fxg4 25 hxg4 h5. Hence, White should prefer 22 ♗c4 instead, with an open outcome.

21	♘xe4	fxe4
22	♗xa6	♗xe5
23	dxe5	♕xa4?!

Black should exchange rooks first. Unfortunately, Black has no possible winning attempt after 23...♖xd1 24 ♖xd1 ♕xa4 25 ♗b5 (White has other opportunities, of course, but 25 ♗b5 is good enough for a draw) 25...♕a5 26 ♗d2 ♕a2 27 ♗c1 ♕a5 (or 27...♔b8 28 ♕f1! ♗c8 29 ♕e2 ♗b7 30 ♕f1) 28 ♗d2. It is hard to see how Black can avoid the repetition of moves without taking major risks.

24	♗xb7+	♔xb7
25	♖a1	♕c6
26	♕a6+	♔b8 (D)

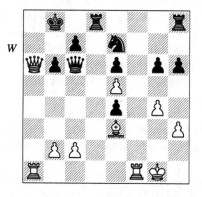

27 ♖f6?

I was probably concentrating too hard during this game, as I could hardly judge the consequences of this move. I must have been too excited that particular day. With nothing special on my mind, and with the use of more time, I would have fairly quickly found the move 27 ♕a7+. White simply gains the advantage after 27...♔c8 28 ♖f7 ♘d5 29 ♗xh6! with a promising ending, for example 29...♕b7 (29...♖xh6 30 ♕a8+ ♕xa8 31 ♖xa8+ ♔b7 32 ♖xd8 ♖xh3 33 ♖e8 yields excellent winning chances, as does 29...♕c5+ 30 ♔h1 ♕c6 31 ♕a8+ ♕xa8 32 ♖xa8+ ♔b7 33 ♖xd8 ♖xd8 34 ♖g7 e3 35 ♔g2 – White answers 35...♖f8 with 36 ♖xc7+ ♔xc7 37 ♗xf8) 30 ♕a8+ ♕xa8 31 ♖xa8+ ♔b7 32 ♖xd8 ♖xd8 33 ♗g5 (more convincing than 33 ♖g7 ♘b4 34 c3 ♘d3 35 ♖xg6 ♘xb2 36 ♖xe6 ♖d3 37 ♔g2 ♖xc3 38 ♖f6 and White is only slightly better) 33...♖a8 34 h4 ♖a1+ 35 ♔f2 ♖a2 36 h5 gxh5 37 gxh5 ♖xb2 38 h6 ♖xc2+ 39 ♔g3 ♖a2 40 ♖f8. It looks like the race ends in White's favour. Still, I think that all this would have been difficult to calculate under the circumstances. After the text-move, 27 ♖f6, the winning chances have gone, but it is still a draw.

| 27 | ... | ♕b7! |

Black defuses any possible liquidations involving ♕a7+ and ♕a8+.

28	♕xb7+	♔xb7
29	♖xe6	♘d5
30	♖e1	

30 ♔f2? would be a mistake since 30...♖df8+ 31 ♔e2 ♖f3 is very unpleasant for White.

30	...	♘xe3
31	♖xe3	♖d2
32	♖xe4	♖xc2
33	♖xg6	♖d8 (D)

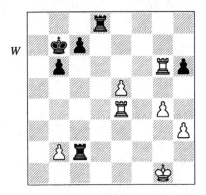

34 ♖e1

The defence with 34 ♖f6 ♖d1+ 35 ♖f1 ♖dd2 is less attractive, because White would have no active rook left. I thought it better to keep one rook available to support the march of my kingside pawns.

34	...	♖dd2
35	♖xh6	♖g2+
36	♔h1	♖h2+
37	♔g1	♖cg2+
38	♔f1	♖xb2
39	♔g1	♖hg2+
40	♔h1	b5
41	e6	♖ge2?!

This is very risky, even though the position remains within drawing margins. I am pretty sure that Maya did not believe in this move as a winning attempt, but she had to try to win at all costs. The correct move is, of course, 41...♖h2+ with a draw.

42	♖xe2	♖xe2
43	♖f6	b4
44	g5	b3
45	♖f1	c5

The alternative 45...♖xe6 46 ♖b1 ♖e3 47 g6 ♖g3 48 g7 draws straight away. Hence, Black sends her second pawn for assistance.

46	g6	♖xe6
47	g7 (D)	

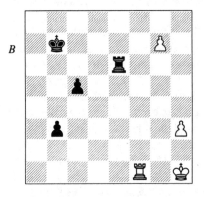

47 ...   ♖e8

After 47...♖g6, White has two ways to make a draw. The first one is the simple 48 ♖g1 b2 49 ♖b1 ♖xg7 50 ♖xb2+ ♔c6 51 ♔h2 and White continues with h4, ♔h3, h5, ♔h4, etc. The rook will be sacrificed on c1, keeping the black king as far away as possible. The second method is a little more complicated: 48 ♖f7+ ♔c8 49 ♖f8+ ♔c7 50 ♖f7+ (50 g8♕? ♖xg8 51 ♖xg8 b2 52 ♖g1 c4 wins for Black!) 50...♔c8 51 ♖f8+, with a draw. In the latter variation, it is important to see that Black's king cannot move to the sixth rank due to ♖f6+, nor can it approach the kingside. One example is 49...♔d7 50 g8♕ ♖xg8 51 ♖xg8 ♔c7 (51...c4 52 ♖b8 ♔e6 53 h4 ♔e5 54 h5 wins) 52 ♖g3 c4 53 ♖c3 and White wins.

48 h4

The last clear road to a draw was now 48...c4 (the only move) 49 h5 c3 50 h6 c2 51 h7 b2 52 g8♕ c1♕! *(D)* (certainly not 52...♖xg8? 53 hxg8♕ c1♕ 54 ♕d5+ ♔b6 55 ♕d3 followed by activation of the white king). A beautiful position has arisen on the board.

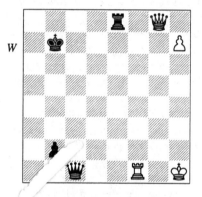

The situation is one of dynamic equilibrium! Neither player can play for a win. White will check the black king, starting with 53 ♕f7+, and Black has no way to avoid the perpetual check. I am not sure whether Maya saw this line right through to the end, but her move...

48 ...   ♖g8??

...lands Black in big trouble.

49 ♖g1   ♔c6

Also 49...c4 50 h5 b2 51 h6 c3 52 h7 ♖xg7 53 ♖xg7+ ♔b6 54 ♖g1 c2 55

h8♕ c1♕ 56 ♕d4+ ♔b5 57 ♕d3+ should win for White, although I would still have to overcome some technical problems.

50 h5   b2 *(D)*

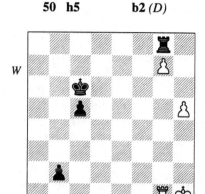

51 ♖b1??

I went for this move, right after I had confirmed at least a thousand times that it would end in a draw. If my brain had been tuned in to any other frequency than how to force the quickest draw, I would have found the line 51 h6! c4 52 ♔h2! c3 53 h7 ♖xg7 54 h8♕ ♖xg1 55 ♕xc3+. I am not sure that I would have accepted a draw offer in that position!

51	...	♖xg7
52	♖xb2	c4
53	h6	♖h7
54	♖h2	♔d5
55	♔g2	♔e4
56	♔f2	♔d3
57	♔e1	♔c3
58	♔e2	♔b3
59	♔e3	c3
60	♔f4	c2

61 Rxc2   Kxc2
62 Kg5

With no more chance to fight for a win, Maya reached out her hand to congratulate me for a good match.

½-½

She did not say much, but it must have been a difficult moment for her. And so, after a long and tiring match, I had become the Seventh World Champion. It was a beautiful present for my 21st birthday.

Real pandemonium broke out after I had won. Never before had an Asian player conquered the World Championship title, and never before had I seen so many happy faces together. The hotel lobby was filled with people and I could hardly move in the direction of my room. It seemed as if the whole City of Manila had turned out to thank me for bringing the title to Asia. And the excitement went on for several more days. Overseas Chinese organized parties, as far as I remember one party every day, and there seemed to be no end to the celebrations. The two journalists who had been with us all the time had already been incorporated into the delegation and rejoiced with us. They had been writing articles since our arrival in Manila and must have been happy, too, that the match was over. After the fifth game – I had just lost two games in a row – one of the journalists had asked the head of my delegation whether it was a good idea to pack his luggage. But now he counted himself lucky that he had made the right decision to stay.

It was a great pleasure that our delegation was invited to come to the Presidential Palace, to meet with President Corazon Aquino. She congratulated me passionately and I received a Medal of Honour from her in person. This is a sweet memory which I will never forget.

Almost two weeks later we returned to Beijing and the reception at the airport was just incredible. My parents had come to welcome me, and also Beijing's vice-mayor, the Head of our Sports Committee and some hundred journalists. I was invited to the City Hall for a further celebration, and I had to give a series of interviews and press conferences. I realized that some things had changed for good. Before the World Championship Match I simply played chess and received some attention, but not too much. Now I was in the limelight and whatever I said was noted and quoted. There was no way back.

A few weeks later I went to Germany to attend the FIDE congress, to which I was invited as the new World Champion. I was celebrated once more and can only remember that it was, again, an extremely hectic time. By the time I returned to China, I was really sick. And for the last time in 1991, I was sent to a hospital to recover.

7 Years of Development (1992-1993)

The next year was extremely difficult. I had to come to terms with my new status as World Champion. From one moment to the next, my life had changed completely and for a while I was not sure where I was or who I was. Before the match against Maya, my life was clearly structured. Now, chaos had set in and it was impossible for me to plan anything. My life had become a whirl of excitement and it took almost half a year before things had normalized. People had put me in a certain position and it was difficult to live up to expectations. In the meantime, I did not play a serious chess tournament for six months and did my very best to focus on other important activities. One of the things I could still hang on to was my course at the university. I had enrolled in 1991 and, between chess events, I stayed there whenever possible. The university had always given me excellent support, and had even arranged special teachers and class-mates to help me with my study. After the match, there was only time to study in the evenings and the weekends but I enjoyed it thoroughly. In terms of chess, I felt like hibernating all winter.

On the whole, 1991 was a big year for chess in China. I became the World Champion and three Chinese woman players qualified for the Candidates tournament. This confidence boost came at a fortunate moment, with the Manila Olympiad coming up soon thereafter. The Olympiad also went well for us. After ten rounds we were even in the lead by half a point. Alas, we failed to finish the job and lost in the last two rounds against Azerbaijan and Kazakhstan respectively. The gold medal went to Georgia, led by an inspired Maya Chiburdanidze, who scored 11½ out of 13. She had her sweet revenge for the Manila match by beating me in round five, although I should add that I ruined an advantageous position by blundering away a piece at move 23. In the final standings China finished in third place, half a point short of the Ukrainian team. I scored 10 out of 13 and received the bronze medal for my individual performance on board one. For all the disappointment, there was the consoling thought that this was probably the strongest Olympiad ever. Admittedly, the Hungarian squad was weakened by the absence of the Polgar sisters. This was amply compensated for, however, by the fact that a total of fourteen teams from newly independent republics of the former Soviet Union and Yugoslavia made their first appearance as FIDE members. It goes without saying that this had an enormous impact on the overall playing level.

Viewed in that light, bronze was not bad after all.

My life quietened down after the 1992 Manila Olympiad and I started to work on chess again. It was in this period that my playing level improved considerably. Until then, I had played quite technically and not too much for combinations. But by the end of 1992, I changed my concept of thinking about chess and after a while I noticed a positive effect. Even though my tournament results were not very impressive, I somehow learned a lot and began to evaluate positions more correctly. Prior to becoming World Champion I had not played abroad a great deal, but suddenly the invitations poured in. I drew up my plan and started to travel... a lot. First there was a grandmaster tournament in Shenzhen, followed by chess events in Budapest, Helsinki, Beijing, Moscow and Baden-Baden.

In between, I even found time to visit the women's Candidates tournament in Shanghai. It was held in a beautiful hotel, and even the President of China had stayed there several times when he visited the city. For the organizers it was a pity that none of the three Chinese players came close to qualifying. In fact, there seemed to be quite a distance between the top players – Zsuzsa Polgar, Nana Ioseliani and Maya Chiburdanidze – and the rest of the field. Zsuzsa was seconded by Bent Larsen and Julio Granda Zuñiga and played a superb tournament. She started off at a furious pace and had a three-point margin at the finish. The fight for second place was won by Nana, who beat Maya by having a better Sonneborn-Berger tie-break. For myself, it was a special feeling that I had only come to watch others play chess. Shanghai is well known for its large shopping areas and there is a lot to see. It proved a popular pastime for many. Most of the ladies arrived in Shanghai with one bag and left with many more.

From all my games in the second half of 1992, I have made a selection of my most memorable ones. The first game was played in the Alekhine Memorial Open Tournament. This was a tough tournament, as I had to find out the hard way. Russia is a country with many strong chess masters, eager for a good result. After a few rounds I realized that I needed to adjust my goal, which was to play in the upper half of the tournament. Amongst my opponents were grandmasters like Oll, Psakhis and Yakovich – rarely had I played such strong opponents before. In fact, the worst feeling was that I played with little confidence due to a poor start. I started to understand the meaning of the word *suffering* during a game. Finally I finished with a 50% score but it had been hard work all along. Yet, there was one day when the sun was shining on me in Moscow...

Game 16
Xie Jun – Andrei Kharlov
Alekhine Memorial Open Tournament, Moscow 1992
Sicilian, Lasker-Pelikan

1	e4	c5
2	♘f3	♘c6
3	d4	cxd4
4	♘xd4	♘f6
5	♘c3	e6
6	♘db5	d6
7	♗f4	

It was already too late to realize that Kharlov comes from the same area as Evgeny Sveshnikov. Being a pupil of the leading expert on this line, he was bound to know a great deal about it.

7	...	e5
8	♗g5	a6
9	♘a3	♗e6

This move is less common than 9...b5.

10	♘c4	♖c8 *(D)*

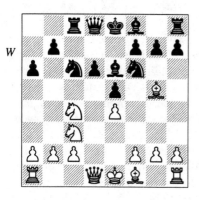

11 ♘e3

In the same tournament, the same year, my opponent played another interesting game with this line. Belikov-Kharlov continued 11 ♘d5 ♗xd5 12 ♗xf6 gxf6 13 ♕xd5 ♘d4 14 ♗d3 with complex play. The main line is 11 ♗xf6, after which play could continue as follows: 11...gxf6 (11...♕xf6 12 ♘b6 ♖b8 13 ♘cd5 ♕g6 14 ♕d3 ♗e7 15 ♘c7+ ♔f8 16 ♘cd5 gives White a big advantage according to Kasparov) 12 ♘e3 ♗h6 13 ♘g4 ♗g7 14 ♗d3 ♕b6 15 ♖b1 ♘d4 16 0-0 f5 17 exf5 ♘xf5 18 ♗xf5 ♗xf5 19 ♘e3 ♗e6 20 ♕h5 with a good position for White – an instructive game with this position was Zso.Polgar-Hjartarson, Reykjavik 1995.

11	...	♗e7
12	♗xf6	♗xf6
13	♘cd5	♗g5
14	c3	0-0
15	♗e2	g6
16	0-0	

I was not feeling at my best that particular day, so I chose the most solid move. I was anxious to see how my opponent would continue.

16	...	♔h8!? *(D)*

Interesting enough. If Black had played 16...f5 at once, the game could have continued 17 exf5 gxf5 18 ♔h1

♘e7! with an unclear position. White can try to block the centre pawns with 19 f4 ♘xd5 20 ♘xd5 ♗h6 (the inferior 20...♖c5?! 21 c4 ♗xd5 22 b4 ♗xc4 23 bxc5 ♗xe2 24 ♕xe2 ♗xf4 25 ♖ad1 gives White the initiative) 21 c4 ♗g7. The exchange of one pair of knights has favoured Black, because White can exert less pressure on the centre.

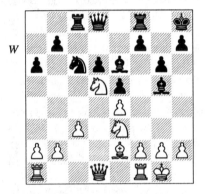

W

17 ♔h1

Now White is better equipped to meet ...f5. The position prior to 17 ♔h1 is not unknown and has occurred in at least one other game. Ciocaltea-Simić, Athens 1981 saw the moves 17 ♕d3 (it was actually 16 ♕d3 here because the game featured 5...e5 instead of 5...e6) 17...f5 18 ♖fd1 ♖f7 19 ♗f3 ♕f8 20 ♘b6 ♖d8 21 ♕e2 ♗h4 22 g3 f4 23 ♗g4 fxe3 24 ♗xe6 ♖xf2 25 ♕xe3 ♖f3 26 ♕e2 ♗xg3, resulting in an unclear position.

17 ...   f5!?

I would prefer 17...♘e7, inviting White to exchange the knights.

18	exf5	gxf5
19	f4	♗h6
20	♗d3	e4?

Again, 20...♘e7 is the right move to make, maintaining maximum flexibility with the pawns. In that case, an unclear position would arise after 21 ♘xe7 ♕xe7 22 ♕h5 ♗xf4 23 ♘xf5 ♕e8! (23...♕g5 is the wrong method to swap queens, as White is much better after 24 ♕xg5 ♗xg5 25 ♘xd6 ♖xf1+ 26 ♗xf1) 24 ♘g7 ♕xh5 25 ♘xh5 ♗g5.

21 ♗c2 (D)

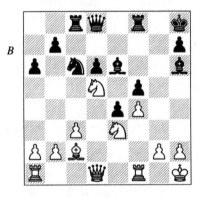

B

With 21 ♗c2 the game has reached a position in which Black has difficulties finding the right plan, if indeed one exists. The position is in a sense blocked, which makes the knights in most cases stronger than the bishop-pair. In addition, Black has too many weak squares in the centre. Lastly, if the game were to reach an endgame, the pawn structure is most promising for White. In short, White has a big advantage.

21 ...   ♛h4
22 ♕e1!

As just mentioned above, I am of the opinion that the endgame can only favour White. If Black refuses the offer to exchange queens, he will have to move his queen to a less active place.

22 ...   ♛h5
23 ♘b6   ♜cd8
24 ♗b3!

Chess looks like a simple game if you find the right plan and when the pieces seem to find the right squares automatically. I think that my play is logical: after the exchange of the light-squared bishops, White will use the d5-square as the basis for all future plans.

24 ...   ♗xb3
25 axb3   ♘e7
26 ♘ed5   ♘g6 (D)

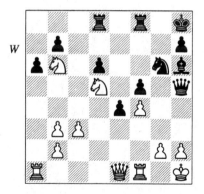

W

The only move to generate counter-play, but Black's hope is short-lived.

27 ♕d1!   ♛h4

If Black chooses 27...♕xd1 28 ♜axd1 ♜de8 29 g3, White wins easily.

The plan is first to put the king on e3, followed by doubling rooks on the d-file. Black is in dire straits.

28 g3

This diverts the black queen into the corner.

28 ...   ♛h3
29 ♘c7   ♜f7
30 ♘e6   ♜e8
31 ♕d4+   ♚g8
32 ♕d5 (D)

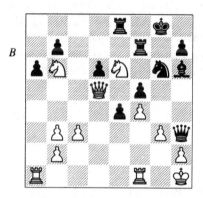

B

Black is in a kind of zugzwang. He has no proper plan and no good moves, even though there are many pieces left on the board. The white queen and knights can act at will. How to break down Black's last defence is now a matter of (not too difficult) technique.

32 ...   ♘f8
33 ♘d4   ♘g6
34 ♘c4   ♗f8
35 ♘e6   ♜xe6
36 ♕xe6   ♚g7
37 ♘e3   ♜f6
38 ♕c8   ♘h4

39	♕xb7+	♔h8		42	♕xa6	♖g6
40	♖f2	♘f3		43	♕c4+	♔g7
41	♕c8	♔g8		44	♖a7+	1-0

The next game was played in Germany, in the town of Baden-Baden, at the end of 1992. I was invited to compete in Group B, where the average Elo rating of the twelve players made it a Category 11 tournament. The oldest participant, Wolfgang Uhlmann, and I were the players with the lowest rating in the group. Up to round six everything went fantastically well. I had won three times (Hickl, Tischbierek and Brunner) and had made three draws (Van der Wiel, Hort and Uhlmann) and could hardly believe I was leading! Unfortunately, the success was too much for me. I began to dream of winning many more games and having a great triumph in the tournament. Moreover, it was now well possible to make a 'male' GM norm and, at the same time, raise my Elo rating to over 2500. But from that moment onwards my play started to deteriorate. First, however, there was this nice game in round seven.

Game 17

Romuald Mainka – Xie Jun

Baden-Baden 1992
Ruy Lopez, Closed with 9...♘d7

1	e4	e5
2	♘f3	♘c6
3	♗b5	a6
4	♗a4	♘f6
5	0-0	♗e7
6	♖e1	b5
7	♗b3	d6
8	c3	0-0
9	h3	♘d7
10	d4	♗f6
11	a4 *(D)*	

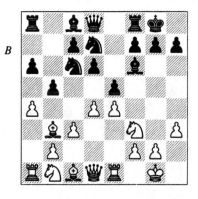

11 ...   ♗b7

This line was very fashionable during the early 1990s. The same position occurred several times in the Kasparov-Karpov match of 1990 and raised the interest of many a grandmaster. Black also has another interesting move at his disposal: 11...♖b8 12 axb5

axb5 13 d5 (Nigel Short tried 13 ♗e3 against Agdestein, Reykjavik 1990, with the follow-up 13...♘e7 14 ♘bd2 c6 15 ♘h2 ♘g6 16 ♘df3 ♕c7 17 g3! ♖e8!?) 13...♘e7 14 ♘a3 and Black has to make a choice. An old example, Suetin-Sokolsky, USSR 1953, featured 14...b4 15 cxb4 ♖xb4 16 ♗d2 ♖b8 17 ♗c3 g6 18 ♘c4. A more recent example is Popović-Agdestein, Belgrade 1989, which saw 14...♘c5!? 15 ♗c2 c6 16 b4 ♘a6 17 dxc6 ♘xc6 18 ♕e2 ♘c7 19 ♖d1 ♗e6 20 ♖b1 ♕d7 21 ♘g5. In all cases, White has a small plus but Black's position seems solid.

12 ♘a3 *(D)*

The variation with 9...♘d7 and 10...♗f6 is full of possibilities. In Lanka-Svidler, European Team Ch, Pula 1997, White played 12 d5 ♘e7 13 axb5 axb5 14 ♖xa8 ♕xa8 15 ♘a3 ♗a6 16 ♘h2 ♘g6 17 g3 ♖b8 18 ♗d2 ♗e7 19 h4 ♘c5 20 ♗c2 ♗c8 21 ♕a1 c6 with an unclear position. I faced the same line myself, as White, in my 13th match game against Maya Chiburdanidze in Manila 1991. There I played 12 axb5 axb5 13 ♖xa8 ♕xa8 14 d5 ♘e7 15 ♘a3 c6?! – new at the time, but dubious – 16 dxc6 ♗xc6 17 ♕xd6 ♘c8 18 ♕d1 ♘c5 19 ♗d5! ♘xe4 20 ♗xc6 ♕xc6 21 ♕d3 ♘cd6 22 ♘xb5, when

Black did not have enough compensation for the pawn.

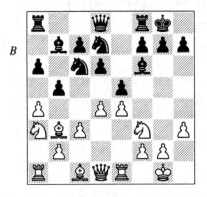

B

12 ...   exd4

Following in Karpov's footsteps. Black has a wide choice, as with every move in this line, but alternatives do not seem to equalize. Here are just a few examples to show what problems Black might face. White has a substantial advantage after both 12...♕b8?! 13 ♗g5! exd4 14 ♗xf6 ♘xf6 15 cxd4, de Firmian-Benjamin, USA Ch 1988, and 12...♘e7 13 ♖b1 c6 14 ♗e3 ♕c7 15 ♘g5! bxa4 16 ♗xa4 d5 17 ♗c2 h6 18 ♘f3 exd4 19 cxd4 dxe4 20 ♗xe4 ♘d5 21 ♗d2 ♖fe8 22 ♘c4, Sax-Korchnoi, Candidates match (2), Wijk aan Zee 1991. The lesser evil is 12...♖e8 13 axb5 axb5 14 d5 ♘e7 15 ♗e3 ♗a6 16 ♘c2 with only a slight plus for White, Ernst-Adams, London 1991.

13 cxd4   ♖e8

It is worth noting that the two big K's had this position twice in their New York/Lyons match of 1990. In game 12, Karpov chose 13...♘a5 14

♗a2 b4 15 ♘c4 ♘xc4 16 ♗xc4 ♖e8 17 ♕b3 ♖xe4 18 ♗xf7+ ♔h8 19 ♗e3 but White was better. Karpov decided to vary with 13...♘b6?! in game 18, but this was certainly not an improvement. Kasparov reacted forcefully and got an even bigger advantage after 14 ♗f4! bxa4 15 ♗xa4 ♘xa4 16 ♕xa4 a5 17 ♗d2!.

14 ♕d2

Besides this move, the other popular line for White is 14 ♗f4. Black managed to equalize with 14...♘a5 15 ♗c2 b4 16 ♘b1 c5 17 ♘bd2 ♘f8 18 e5 dxe5 19 dxe5 ♗e7 20 ♕e2 ♕b6 21 ♗d3 ♖ad8 22 ♘c4 ♘xc4 23 ♗xc4 ♕c6 24 b3 ♘e6 in Onishchuk-Piket, Wijk aan Zee 1997, but there are ample chances to deviate. What about moves like 14 ♗c2, 14 d5, 14 axb5, etc.?

14 ...   ♖e7 (D)

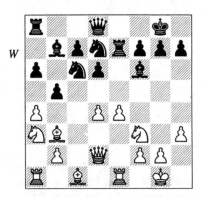

W

15 ♖b1

Actually, the earliest game I was able to find with this particular position was Adams-Short, British Ch

(Swansea) 1987. Black was on top after 15 ♗c2 ♛e8 16 b3 bxa4 17 bxa4 a5 18 ♗b1 ♘c5!? 19 e5 dxe5 20 ♕c2 e4 21 ♗g5 ♗xg5 22 ♘xg5 ♘d3 and went on to win after 43 moves.

15 ...   bxa4

Was this a novelty? I am not sure, but my opponent used a lot of time to ponder the position. This surprised me slightly: what else is there but to take on a4? After 15...b4 16 ♘c4, White has the better game.

16 ♗xa4   ♘b6
17 ♗c2   a5 (D)

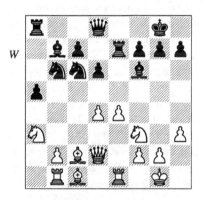

With the plan of playing ...♘b4, attacking the e-pawn.

18 ♕c3   ♘b4

Had I foreseen White's next move and its consequences, I would probably have opted for 18...h6!? 19 ♗f4 ♘b4 20 ♖a1 c5 with the initiative. In contrast, 18...♘xd4?! is weak and does not meet the demands of the position. White obtains a plus with 19 ♘xd4 c5 20 ♗e3 cxd4 21 ♗xd4 ♖c8 (or 21...♗xd4 22 ♕xd4 ♖c8 23 ♕d3) 22

♗xf6 ♖xc3 23 ♗xe7 ♕xe7 24 bxc3. Now White finds a strong reply.

19 ♗g5!

A strong move. The exchange of the dark-squared bishop is an absolute necessity for White. Other moves lead to a passive position.

19 ...   ♘xc2

I did not like the position after 19...♗xg5 20 ♘xg5 ♕e8 21 ♗b3, for example 21...h6 22 ♘xf7 ♖xf7 23 ♗xf7+ ♕xf7 24 ♖e3. White has active play, whereas the accumulated black pieces on the b-file do not cooperate well.

20 ♕xc2   ♖xe4!

As a result of my move, White sank into deep thought again. He spent more than half an hour on his 21st move. I started having doubts whether Mainka had foreseen the text-move prior to making his move 19 ♗g5!.

21 ♖xe4

It is also possible that my opponent had planned, at first, to play 21 ♗xf6 ♖xe1+ 22 ♖xe1 ♕xf6 23 ♕xc7 ♗xf3 24 ♕xb6 ♕g6 25 g3 ♕f5 26 ♕b5, when the position is equal since Black has to exchange queens in view of the mating threat on e8. Maybe he realized in time that Black has in fact the much stronger reply 22...gxf6! 23 ♘h4 ♔h8. Black is happy with the extra pawn and the open g-file.

21 ...   ♗xe4
22 ♕xe4   ♗xg5
23 ♘xg5

Rather than the text-move, I was expecting 23 ♕c6 ♗f4 24 ♘b5 d5 25 g3 ♗d6 26 ♖e1, with some compensation for the pawn.

| 23 | ... | ♕xg5 |
| 24 | ♕c6 | ♕d5! |

The queen is excellently placed in the centre and has taken up a dominant position.

| 25 | ♕xc7 | ♕xd4 |
| 26 | ♖e1? | |

There was still a chance to fight for a draw with 26 ♘b5!? ♕c5 27 ♕xc5 dxc5 28 ♖c1 ♘d7 29 ♘d6 ♖b8 (not 29...♔f8 30 ♘b7) 30 ♖c2 ♔f8, although Black should be able to generate some winning chances.

| 26 | ... | g6! |

This prevents any tricks that White might have and keeps up the pressure.

| 27 | ♘b5 (D) | |

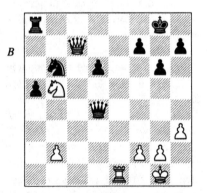

I could almost smell that there was a winning continuation somewhere, but proving it was quite something else. I spent a lot of time deciding on my next move and chose the wrong one in the end. Of course, I should have played 27...♕b4! 28 ♘c3 ♖c8 29

♕b7, with two possible winning ideas. The first one is 29...d5! but, to tell the truth, I was a bit too lazy to calculate all the possibilities. The following lines are the most relevant ones, though not at all forced: 30 ♖e7 (30 ♖d1 ♕xb2 31 ♘xd5 ♖c1 32 ♘f6+ ♔g7 33 ♘e8+ ♔f8 and Black wins) 30...♕xb2 31 ♘xd5 (31 ♖xf7 ♕xc3 32 ♖xh7 ♕c1+ 33 ♔h2 ♕f4+ 34 g3 ♕xf2+ 35 ♔h1 ♖c1# is mate) 31...♕c1+ 32 ♔h2 ♘xd5 33 ♖xf7 ♖c7 and wins. But to check all the branches of the 'variation tree' would require much energy, and, therefore, I looked at a safer and simpler line. I started by looking in the right direction with 29...♕xb2 30 ♘d5 ♖c1 31 ♘f6+ ♔g7 32 ♘e8+ ♔h6. Unfortunately, that is where I stopped calculating and thought it too risky to expose my king in this way. Had I continued, and looked only two moves further, I would have seen that it is not as dangerous as it looks. White can resign after 33 ♕e4 ♖xe1+ 34 ♕xe1 ♘c4, being two pawns down.

27	...	♕c5?
28	♕xc5	dxc5
29	♖c1 (D)	

Black still is one pawn up but the win has become problematic. For instance, after 29...♖b8 30 ♘d6 (better than 30 ♖xc5 ♘a4) 30...♘a4 31 ♘c4 ♔f8 32 ♖a1 White defends well. So I tried...

29	...	c4!?
30	♘a3	♖c8
31	♔f1	♔f8
32	♘b5!	

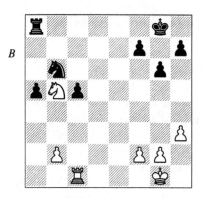

A clever defence. White takes the d6-square under control. If the black king approaches the centre, then White would be lost: 32 ♔e2 ♔e7 33 ♔d2 ♔d6 34 ♔c3 ♔c5.

32   ...   ♖c6?!

Inaccurate. I do not understand why I did not pay more attention to the better choice 32...♖c5! 33 ♘c3 ♖e5.

33   ♘c3   ♖d6??

Another bad move. For no reason whatsoever I picked this move, but 33...♖e6 would have isolated the white

king. That was one of the last winning chances for me.

34	♔e2	♔e7
35	♖a1	♖e6+
36	♔d2	♖e5
37	f4	♖f5
38	g3	g5?

I could have retained the material plus with 38...h5, and this may yield some chances later. This is easier said than done, though. In all seriousness, I do not see how Black can improve her position any further.

39	♔e3	gxf4+
40	♔e4	♔e6
41	g4	♖e5+
42	♔xf4	f5

In spite of the extra pawn there is no win any more.

43	♖d1	fxg4
44	hxg4	♘d5+
45	♘xd5	♖xd5
46	♖h1	♖d2
47	♔e4	♖xb2

½-½

I did not feel pleased the moment that I had to agree to a draw. I was dominating during most of the game and, in addition, the result was not in accordance with my plan. But somehow, I really like this game and will remember it for a long time. However, I had failed to see the warning and continued to dream of winning the tournament. Then, the nightmare began. I could not set myself free from my daydream and I lost the last four games. In every game I had good chances at some point. I did not really blunder but failed each time to discern the winning plan. My final score was minus one, while the overall winner only had plus two. Yet, the lesson was learned: never daydream during a tournament, at least not during the day.

My rating had not improved that much in 1992, but I felt that I was building up for the coming period. In 1993, I did not play a great deal. Only once did I travel abroad, to participate in the Ladies against Veterans tournament, but for the rest I spent my time in China. I enjoyed the period of relative calm and could now prepare well for the next World Championship. It had been known since the beginning of 1993 that the World Championship match would be played in October, in Monaco, and that my opponent would be Nana Ioseliani. Nana had played 4-4 in the match against Zsuzsa Polgar and four additional games with an accelerated tempo had also failed to bring about a decision. In the end, the decision was made by the drawing of lots and Nana was the lucky one. But the fact that she had qualified did not come as a surprise to me. I knew that Nana was a fighter and she would not surrender until the very end. With more than half a year to go, I had ample time to prepare. Aided by my seconds, and with the help of the chess association, I started to work. During the first half of 1993, I worked harder than ever before on my chess. I can remember that, at times, I also started to realize how much there was still to learn. Perhaps this is the side-effect of progress made. The more you know, the more you realize how weak you are.

Outside chess, life had a few surprises in store. In the beginning of 1993, I was informed that I was elected as a Member of Parliament and I was asked to attend the National Congress in March. In China, this is considered a great honour. All the more so in my case, because I was one of the few sportspeople in parliament and was even appointed a member of the so-called Presidential Group. It was all part of the new Chinese policy to select younger people for political functions. Of course, I was very proud but also overwhelmed by the appointment. It was a tremendous experience for me – do not forget that I was only twenty-two years old – and a nice break from chess.

In the world of chess I also had a new experience. For the first time I was able to participate in the annual Ladies against Veterans tournament, sponsored by chess benefactor Mr van Oosterom. This tournament is usually held in June, and it is charming that the event always takes place in a different city, usually in Europe. The tournament's name is taken from the name of the local dance, and on this occasion the choice of *Vienna Walzer* was obvious. Most of the other players had already played in the first edition. I felt that it would be wonderful to play against these grand old maestros, some of them former World Champions and all top players in their best time. I only knew the names of the players from studying their games and watching them play at the Olympiads. But now I could sit opposite these 'legends' at the chess board. I really looked forward to the event and expected to learn a lot.

Over the years, the Ladies versus Veterans has become one of my favourite tournaments. The atmosphere is great and the organizers are friendly yet very professional. I cannot think of any other tournament where the conditions are so excellent and, what is more, where the opponents are such true gentlemen. One can easily be fooled by the age of the men, but here the greatest caution should be exercised. Most of the veterans could have been our fathers, or even grandfathers, but what fighting spirit they have! Take Smyslov for example. At the board he sits as if he has almost fallen asleep, deceptive indeed, yet his brain works like a young man's. The moment you make a mistake, his eyes open and he is down on it in a flash to teach you a lesson.

Game 18

Xie Jun – Vasily Smyslov

Ladies against Veterans, Vienna 1993

French, Tarrasch with 4...♕xd5

1 e4

In my preparation for this game, I noticed that there was little use in focusing on particular lines: the man with the black pieces had tried almost every opening in his life. So, in the end, I decided just to save my energy for the game itself and see what would happen.

1 ... e6

The French Defence was a surprise indeed. This was one of the few openings which I could not have expected.

2	d4	d5
3	♘d2	c5
4	exd5	♕xd5
5	♘gf3	cxd4
6	♗c4	♕d6
7	0-0	♘f6
8	♘b3	♘c6
9	♘bxd4	♘xd4
10	♘xd4	a6 (D)
11	♖e1	

I have some experience with this line and played 11 c3 in several games. It usually leads to a solid position, for instance after 11...♕c7 12 ♕e2 ♗d6 13 h3 0-0 14 ♖d1, with equal chances for the two sides.

11 ... ♗d7

The more common move is 11...♕c7 with the idea ...♗d6 or ...♗c5 and

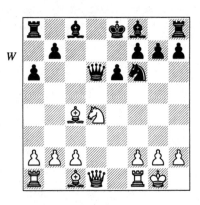

castling kingside. Smyslov's idea is interesting, and a remarkable decision for someone who is 72 years of age.

12 c3 0-0-0

I have not been able to find this move in my database, so it may have been a theoretical novelty. The main theoretical line goes 12...♕c7 13 ♕e2 (13 ♗b3 was played in the game Marciano-Rozentalis, Belfort 1997, leading to a small plus for White after 13...0-0-0 14 ♕e2 ♗d6 15 h3 h6 16 a4 ♖he8 17 ♗e3 ♔b8 18 ♘f3 ♗c6 19 a5) 13...♗d6 14 h3 (14 ♘f5!? is interesting) 14...0-0 15 ♗g5. Then Palac-Savchenko, Erevan Olympiad 1996 featured 15...♗h2+ 16 ♔h1 ♗f4 17 ♗xf4 ♕xf4 18 ♔g1 ♖fe8 and soon ended in a draw.

13 ♕e2 ♕c7

14 h3   ♗d6
15 a4

It seems that I have achieved more in comparison to the game Marciano-Rozentalis as mentioned above. Not only has White gained one tempo by omitting the move ♗b3, but it is also easier for White to push the b-pawn and ♗xa6 might become a threat at some point. Needless to say, I was quite optimistic about my position here, but my great opponent found a sharp plan which leads to tremendous complications.

15 ...   e5!
16 ♘c2   ♗f5
17 ♘e3   ♗g6
18 b4   e4
19 ♗a3?

Too slow! If I had the fighting spirit of my opponent – castling queenside! – I would have found the sharpest continuation at this moment. The right plan is 19 b5 a5 20 b6! ♕xb6 21 ♗a3 ♗xa3 22 ♖xa3 ♖d7 23 ♖b3 ♕d8 24 ♖eb1 with a strong attack. It is hard to find a decent defence for Black. All his pieces are positioned on the wrong side of the board.

19 ...   ♗h2+
20 ♔h1   ♗f4
21 b5   ♗xe3
22 fxe3 (D)

I was happy with my position and was calculating how to continue the attack. But Smyslov's next move spoils all my plans.

22 ...   ♖d3!!
23 ♕a2

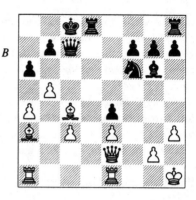

A pawn on d3 would suit Black well. He would take over control after 23 ♗xd3? exd3 24 ♕b2 ♘e4 25 bxa6 bxa6 26 ♖ad1 ♖d8.

23 ...   h5
24 ♔g1   ♘g4!

Am I really playing a man who is in his early seventies? Even though all these moves cost Mr Smyslov quite some time, I expected the worst outcome for myself. What could I do against such a fearless fighter?

25 hxg4   hxg4
26 g3?

After the game, Lev Polugaevsky, captain of the ladies' team, showed us the moves that I should have made: 26 ♗xd3! exd3 (26...♕h2+ 27 ♔f2 g3+ 28 ♔e2 exd3+ 29 ♔d1 leaves White a rook up) 27 ♗d6!! – this is what I had overlooked! – 27...♕xd6 28 ♕c4+ ♔b8 29 ♕f4 and the endgame is easier to play for White. By the way, the post-mortem was a special experience. Mr Smyslov could not believe that his fantastic sacrifice was not working, and he kept trying to find improvements for Black. He and Lev Polugaevsky took opposite points of view, and they kept on discussing the position like two eighteen-year-olds. I just sat there and listened carefully, suffering from the feeling that I had left part of my brain on the board. I was so astounded at seeing so much enthusiasm in these venerable gentlemen, that I simply could not keep my thoughts straight. Let us get back to the game.

26   ...   ♕xg3+
27   ♕g2   ♖xe3 (D)

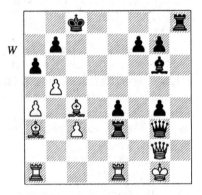

W

28   ♕xg3?
Better is 28 ♗f1, which I had missed as well. A possible continuation is 28...axb5 29 axb5 ♖h3 30 ♗b4 ♖xe1 (30...♕h4 31 ♖a8+ gives White an enormous attack) 31 ♖xe1 f5 32 ♕xg3 ♖xg3+ 33 ♔h2 ♖f3 with an unclear position. As a weak excuse I can only say that both of us were, by now, under terrible time-pressure.

28   ...   ♖xg3+
29   ♔f2   ♖hh3?!

Why not take one more pawn with 29...♖xc3 30 ♖ac1 ♖h2+ 31 ♔g1 ♖hc2 32 bxa6 (32 ♖xc2 ♖xc2 33 ♖c1 ♖xc1+ 34 ♗xc1 axb5 35 axb5 ♔d7 is better for Black) 32...♖g3+? The reason that Mr Smyslov did not choose this line is that he desperately wanted to win!

30   bxa6   bxa6?!
For the same reason, Mr Smyslov probably rejected the line 30...e3+ 31 ♖xe3 (31 ♔e2 ♖g2+ 32 ♔d1 ♖d2+ 33 ♔c1 bxa6 34 ♗xa6+ ♔c7 35 ♗b4 ♖c2+ 36 ♔d1 ♖d2+ draws) 31...♖xe3 32 a7 ♖hf3+ 33 ♔g2 ♖g3+ 34 ♔h2 and so on. That was yet another way to force the draw.

31   ♗xa6+   ♔c7
32   ♗c5 (D)

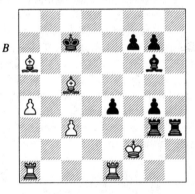

B

Black should now make it a priority to clear away the remaining white pawns as quickly as possible. Therefore 32...♖xc3! was called for. Play could have proceeded 33 ♗d4 ♖cf3+ 34 ♔e2, leading to two main lines. The first one is bad for Black: 34...♖h2+?

35 ♔d1 f6 36 ♗e2 ♖b3 37 a5 g3 38 a6 ♗h5 although White can go astray here. After 39 a7? ♗xe2+ 40 ♖xe2 ♖d3+ 41 ♔c1, the sobering 41...♖xe2, followed by ...♖e2-e1-e2, etc., saves the draw. Instead, 39 ♗xh5 secures the win for White. The better defence is 34...f6 35 ♖ac1+ (35 ♖ed1 ♖h2+ 36 ♔e1 e3 37 ♖ac1+ ♗c2 38 ♗d3 ♖h1+ 39 ♔e2 ♖h2+ is a draw) 35...♔d6 36 ♖ed1 ♖h2+ 37 ♔e1 ♖h1+ 38 ♗g1+ (or 38 ♔d2 ♖h2+ 39 ♔e1 ♖h1+ equalizing) 38...♔e5 39 ♔e2. White is slightly better, although it must be said that this is all far too complicated to see while in time-trouble.

| 32 | ... | ♖f3+ |
| 33 | ♔e2 (D) | |

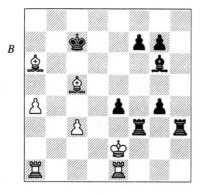

| 33 | ... | ♖h2+? |

Here, Black makes a huge mistake. His last chance was 33...♖xc3 34 ♗d4 ♖c2+ 35 ♔d1 ♖c6 36 ♗e5+ ♔b6 37 ♗b5 ♖e6 38 ♗xg7 and, although White is better, Black can still make his opponent's task very difficult.

| 34 | ♔d1 | ♖xc3 |

The last practical chance would have been 34...f5, but the outcome is not in doubt if White plays 35 ♗d4 ♔c6 36 ♗b5+ ♔d5 37 a5 and the a-pawn marches on.

| 35 | ♗d4 (D) | |

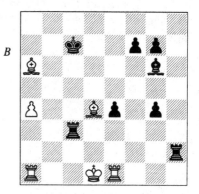

Suddenly it becomes apparent that Black's rooks are on the wrong squares and so Black will lose the exchange. Finally, I saw that victory was waiting for me at the finish. The rest of the game was relatively easy.

35	...	♖cc2
36	♗e5+	♔b6
37	♗xh2	♖xh2
38	♗e2	f5
39	a5+	♔a7
40	♖c1	♗e8
41	♖c7+	♔b8
42	♖xg7	♗a4+
43	♔c1	e3
44	a6	♖h6
45	♔b2	♖d6
46	♔a3	♗c6
47	♖b1+	♔a8
48	♖b6	1-0

I was doing quite well in the first leg of the tournament but then I had to play Larsen as White. I felt quite confident during this game, and that may well have been the reason why I hardly realized how delicate my position had become in the course of the middlegame. After move 20 I thought that it was not easy for White to find a plan, but not at all that I was worse. By the time that I thought that Black was possibly slightly better, my position was already close to losing. The game is without a doubt one of my most memorable ones. I saw clearly that there was a huge distance in positional judgement between myself and one of the great masters of chess history.

Game 19

Xie Jun – Bent Larsen

Ladies against Veterans, Vienna 1993
Sicilian, Kupreichik's 5...♗d7

1 e4	c5
2 ♘f3	d6
3 d4	cxd4
4 ♘xd4	♘f6
5 ♘c3	♗d7!? *(D)*

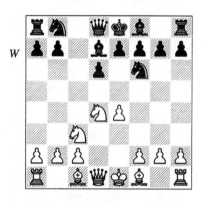

A typical Larsen move. He often tries to do something out of the ordinary.

6 ♗e2

Alternative moves such as 6 ♗e3 and 6 ♗g5 seem perfectly playable.

6 ...	g6
7 0-0	♗g7
8 ♗g5	♘c6
9 ♘b3	a6
10 a4	

The standard reaction. I am unsure, however, whether this move really helps to restrict Black's queenside play. On the other hand, it may leave some weak squares in White's camp. 10 ♖e1 and 10 f4 both seem to be better.

10 ...	♖c8
11 ♔h1 *(D)*	

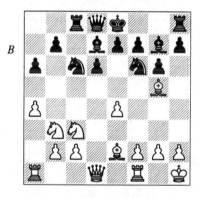

11 ...	♗e6

At first sight, it looks as if the game has reached a position similar to the Dragon, but the appearance is deceptive. Black has wasted one tempo by moving his light-squared bishop in two moves to e6, and Black has not yet castled, whereas White has willingly pushed the a-pawn to a4. Surprising as it may seem, it is conceivable that these minor changes favour Black.

12 f4	♘d7
13 f5?!	

During the game, I thought that this was a strong move, because Black is 'forced' to surrender his bishop-pair. I felt at the same time that giving up the e5-square had to be of minor importance. A sound move would have been 13 ♖b1, with the idea of ♘d5.

13	...	♗xb3
14	cxb3	♘f6
15	♖c1	♘e5
16	♕d2?	

In the belief that I had prevented Black from castling, I continued with my piece development. The right plan was 16 b4, followed by b5, when White has the initiative on the queenside.

| 16 | ... | 0-0 (D) |

A blunder, so I thought, and without much thought I went for the 'refutation'.

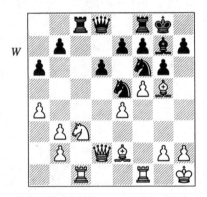

17	♗xf6	♗xf6
18	♘d5	♖xc1
19	♘xf6+??	

This was the reason why I assumed that Black could not castle on move 16. How on earth could I have imagined

that Larsen, with all his experience, had overlooked such a simple plan? In fact, I am the one who has fallen into a trap! Within a few moves it becomes apparent that Black has the superior position. He has a wonderful knight on e5, compared to the crippled bishop on e2, and the pawn structure is definitely in his favour. 19 ♖xc1 was the right move, of course, when the position is about equal.

19	...	exf6
20	♖xc1	♕d7
21	h3	♔g7 (D)

Always a useful move.

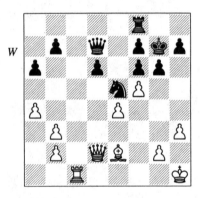

22 ♗c4?

The modest 22 ♔h2 was a good move, to stop Black playing ...♖c8. The problem was that I did not realize yet that I had an inferior position. There are weaknesses on both sides, and White can still defend the position with careful play. Black can, of course, always take on f5 but this compromises his position and involves unnecessary complications.

22 ...   🜚c8
23 ♗d5

So I got what I wanted – a strong bishop on d5. But it will become painfully clear that I did not understand the position very well. Larsen did. After the exchange of rooks, the relative value of the remaining pieces is more important than anything. Here, the knight is by far superior to the bishop.

23 ...   🜚xc1+
24 ♛xc1   b5
25 ♛f1 (D)

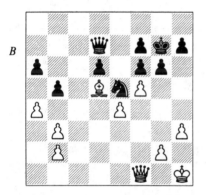

25 ...   g5!

This move came as a shock to me. I realized instantly that it was not me who was playing for a win now, but Larsen. First I stared at my pawn structure, and a moment later at my bishop. Then I understood that my opponent had simply lured me into a bad ending. There is no choice but to defend.

26 ♛d1?

I did not see a proper plan and just played on. As far as I could see the d5-bishop was now deadwood. I felt quite sad about it. Still, there was a better option. White could have left the queen on f1, keeping an eye on the b5-square. It is not all that easy for Black to make progress in that case, although I am pretty sure that Larsen would have come up with some constructive ideas. One line of defence could have been 26 g3, for instance 26...h5 27 ♔g2 ♔f8 28 ♛e2 g4 29 h4 ♔e7. For sure, Black is better but White can fight on. Now the position goes down rapidly.

26 ...   ♛a7
27 ♛e2   ♛c5

Black improves his position with remarkable ease.

28 ♔h2 (D)

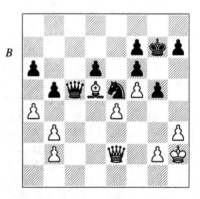

28 ...   b4!

Black assures himself of a large advantage by fixing the queenside pawns. White cannot take the pawn on a6 due to 29 ♛xa6 ♛f2 30 ♔h1 g4 with mate to follow.

29 ♗c4   a5
30 g4

30 g3!? was certainly more flexible.

| 30 | ... | ♛d4 |
| 31 | ♗b5 | |

In view of my upcoming time-trouble, I decided to play a waiting move.

31	...	♚f8
32	♗c4	♚e7
33	♔g2	♘d7
34	♗d5	♚f8 (D)

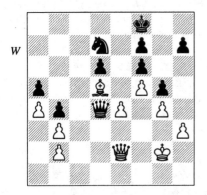

35 ♛a6

I could not stand it any more that Black was strengthening his position all the time, so I chose to sacrifice the b2-pawn rather than to try to defend it. What else is there to prevent Black's queen from invading the dark squares? The line 35 ♗c4 ♘c5 36 ♔f3 ♚e7 37 ♛c2 ♛e5 is an example of my troubles. The black pieces have taken up ideal positions and White has too many squares to guard.

35	...	♛xb2+
36	♔f1	♛c1+
37	♔e2	♛c2+
38	♔f1	♛d1+

38...♛c5 was also good, but Black has better.

39	♔g2	♘e5!
40	♛xd6+	♚g7
41	♛c5	♛f3+
42	♔h2	♛e2+
43	♔g3	♘d3
44	♛a7	♛e1+
45	♔h2	♛d2+
46	♔g1	♛c1+
47	♔h2	♛f4+
48	♔h1	♘e5
49	♔g2	♛f3+
50	♔h2 (D)	

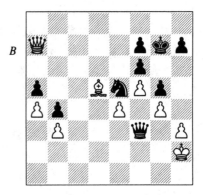

50 ...   h5!

Just when I had started to relax somewhat, Larsen uncorks an unexpected attack.

51	gxh5	♛xh5
52	♔g2	♘d3
53	♛e3	♘f4+
54	♔h2	♛d1
55	♛f2	♛d3

Of course, Black has an easy win with 55...♘xd5 56 exd5 ♛xd5 57 ♛c2 ♛f3, but my formidable opponent decides to beat me in another type of endgame. He wants to emphasize once more the superiority of his knight over my bishop.

56	h4	♕h3+
57	♔g1	♕g4+
58	♔h2	♕xh4+
59	♕xh4	gxh4
60	♗c4	♔f8
61	♔g1	♔e7
62	♔f2	♔d6
63	♔f3	♔e5
64	♗xf7	h3
65	♔g3	♔xe4

66	♗e6	♔e5
67	♗d7	♘e2+

I saw that there was no way to save the game and congratulated Larsen on his victory.

0-1

It is not easy to forget a game which you lose in such a way, and it really made me feel sick for a while. I had to wait one year before I could take revenge (see Game 24). Sometimes, this is the only way to wipe out a horrid memory...

In this edition of the Ladies against Veterans, I played quite well in the beginning and won some nice games. Then I lost a few, and recovered again later on. It was a convincing win for the ladies in 1993, with, in particular, Maya Chiburdanidze and Zsuzsa Polgar in good form. I was not happy with my own performance of 7 out of 12, but I had a good overall feeling. I had met lots of nice people involved with organizing the tournament and the chief arbiter Geurt Gijssen turned out to be an amiable man as well. The Ladies against Veterans tournaments have given me many cherished memories.

Between this tournament and the World Championship Match against Nana Ioseliani I played in the National Championship 'for men'. It was the last time that this tournament was held as a round-robin event, as in 1994 the Swiss system was introduced. I was rated amongst the top ten chess players in China and had qualified on that basis. I did not play so badly and finished in third place. In psychological terms it was even more important for me that my national rating went up to just over 2500 as a result. My new Elo rating was 2503, to be precise, and this gave me plenty of confidence for the forthcoming match against Nana.

8 My Second World Championship Match (1993)

In October 1993, my team and I flew to Monaco for the match against Nana Iose-liani. The number of journalists that accompanied us had increased somewhat, to four or five, but the rest of the team consisted of the same people that joined me during my first match in Manila.

Monaco was beautiful and the October weather lovely. Very quickly I had found the right daily routine, to which I adhered until the end of the match. In the morning I would prepare for the game with my seconds, and at regular times I went for a walk with my doctor. He used to have his typical joke. I was born in 1970, the Year of the Dog according to the Chinese calendar, and if anyone asked him what we were going to do, he instantly replied "I am going to walk the dog". It was an enjoyable stay, also because the organizers took great care of every detail and had left nothing to chance. One example was, again, the problem of Western food. Chinese people who travel abroad face difficulties due to the fact that the food differs greatly from that in China. The organizers solved this problem by giving us pocket money to eat in Chinese restaurants. Of course these are all small matters, but they were extremely important in order for us to feel comfortable during those weeks.

It was logical that I had little to complain about, due to the fact that the match turned out to be a one-sided affair. Luck was on my side in the first game. I sacrificed a piece, although the compensation should not have been sufficient. However, Nana was already in time-trouble and blundered, giving me the opportunity to finish off in beautiful fashion. This came as a shock to Nana, from which I don't believe she ever recovered. I managed to win the second game as well and, from that moment onwards, everything just went my way. I felt in great shape and winning four out of the first five games was beyond my wildest dreams. For me it was the ideal result, but for Nana it must have been horrible never to get into the match.

Below is the seventh game of the match, when I was leading 4½-1½. The situation had just turned a little less rosy. I had lost the sixth game, with the white pieces. It had been a terribly long game – a fact that usually leaves nice memories for the winning side. If I allowed Nana another win, she would have had a real chance to recover from her bad start. In that case, I would have had to step up the pace once more and fight against a revitalized Nana. However, things turned out well and game seven saw what was probably one of my best performances in this match.

Game 20

Nana Ioseliani – Xie Jun

World Ch Match (7), Monaco 1993
King's Indian, Classical Main Line

1	d4	♘f6
2	♘f3	g6
3	c4	♗g7
4	♘c3	0-0
5	e4	d6
6	♗e2	e5
7	0-0	♘c6
8	d5	♘e7
9	♘d2 *(D)*	

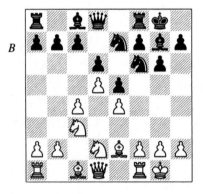

This was the third time in the match that we played this line. Every time Nana tried some new approach in this system, but on no occasion did she gain much from the opening.

9	...	a5
10	a3	♘d7
11	♖b1	f5
12	b4	♔h8
13	f3	axb4

14	axb4	c6!?

This is a very 'Chinese' move as it originates from my long-time trainer, Ye Jiangchuan, who developed it during this match. The idea stems from a similar position after 12...♔h8 13 ♕c2 ♘f6 14 f3 axb4 15 axb4 c6, as in Lputian-Dolmatov, Rostov 1993.

Usually Black plays 14...♘g8 here, Judit Polgar being one of the move's most loyal adherents. The following example shows how well she understands this line: 15 ♕c2 ♗h6 16 c5 dxc5 17 ♘b5 c6 18 dxc6 bxc6 19 ♘d6 cxb4 20 exf5 ♘df6 21 ♘xc8 gxf5 22 ♘c4 ♗xc1 23 ♖fxc1 ♖xc8 24 ♖xb4 ♕d4+ 25 ♔h1 ♖cd8 26 ♖b7 ♘h5 and Black had a great position in Khalifman-J.Polgar, Dos Hermanas 1993.

15 ♔h1!?

In the third game Nana had played 15 dxc6 instead, with the continuation 15...♘xc6 16 ♘b3 ♘xb4 17 ♕xd6. The game later ended in a draw. The text-move must have been Nana's home preparation for this particular game.

15	...	♘f6
16	♘b3 *(D)*	
16	...	cxd5!

The placement of the knight on b3 is the signal for Black to fix the pawn

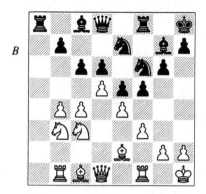

structure on the queenside. This considerably simplifies the defence of Black's queenside, as will be apparent later on.

17 cxd5

The alternative 17 exd5 would lead the game into extremely complicated paths, as both sides would have an advantage on a different side of the board.

17 ...   f4
18 ♘a5!

In the strong conviction that the c4-square is now the best place for the knight. Whenever I face players from the former Soviet Union, I have the feeling that they really play with an iron belief and stick to their points of view – proof of a good chess education.

18 ...   g5
19 ♘c4   ♘g6

19...♖g8 is the other good move for Black. In that case, Black may have more choice later with regard to the future of the e7-knight.

20 b5!?

20 ♗d2, to prepare ♗e1-f2, is a more direct plan for White.

20 ...   ♖g8
21 ♗d2

21 ♘a4, intending ♘b6, is premature. It allows an immediate 21...g4, when Black's attack comes first. There was a serious alternative in 21 b6, but Black gets good attacking chances after 21...♗f8 22 ♘b5 ♘e8 23 ♗a3 ♗d7 24 ♕b3 ♕f6 25 ♖fc1 h5.

21 ...   ♗f8 (D)

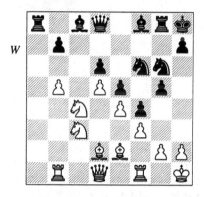

22 ♗e1   h5
23 ♖a1   ♖b8!

The open a-file is less important for the moment. Black will now concentrate on the attack on the white kingside, while the queenside belongs to White. The result of the game depends solely on which attack reaches its target first.

24 ♘a4

White had to choose the right plan to get the initiative on the queenside. Besides the text-move, it was also possible to play 24 b6 g4 25 ♘b5 g3 26

♘c7 ♘h7 27 hxg3 fxg3 28 ♗xg3 ♘f4
29 ♗xf4 exf4 30 ♕e1 ♖g3 31 ♔g1
♘g5 32 ♔h2 with a complex position.
Maybe Deep Blue is the only 'player'
able to calculate these variations until
the very end.

   24 ...   **g4**
   25 ♘ab6 (D)

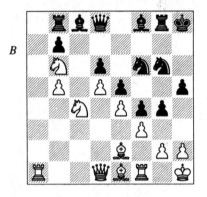

     25 ...   **g3!!**
I felt so happy to hear after the
game from my trainer Ye Jiangchuan,
that he was of the opinion that 25...g3
was worth two exclamation marks. It
has not happened too often that he
applauded one of my moves, but I
believe him in this case. The move
25...gxf3 is more alluring as it opens
the g-file, but it also facilitates White's
defensive task.

   26 ♘xc8
White has no choice, as she would
come under a severe attack after 26 h3
♗xh3 27 gxh3 ♘h4 28 ♖g1 ♘d7. Then,
29 ♘xd7? would allow 29...♕xd7 30
♗f1 g2+ 31 ♗xg2 ♖xg2 with mate to
follow.

   26 ...   **♖xc8**
   27 ♗a5   **♕e7**
   28 h3   **♘h7**
   29 ♕d3   **♘g5**

29...♕h4? is a mistake in view of
30 ♖fc1 ♘g5 31 ♗f1, when White defends successfully. Black has no material left to sacrifice.

   30 ♖g1   **♘h4**
This is a more subtle way to con-
duct the attack. Now the only move for
White is 31 ♗f1!, which I planned to
answer by 31...♕f6 pressuring the
kingside. In my view, the chances
should be about equal. Both Black and
White have to keep their eyes open,
watching all sides of the board. Unfortunately for Nana, she missed my
coming assault and played...

   31 ♘b6?? (D)

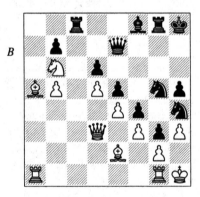

   31 ...   **♘xh3!**
A decisive blow. The rook cannot
be taken on account of 32 ♘xc8?
♘f2#.

   32 gxh3   **g2+**
   33 ♖xg2

33 ♔h2 leads to a beautiful mate after 33...♕g5 34 ♗e1 (34 ♖gb1 ♕g3+ 35 ♔g1 ♕xh3 36 ♘xc8 ♕h1+ 37 ♔f2 ♕h2 does not help either) 34...♕g3+ 35 ♗xg3 fxg3#.

33	...	♘xg2
34	♖g1 *(D)*	

Taking the rook was once more impossible, this time due to 34 ♘xc8 ♕h4.

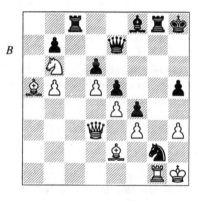

34	...	♖c1!

The whole combination hinged on this move. White has no choice but to accept the Greek gift because her position would collapse after 35 ♗d1 ♘e3.

35	♖xc1	♕h4

White is completely lost.

36	♗f1	♕xh3+
37	♔g1	♘e1+
38	♔f2	♕g3+

The reason that I preferred the text-move over 38...♘xd3+, with a much easier finish, was that I wanted to prolong the game as long as possible. I simply hoped that this would leave a deeper impression in my opponent's memory, which might have a bad influence on her later in this match. Childish logic, as I see it now.

39	♔e2	♘xd3
40	♔xd3	♕xf3+

It was pity that Nana did not want to play on. Instead, she resigned.

0-1

The score had changed to 5½-1½ in my favour and the Chinese delegation was relieved. I was not far from overall victory. At the start of the eleventh game my lead had increased to 7½-2½ and I needed half a point more to finish the match. Prior to the game, the members of my group gathered in the playing hall and all of them were dressed quite formally. Although no one had explicitly mentioned it to me, it was clear that they thought that the match would end on that particular day. I felt the same desire but first there was ... the game.

Game 21

Nana Ioseliani – Xie Jun

World Ch Match (11), Monaco 1993
King's Indian, Gligorić

1 d4	♘f6
2 c4	g6
3 ♘c3	♗g7
4 e4	d6
5 ♘f3	0-0
6 ♗e2	e5

I was very happy to see 'my' King's Indian again as I had already scored 4½ points out of my five black games with it.

7 ♗e3	c6
8 d5	♘g4
9 ♗g5	f6
10 ♗h4 *(D)*	

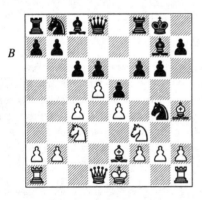

10 ... h5!?

Karpov-Kasparov, World Ch match (19), New York/Lyons 1990 saw Black try 10...♘a6 11 ♘d2 ♘h6 12 a3 ♘f7 13 f3 ♗h6 (13...h5 would transpose to our game) 14 ♗f2 f5 15 ♕c2 ♗d7 16 b4 c5 17 ♖b1 b6 18 ♘f1 ♗f4 19 g3 ♗h6 20 h4 ♘c7 with an equal position.

11 ♘d2	♘a6
12 a3	♘h6
13 f3	♘f7
14 dxc6?!	

This is not accurate because it gives away the e6-square. It was better to consolidate the position with 14 ♗d3.

14 ...	bxc6
15 b4	♘c7 *(D)*

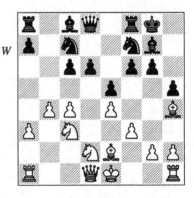

Black's plan is crystal clear: the knight heads for the excellent f4-square.

16 ♘b3	♘e6
17 0-0	♘f4
18 ♖e1	♗e6

Yet another piece makes use of the e6-square. In the meantime, White has hardly managed to put any pressure on Black's position.

19   &f1   g5
20   &f2 *(D)*

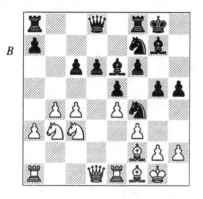

       20   ...   f5?!
Now it is my turn to make a dubious move. 20...g4 was indicated, with increasing pressure on the kingside.

       21   ⓝa5
White could have refuted Black's 20th move with 21 g3! fxe4 (21...ⓝg6 is possible, of course, but Black's attack has lost momentum altogether) 22 gxf4 exf4 23 ⓝxe4, when White has a large advantage.

       21   ...   ♛d7?!
Again, there was a better move in 21...♜c8. The black queen can later move to a more active square such as g5.

       22   c5!?
White misses her last opportunity to play 22 g3.

       22   ...   d5!

23   g3? *(D)*
Too late now! White should have continued with 23 exd5 cxd5 24 c6, with at least some initiative on the queenside. Still, I like Black's dynamic position with five pawns on the fourth rank.

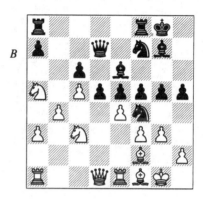

       23   ...   fxe4!
Of course! 23...ⓝg6 is inferior due to 24 exd5 cxd5 25 &b5, when White has a substantial plus.

       24   fxe4
Not much better is 24 gxf4 exf4 25 &d4 ⓝe5 26 fxe4 &g4 27 &e2 f3 with a superior position for Black.

       24   ...   d4
       25   gxf4   exf4
       26   ⓝxc6
After 26 ⓝa4 ⓝe5 Black would have more than enough compensation. Nana now decides to return the piece in the hope of saving the endgame. But Black has lost none of her advantage. The threats on the kingside are more serious than White's counterplay, even without queens.

| 26 | ... | dxc3 |

The simplest method of maintaining the advantage and much better than 26...♕xc6 27 ♘d5!.

27	♕xd7	♗xd7
28	♘e7+	♔h7
29	♖ac1 *(D)*	

29 ♘d5 ♘e5 is much better for Black.

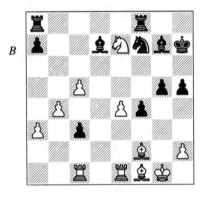

| 29 | ... | g4! |

Also in a typical King's Indian endgame it is important to fight for the initiative. The black knight jumps to g5 with devastating effect.

| 30 | ♖ed1 | ♗e6 |
| 31 | ♘d5?? | |

This effectively ends the game, because it does not create any counterplay. What else is there? During the game I tried to study the consequences of the daring 31 ♖d5!?. It is clear that White has certain play when Black decides to take the rook: 31...♗xd5 32 exd5 is the best White could have hoped for. The situation is unclear.

| 31 | ... | ♘g5 |
| 32 | ♘xc3 | h4 |

From now on, the position plays itself.

33	♖d3	g3
34	♗e1	♗e5
35	♗d2	♘h3+
36	♔g2	♖ad8
37	♘d5	♗g4

37...♘f2 would have won as well. In this lost position, Nana could no longer make her 38th move in time and she decided to resign.

0-1

It is not easy to comment on the course of such a match. Naturally it had been easier than my first World Championship Match. I was more experienced this time and, moreover, things went extremely well straight from the beginning. It all seemed effortless and I could not help feeling that the match was over too quickly. There was one group in particular who had reason to complain about the exceptional 8½-2½ score: the journalists. With little tension in the match, they clearly had problems writing exciting copy. Half-way through the match, one of the journalists even joked that I could at least make some more draws. A match that went up and down would have given them a lot of topics and interesting articles. To be honest, their problems did not concern me in the least.

9 Sabbatical Years (1994-1995)

In the summer of 1994, having been away from the game for half a year, I started to play serious chess again. After the match with Ioseliani I needed a break and I spent most of my time at the university. Then, I travelled to Indonesia and from there on to India, where I was invited to act as commentator in the Timman-Salov match. Sanghi Nagar proved to be a very remote place, nowhere near a big city. The whole area of 400 square kilometres was owned by one man – quite impressive. It was a strange feeling, being so isolated from the rest of the world. For me, it was a relaxed time and a nice job for a change. It was also the first time that I realized how much pressure the male players had to contend with. Anand was two points up against Kamsky, and lost. Kramnik blew it in the last round against Gelfand and the match Timman-Salov was very tense as well. In the beginning, Timman was lucky to save a few lost positions. Later, he himself got the good positions but started to lose. How tough life must be as a chess professional, I thought.

It was in the summer that I received the 'male' International Grandmaster title. I do not remember exactly when, but I think that the notification came just before my trip to Amsterdam. In the early days, there was the rule that the World Championship title for women counted as one 'male' GM norm over nine games. I had gained the title twice and had scored 'male' GM norms in Monaco and Amsterdam as well. Later, I understood that the rules had been changed and that winning the World Championship twice would automatically lead to an GM title. I am not sure whether I was awarded the GM title under the old or the new rules, but it certainly gave me great satisfaction.

During the year 1994, my overall performance was quite good and my international Elo rating went up accordingly, first to 2515 and later to 2555. This did not come as a surprise to me. I had invested a lot of time in preparing for my match against Ioseliani and the investment started to pay off. The second half of 1994 was a period when I loved to play and was full of energy. Travels took me to Amsterdam, Tilburg, Jakarta, Kuala Lumpur, Cap d'Agde, Monaco and Moscow. From that particular period, I have selected some of my most memorable games.

The first tournament after my sabbatical period was Amsterdam, where I competed in the Donner Memorial. Jan-Hein Donner was a Dutch grandmaster who reached his peak in the 1960s. His greatest successes included a triumph in

Beverwijk 1963, ahead of Bronstein, Parma and Ivkov, and a first place in Venice 1967. In the latter tournament, he even surpassed the reigning World Champion Petrosian. I learned that Donner used to be extremely popular amongst Dutch chess aficionados. Not necessarily for his play, but all the more so for his writing. He left a huge legacy in countless articles, some of which were quite controversial. One of his pet subjects was the combination 'women and chess'. Women were not able to play chess, Donner used to declare enthusiastically, because they lacked intuition. This probably explains the eagerness of the chess organizers to ensure that there was at least one female contestant in their tournament.

Thus far, Amsterdam had been my strongest tournament ever. With the likes of Piket, Adams, Yusupov, Timman, Lautier and Ivan Sokolov amongst the participants, it reached Category 15. The rating average of the other nine players was 110 Elo points higher than my own. Hence, when I agreed to accept the invitation, I was not sure how many defeats were awaiting me. Things turned out rather better than expected. After a slow start, I started to make some points and in the end managed to score 50%. If I had won in the last round against Piket, instead of losing, I would even have shared first place. But Piket played a good game and won deservedly. The quality of my games was far lower than could have been expected in view of the level of this tournament. Nevertheless, they were very interesting. Here is one of my better games.

Game 22
Paul van der Sterren – Xie Jun
Donner Memorial, Amsterdam 1994
English, Anti-Grünfeld

1	♘f3	♘f6
2	c4	g6
3	g3	♗g7
4	♗g2	0-0
5	♘c3	d5
6	cxd5	♘xd5
7	0-0	♘c6
8	♘xd5	

I was quite surprised by my opponent's opening choice. White just wants to skip the middlegame stage, intending to steer the game directly into the endgame. It is more common to play 8 d4. Then the game transposes to one of the main lines of the Grünfeld, with a lot of choices for both sides.

8	...	♕xd5
9	d3 (D)	

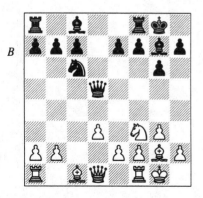

9 ...   ♕b5!

Van der Sterren used quite some time to decide upon his next move. Maybe he had expected me to follow Ribli-K.Honfi, Hungarian Ch 1974, which proceeded 9...♕h5?! 10 ♕b3! and White was slightly better. Black had a problem there because the queen is not well placed on h5.

10	♖b1	a5
11	♗e3?!	

This is a dubious move. White would have done better completing his development with 11 b3. Some vital pieces will soon disappear from the board after 11...a4 12 ♗b2 ♗xb2 13 ♖xb2 ♗e6, leading to an approximately equal position, as in Bertholee-Hellers, Amsterdam 1990. White has another try in 11 a4 ♕a6 12 ♗e3 e5 13 ♕c1 e4 14 dxe4 ♕xe2, Valcarcel-Portisch, Las Palmas 1972, but Black is OK in this line, too. All in all, I doubt whether the set-up with 8 ♘xd5 promises White any advantage.

11	...	a4
12	♕d2	

12 ♘g5 was tried in Andersson-Agdestein, Haninge 1988. That game continued 12...♘d4 13 ♖e1 ♗d7 14 ♘e4 c5 15 ♕c1 ♖ac8 16 ♗h6 ♖fd8 17 ♗xg7 ♔xg7 18 b3 axb3 19 e3 and

now Agdestein played an interesting piece sacrifice: 19...♕xd3 20 exd4 bxa2 21 ♖b2 cxd4 22 ♕a1 ♗e6 23 ♘g5 ♗b3. The position is difficult to evaluate.

12 ...   ♗e6 (D)

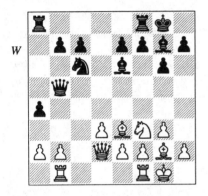

13 a3

After the appearance of the weak b3-square, Black will find it quite easy to decide upon a plan. It was impossible for White to play 13 b3, however, on account of 13...axb3 14 axb3 ♖a3, when Black has a big advantage.

13 ...   ♘a5
14 ♗h6

During the game I was not sure how to meet 14 ♘d4!?, but later I found the way to improve Black's position: 14...♗xd4 15 ♗xd4 ♘b3 16 ♕e3 ♘xd4 17 ♕xd4 ♖fd8 18 ♕c3 c5! followed by ...♖ac8 and ...b6. Black has an easier game and more space. On the other hand, White has quite a solid position and should be able to defend successfully.

14 ...   ♘b3

15 ♕e3   ♖fd8
16 ♗xg7   ♔xg7
17 d4?!

Realizing that Black has a clear plan to strengthen her position, White loses his patience. A better move would have been 17 ♘g5, which I planned to answer with the logical 17...♖a6. In that case, White has two reasonable moves. Firstly 18 ♖fe1, which Black meets with 18...h6 (better than 18...♘d4 19 ♕c1) 19 ♘e4 ♕e5 20 ♘c3 ♕xe3 21 fxe3 c6 with the idea of ...b5, ...♖b8 and ...b4. Black is better but White has survived thus far. The second try is 18 ♖bd1, when Black can reply in the same, favourable way with 18...h6 (18...♘d4 is interesting) 19 ♘e4 ♕e5 20 ♘c3 ♕xe3 21 fxe3 c6. Black has some advantage in these lines. Nevertheless, 17 ♘g5 is better than the text-move, which creates yet another weakness.

17 ...   ♖d7
18 ♕c3 (D)

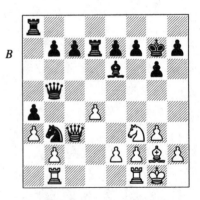

18 ...   ♕a5!

This powerful move secures the advantage. Alternatives would only allow White to push his central pawns, for instance 18...♔g8? 19 e4 c6 20 ♖fd1 ♕a5 21 ♕e3 ♗g4 22 h3 ♗xf3 23 ♗xf3 ♖ad8 24 d5 and White has somewhat improved his position.

19 ♖fe1   f6

I would have played the same move in response to 19 ♖bd1.

20 ♕xa5?

White escapes into an ending, but it soon becomes clear that this one is extremely unpleasant for him. I had expected the natural move 20 ♖bd1 and planned to reply 20...♖a6, gradually, albeit slowly, improving my position.

20 ...   ♖xa5
21 ♖bd1   ♖b5
22 e3   ♘a5 *(D)*

The b2-pawn cannot be defended any longer. But White has a nice trick up his sleeve.

consequences appear good for me. It is unlikely that any other move would have saved the game for White. Still, he could have chosen a continuation that would have put me more to the test. Not 23 ♖e2 because of 23...♘c4, when Black is much better. Most difficulties would have been posed by 23 ♖d2!? ♘c4 24 ♖c2 ♖xb2 (not 24...♘xb2? 25 ♖b1) 25 ♖xb2 ♘xb2 26 ♖b1 ♘c4 27 ♖xb7 c6! (it is too early for 27...♘xa3 due to 28 ♖a7 ♗b3 29 ♘d2 followed by ♗c6) 28 ♖b4 ♖a7 29 ♘e1 ♘xa3 30 ♗xc6 ♗b3 31 ♔g2 (31 f4 deserves deeper analysis as it makes way for the white king) 31...♖a6! (31...♘c4 fails tactically to 32 ♗xa4!, restoring the material balance after the forced 32...♘xe3+ 33 fxe3 ♗xa4) 32 ♗b7 ♖a5 33 ♗c6 ♘c2. I think that the final position is won for Black, but it may have been laborious to find during the game.

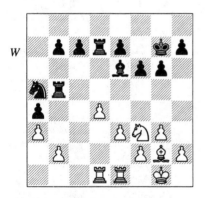

23 d5? *(D)*

A nice move – which I overlooked, I must admit – but fortunately the

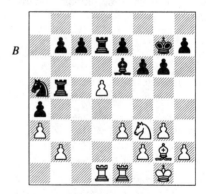

23 ...   ♗f7!

I established quickly that the pawn on d5 was poisoned. Black cannot take it with any of the pieces. Both 23...♖bxd5 and 23...♖dxd5 are punished by 24 ♘d4 and, even more remarkably, 23...♗xd5 fails to the same move. After 24 ♘d4! ♖c5 25 e4! ♗f7 26 ♘f5+ gxf5 27 ♖xd7, White would be an exchange to the good.

24	♖d4	♖xb2
25	♖xa4	♖xd5 (D)

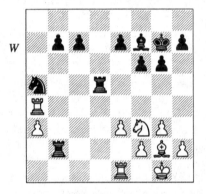

Black is a healthy pawn up, which should normally be enough for victory.

26	e4	♖db5
27	♗f1	♖c5
28	e5	

White tries to drive a wedge into the black pawn structure. He would be worse off after 28 ♖b4 ♖a2, with an easy win for Black.

28	...	♘c6
29	exf6+	exf6
30	♘d4?! (D)	

In addition to his material deficit, White's pieces are badly placed as well. This all makes it difficult to find a proper defensive move. The text-move allows Black to execute a 'petite combinaison'.

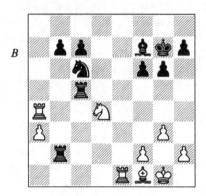

30	...	b5!
31	♘xb5	♖bxb5
32	♗xb5	♖xb5
33	♖c1	♗d5
34	♖a6	♘d4

34...♖b6 would have been the safest way to win.

35	♖xc7+	♔h6
36	f4	♖b2
37	♖aa7	♘f3+
38	♔f1	♗c4+
39	♖xc4	♘d2+
40	♔e2	♘xc4+
41	♔d3	♘d6
42	♖d7	♖b3+
43	♔c2	♖b6
44	a4	♘e4
45	a5	♖a6
46	♖d5	♘d6
47	♔c3	♘b7
48	♔b4	f5
49	♖b5 (D)	

I took my time to calculate the resulting pawn ending right to the end.

To my great relief it proved to be a straightforward win.

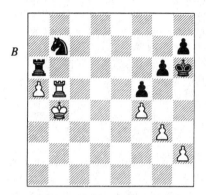

49 ...   ♘xa5!

A nice way to finish the game.

50 ♖xa5   ♖xa5
51 ♔xa5   g5! *(D)*

The pawn endings are interesting and study-like. When I calculated some candidate moves during the game, I realized that not every line wins. The text-move is the most convincing way. Black can also win with 51...♔h5, although care is needed. White can only play 52 h3, after which Black can choose between two different winning lines:

a) 52...g5 53 fxg5 ♔xg5 54 ♔b4 h5 (not 54...f4? 55 h4+! ♔g4 56 gxf4 ♔xf4 57 h5 ♔g5 58 ♔c3 ♔xh5 59 ♔d3 ♔g4 60 ♔e2 ♔g3 61 ♔f1, drawing) 55 ♔c3 h4 56 gxh4+ ♔xh4 57 ♔d2 ♔xh3! (the only move as 57...♔g3? 58 ♔e2 ♔g2 59 ♔e3 ♔g3 60 ♔e2 f4 61 ♔f1 draws once again) 58 ♔e3 ♔g3 59 ♔e2 f4 60 ♔f1 ♔f3 gives Black the opposition on the sixth rank.

b) The second win follows after 52...h6 53 ♔b4 g5 54 fxg5 hxg5 55 ♔c3 g4 (55...f4? 56 gxf4 gxf4 57 ♔d2 ♔h4 58 ♔e2 ♔g3 59 ♔f1 is equal) 56 h4 (56 hxg4+ ♔xg4 57 ♔d2 ♔xg3 58 ♔e2 f4 59 ♔f1 ♔f3 wins) 56...f4 57 ♔d3 (not 57 gxf4 g3) 57...fxg3 58 ♔e2 ♔xh4 59 ♔f1 ♔h3 60 ♔g1 g2 61 ♔f2 ♔h2.

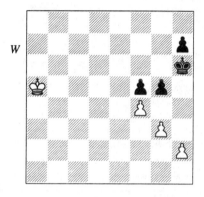

52 ♔b4

The unfortunate white monarch hurries back to the kingside, but to no avail. Other moves lead to the same result, e.g. 52 fxg5+ ♔xg5 53 h3 (53 ♔b4 ♔g4 54 ♔c4 ♔h3 55 ♔d4 ♔xh2 56 ♔e5 ♔xg3 57 ♔xf5 h5 58 ♔g5 h4) 53...h5! (this is easier than 53...f4 54 h4+ ♔g4 55 gxf4 ♔xf4 56 h5 ♔g5 57 ♔b4 – if the white king can reach the f1-square, the game will end in a draw, but Black is just in time to prevent this – 57...♔xh5 58 ♔c3 ♔g4 59 ♔d2 ♔f3 60 ♔e1 ♔g2 61 ♔e2 h5 and Black wins) 54 ♔b4 h4 55 gxh4+ ♔xh4 56 ♔c3 ♔xh3, winning easily.

52 ...   gxf4

53	gxf4	♔h5
54	♔c4	♔g4
55	♔d3 (D)	

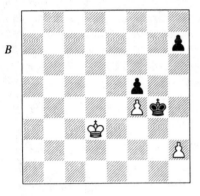

B

55 ...   ♔f3

There is only one obvious way to go wrong. If I had gone directly for the h-pawn, White draws with 55...♔h3? 56 ♔d4 ♔xh2 57 ♔e5 ♔g3 58 ♔xf5 h5 59 ♔g5. But the f-pawn could be taken without objection: 55...♔xf4 56 ♔e2 ♔e4 57 ♔f2 f4 58 ♔e2 f3+ 59 ♔f2 ♔f4 60 ♔f1 ♔e3 61 ♔e1 f2+ 62 ♔f1 ♔f3 63 h4 h6 64 h5 ♔e3 wins.

Here Van der Sterren resigned.

0-1

The main line shows the reason why: 56 ♔d2 (56 ♔d4 ♔xf4, or 56 h3 ♔xf4 57 ♔e2 ♔g3) 56...♔g2 57 ♔e3 ♔xh2 58 ♔d4 ♔g3 59 ♔e5 ♔g4.

The next game was played in the South of France, in the last round of a five-round mini-tournament, a strange Swiss system with ten players. The event itself was quite strong, featuring big names such as Gelfand, Topalov, Adams, Lautier and the youngest grandmaster at the time, Leko. As it was arranged, the winner would play a mini-match of two games against another big shot: Anatoly Karpov. I do not have to add that I had little hope of winning the tournament. But, at least, I tried my very best.

Game 23
Boris Alterman – Xie Jun
Cap d'Agde 1994
King's Indian, Averbakh

1	d4	♘f6
2	c4	g6
3	♘c3	♗g7
4	e4	d6
5	♗e2	0-0
6	♗g5	♘a6
7	♕d2	e5
8	d5	c6
9	f3	

9 h4 was played in my game against Gaprindashvili, Borzhomi 1990 (see Game 8).

9	...	cxd5
10	cxd5	♗d7
11	g4	h6
12	♗e3	h5
13	h3	♘c5

Recently I tried another move here: 13...♕b8 14 ♗b5 ♕e8 15 ♗xd7 ♕xd7 16 a4 ♖fc8 17 ♘ge2 ♘c5 18 ♕d1 ♕d8 19 b4 ♘cd7 20 a5 a6 21 ♘a4 ♘h7 was the game Wagner-Xie Jun, Cannes 1997.

| 14 | 0-0-0 *(D)* | |
| 14 | ... | ♕b8 |

This was a new move, deviating from Alterman-Gelfand, played two rounds earlier in the same tournament. That game continued 14...♕b6 15 ♔b1 a5 16 ♗d3 a4 17 ♘ge2 ♖fc8 18 a3 ♗e8 19 ♘c1 ♕d8 20 ♗g5 ♕b6 21 ♗e3 ♕d8 22 ♗g5 ♕b6 and the

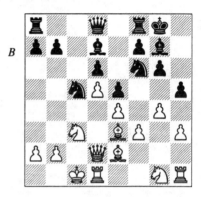

players agreed to a draw. Alterman, who comments on this game in *Informator*, assesses the position after 22 ♗c2 b5 23 ♘3a2 as slightly better for White. My trainer Ye Jiangchuan did not like the queen sortie to b6, for the reason that it stands in the way of the b-pawn. So we decided to try a novel idea.

| 15 | ♔b1 | ♖c8?! |

I contemplated the move 15...b5 for a while, but rejected it because I disliked 16 b4 ♘a4 17 ♘xa4 bxa4 18 ♔a1 ♖c8. I was not sure about this position. In the post-mortem, after some analysis, we agreed that it is about equal.

| 16 | ♖h2? | |

This rook manoeuvre is too slow for this kind of position. Later I found an analysis in *Informator*, written by Alterman, claiming that 16 ♗b5 ♗xb5 17 ♘xb5 a6 18 ♘a3 b5 19 ♖c1 is very advantageous for White. I do not agree with this assessment, because Black plays 19...♕b7, with the idea ...♖c7 and ...♖ac8. I think that the position is about equal.

16   ...   b5 *(D)*

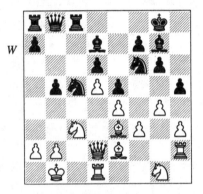

17   ♖c1?

It seems natural to put a rook on the open file. But, in fact, after this move White is in serious trouble. The only move was 17 b4, hoping to slow down Black's attack and to get some counterplay.

17   ...   a5

Black has already taken control. The position of the knight on c5 guarantees Black the more promising position.

18	♗d3	♖a7
19	♘ge2	♖ac7
20	♘d1	a4
21	♘f2	b4?!

Here, the most precise move was 21...h4!? with the idea of continuing

...♘e8. Only then, when everything is ready, should Black push ...b4.

22   ♗xc5 *(D)*

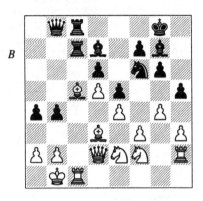

22   ...   dxc5!

A good strategic decision! If you have a space advantage, you should keep as much material on the board as possible. The opponent will always face the problem of finding the right squares for his pieces. Inferior would be 22...♖xc5 23 ♖xc5 dxc5 (23...♖xc5 24 ♖h1 followed by ♖c1 defuses the attack) 24 ♗c4 ♗b5 25 ♗xb5 ♕xb5 26 ♘d3 and White is back in the game.

23   ♗c4

Not bad in itself, but White could have gained one more tempo to re-arrange his pieces: 23 ♗a6! seems better because the black rook is much better placed on c8 than on d8. Play could continue 23...♖d8 24 ♗c4 ♗b5 – the blockade must be removed – 25 ♘d3 ♗xc4 (Black should not open the h-file with 25...hxg4 26 hxg4 ♗xc4 27 ♖xc4 ♕b5 28 ♖c1, when White takes over the initiative) 26 ♖xc4 ♕b5 27 b3 (27 ♖c1? is a mistake due to 27...♗h6 with an advantage) 27...♖a8 (this seems better than 27...♘e8 28 gxh5 ♘d6 29 h6 ♗f8 30 ♘xe5, with good play for White) 28 ♕b2 axb3 29 axb3 ♘d7. Although I still prefer Black's position, it is clear that White has more counterplay here than in the game.

23	...	♗b5
24	♘d3	♗xc4
25	♖xc4	♕b5
26	b3	

26 ♖c1 is, again, met by 26...♗h6. The other rook move, 26 ♖c2, provokes 26...b3 27 axb3 axb3 28 ♖c3 c4 and the attack is unstoppable.

26	...	♘e8 *(D)*

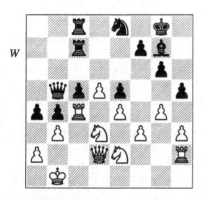

W

27	♖h1

The second rook comes to the rescue. White did not have the time to disrupt Black's kingside pawn structure: 27 gxh5 ♘d6 28 h6 axb3 29 axb3 ♘xc4 30 bxc4 ♕xc4 31 hxg7 ♕b3+ 32 ♘b2 ♕xf3 would give Black a big advantage.

27	...	♘d6
28	♖hc1	hxg4
29	hxg4	axb3
30	axb3	♘xc4
31	♖xc4	

I did not think very much of this position for White. However, once it appeared, it dawned upon me that, if Black could not find a swift method to crack White's position, I would even be worse. The two white knights can come to life very quickly.

31	...	♕a6
32	♘ec1 *(D)*	

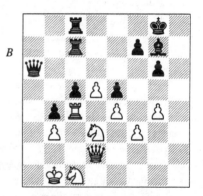

B

32	...	♕f6!

I like this move, which extends the power of the queen to the maximum. Now my plan is to occupy the a-file with the two rooks. In the meantime, the queen will attack from the other side of the board.

33	♕e3	♕h4

Threatening 34...♗h6.

34	g5	♕h3

Alterman was already in serious time-pressure, while I had plenty of time left on my clock. Moreover, my position is much easier to play.

35 ♘f2

It was hard to find a move for White. Taking the pawn on c5 was no solution either, because it gives Black yet another open line. I had foreseen 35 ♖xc5 ♖xc5 36 ♘xc5 ♗f8 37 ♘5d3 ♕g2 38 ♘e2 ♕f1+ 39 ♘ec1 ♖c3, when White runs out of moves.

35 ...   ♕f1
36 ♘g4   ♖a8

37 ♕f2   ♕h1

The position is won. The rest requires no further comment.

38 ♔c2   ♖a1
39 ♔d2   ♖b1
40 ♘e3   ♗f8
41 ♕g3   ♖a7
42 ♕xe5   ♕xf3
43 d6   ♕f2+
44 ♔d3   ♖b2
45 ♘c2   ♖d7

0-1

With this win, I shared second place with 3 out of 5, together with three other players. In order to decide the final standings, a double-rounded tie-break was held between the four of us. I will never forget how I suffered in those six rapid games and, finally, I ended in fifth place. Gelfand came out the winner, with 4 points, and went on to beat Karpov.

After Cap d'Agde, it was time again for the Ladies against Veterans tournament – my second time in this event. This time it was held in Monaco, the same place where I had defended the World Championship title 18 months earlier against Nana Ioseliani. For me personally, this second visit to Monaco was the fulfilment of a long-time dream. For the first time I travelled in the company of my mother. To understand what this means, the reader should realize that Chinese people between 50 and 70 years of age grew up in a completely different era. Even though they witnessed great changes in Chinese society, almost none of them have ever had an opportunity to travel abroad. My mother had never been to any other part of the world and she enjoyed every minute of it. To me it was also a new experience, to be accompanied by one of my closest relatives during a tournament. This was all thanks to the generosity of the organizers, I would like to add, who allowed the participants to bring along a partner. It was a thrill to watch my mother's delight during our stay in Monaco, and it gave me the feeling that I had really accomplished something great.

Game 24
Xie Jun – Bent Larsen
Ladies against Veterans, Monaco 1994
Pirc, Classical

1 e4	g6
2 d4	♗g7
3 ♘c3	c6

Black has several options if he develops his pieces via this move-order. It is possible to choose between ...d6 and ...d5. In the latter case, the game will transpose to the Caro-Kann Defence.

4 ♘f3   d6

I faced the move 4...d5 in my game against Nona Gaprindashvili at the Novi Sad Olympiad 1990, which continued 5 h3 ♘h6 6 ♗f4 ♛b6!? 7 ♛c1 dxe4 8 ♘xe4 ♘f5 9 c3 ♗e6 10 ♗d3 ♗d5 11 0-0 0-0 12 ♖e1 ♘d7 13 ♘ed2 ♖fe8 14 ♗xf5 gxf5 15 ♘e5 with the easier game for White.

5 h3	♘f6
6 a4	0-0
7 ♗e3	♘bd7
8 ♗e2	e5 *(D)*

8...a5 is a reasonable alternative.

9 dxe5!?

The reason for fixing the pawn structure is that I did not want to allow Black to play ...d5 on the next move. This would have happened if I had castled, e.g. 9 0-0 d5 10 exd5 e4 11 ♘d2 cxd5 12 ♘b5 ♘e8 13 c3 f5 with a complicated position.

9 ...   dxe5

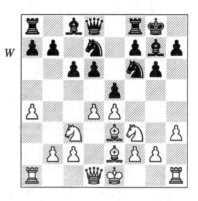

10 0-0

When I checked my database afterwards, I found the same position in one of Spassky's games. He decided to play the knight to c4: 10 ♘d2 ♛e7 11 ♘c4 ♖d8 12 ♛d6 ♗f8! 13 0-0-0 ♛xd6 14 ♘xd6 ♘b6 15 ♘c4 ♖xd1+ 16 ♖xd1 ♘xc4 17 ♗xc4, with a slight edge for White in Spassky-Chabanon, French Ch 1991. The game later ended in a draw.

10 ...	♛e7
11 ♛d3	a5!?

This move prevents White from gaining more space on the queenside, but it does weaken the dark squares. 11...♘h5 was Black's choice in Franzoni-Gavrikov, Zurich 1992. The players agreed to a draw after 12 ♖fd1 ♘f4 13 ♛d6 ♘xe2+ 14 ♘xe2 ♛xd6 15

♖xd6 ♘f6 16 ♘c3, so this game does not tell us very much. I believe that White should have played 12 ♕d2, instead of 12 ♖fd1, to prevent the black knight from landing on f4. After 13 ♖fd1 he would have been better.

12 ♕c4

12 ♖fd1 ♖e8 13 ♕d6 ♗f8 gives Black a solid position.

12 ...   ♖e8

13 ♖fd1 (D)

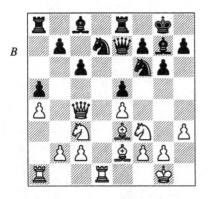

13 ...   h6?!

Larsen's idea is to transfer the knight via h7 to g5, where it will be more active. In the future, the knight might even eye the squares d4 and f4 – from e6 – but it is quite obvious that this plan is time-consuming. More sensible would be 13...♕b4 14 ♘g5 ♖f8 15 b3 ♕xc4 16 ♗xc4 h6 17 ♘f3 ♖e8 18 ♘h4 (18 ♖d2 ♗f8 is unclear) 18...♘f8 19 ♖d6 ♗e6 20 ♘f3 ♗xc4 21 bxc4 ♘e6 22 ♖b1 with some initiative for White. However, the doubled c-pawns are not pleasant and guarantee Black counterplay.

14 ♘d2   ♘h7?!

Once Larsen has made up his mind and decided upon a certain plan, he finds it very hard not to carry on with it. It was not too late for 14...♕b4 15 ♘b3 (15 ♕b3 permits Black to develop his pieces rapidly with 15...♗f8 16 ♘c4 ♕xb3 17 cxb3 ♘c5) 15...♗f8 16 f3 (better than 16 ♖d2 ♘b6) 16...♕xc4 17 ♗xc4 b6 18 ♖d2, with only a small plus for White.

15 ♕b3

The threat ♘c4 becomes a nuisance.

15 ...   ♘g5

Larsen proceeds with his plan. As a result, he forfeits his last opportunity to exchange queens, with 15...♕b4 16 ♘c4 ♗f8 17 ♕a3!? ♘hf6 18 ♘d6 ♖d8 19 ♘xc8 ♕xa3 20 bxa3 ♖axc8 21 ♖ab1. Thanks to the bishop-pair, White maintains an edge.

16 ♘c4   ♘c5?

A careless move. Black will be forced to exchange queens, only now under less favourable conditions. The white knight will invade on d6 or b6, with devastating effect. I suggest 16...♘e6 as the better move.

17 ♕a3   ♘ce6

18 ♕xe7   ♖xe7

19 ♘b6   ♖b8

20 ♗g4!

It is important to keep the c8-bishop incarcerated. The powerful knight on b6 restricts all Black's activities.

20 ...   ♖e8 (D)

We have arrived at the critical moment in the game. Black has played his rook back to e8 in order to free his cramped position. He is ready for 21...h5, which was impossible with the rook on e7 (20...h5? 21 ♗xg5). So what can White do to consolidate the firm grip?

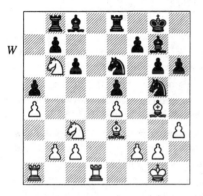

21 ♗xg5!

The right answer! The text-move resolves the ...h5 issue, yet there remains one other problem to solve: how is White to deal with the freeing manoeuvre ...♗f8-c5?

21 ...   hxg5
22 ♘b1!

The combination of my 21st and 22nd moves decides the result of the game. Black has no counterplay whatsoever.

22 ...   ♗f8
23 ♘d2   ♗c5
24 ♘dc4

The second knight arrives just in time.

24 ...   ♗xb6
25 ♘xb6   ♔f8
26 ♖d2   ♔e7

27 ♖ad1   ♖f8 (D)

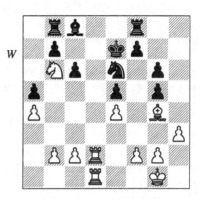

28 ♘xc8+   ♖fxc8
29 ♖d7+   ♔f6

29...♔f8 30 ♗xe6 fxe6 31 ♖h7 will also suffice for a win.

30 ♗xe6   fxe6
31 g4!! (D)

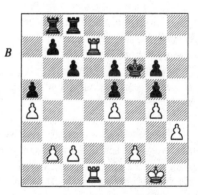

A lovely position. I was just wondering whether Larsen would go as far as to allow me to play 32 ♖d3 and 33 ♖f3, with mate 'between the posts'. He did not, and resigned instead.

1-0

The final position created considerable commotion amongst people in the analysis room. Some of my colleagues even joked that we had produced the position deliberately. Well, this is a question only my opponent can answer. I never asked Larsen why he went for this finale. Maybe he just thought that it would make a nice diagram. In any case, it was the first time I ever managed to win a game like this, and it is indeed one of my sweetest chess memories – espcecially since my opponent was one of the great players of all time.

Some months later, the Olympiad was held in Moscow but I did not perform well. I found it hard to focus on chess and, all the time, I instinctively felt that something was wrong at home. Perhaps this was a kind of telepathy, because when I returned to China I found out that my mother had been taken into hospital. She had undergone major surgery and was treated with chemotherapy. I was shocked and felt extremely sad. For the next two and a half months, my father and I took care of my mother. We did not have time to do anything else. The health care system in China is different compared to Europe and America, where patients usually only see their relatives during visiting hours. Family members in China, in contrast, take care of each other, even in hospital. My father and I spent a lot of time cooking for my mother and we stayed with her as much as possible. She could not eat much and we had to divide the meals over the day. These events affected me deeply and sent me into a period of reflection. I started to wonder about the meaning of life, and chess did not seem all that important any more. There were other priorities. It is needless to say that my chess schedule was severely disrupted by all this and, moreover, I had lost some of my interest. Initially I had planned to participate in the tournament in Groningen in December, but now my chess federation had to cancel my entry. Instead, I stayed at home with my family.

In March 1995, I travelled to Switzerland for the first leg of a twelve-game match against Lucas Brunner and then, in April, to San Francisco. I felt obliged to do so, because I had promised to compete, even though I did not feel much like playing. My mother was still in hospital. On both occasions I was not in great shape, but the results were not too bad. The performance in San Francisco was solid, but I suffered a disaster in the last round when I failed to convert a winning position against Robert Hübner.

Game 25
Dr Robert Hübner – Xie Jun
San Francisco 1995
Ruy Lopez, Flohr/Zaitsev

1	e4	e5
2	♘f3	♘c6
3	♗b5	a6
4	♗a4	♘f6
5	0-0	♗e7
6	♖e1	b5
7	♗b3	d6
8	c3	0-0
9	h3	♗b7
10	d4	♖e8
11	♘bd2	♗f8
12	a3	h6
13	♗c2	♘b8
14	b3	♘bd7
15	♗b2 (D)	

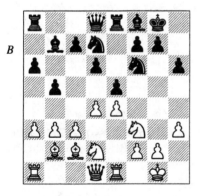

15 ...   c5

A theoretical novelty, as far as I am aware. Previously, every plan for Black started with the move ...c6, aiming for ...d5 or ...a5 in accordance with the requirements of the position. A well-known example in this line is Anand-Ivanchuk, Novi Sad Olympiad 1990, with the continuation 15...g6 16 a4 ♗g7 17 ♗d3 c6 18 ♕c2 ♕c7 19 b4 d5.

16	d5	♕c7
17	♗d3	

White had another move which tries to weaken the pawn on b5, or the b5-square itself. That line goes 17 ♕e2!? ♘b6 18 a4 bxa4 19 bxa4 a5 20 ♗d3, when Black has to be careful, and avoid 20...♖ec8 21 ♗b5 ♘e8? (to prepare ...♘c7, but 21...♘fd7!? is better) 22 c4 ♗a6 23 ♗c3 ♗xb5 24 cxb5, when White has a big advantage. The a5-pawn is weak and White will place his knight on c4. Instead, I would have opted for the more active 20...♖eb8!?, for instance 21 ♗b5 ♘fd7 22 c4 ♗a6 23 ♗c3 ♗xb5 24 cxb5 c4 with an unclear situation.

17	...	♘b6
18	♕e2	♗c8!
19	♘h2?!	

I do not like this move. 19 a4? is also poor due to 19...c4. However, White could have prevented any counterplay with 19 c4!?.

19	...	♗d7
20	c4	bxc4

Maybe I should have taken more time to consider 20...♖eb8!?, because White would be ill-advised to take on b5: after 21 cxb5?! axb5 22 ♗xb5? ♗xb5 23 ♕xb5 ♘a4 24 ♕d3 ♘xb2 25 ♕c2 ♘a4, Black is more than OK. I rejected 20...♖eb8 when I saw 21 ♖ec1, when I was at a loss for a good plan. That was the reason that I chose to keep the rook on e8.

21 ♘xc4   ♗b5
22 ♘d2 (D)

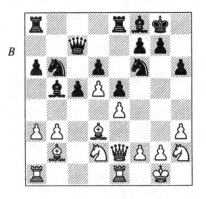

22 ...   ♖ab8?!
During the game I was uncertain about the evaluation of the position after White takes twice on b5. My change of opinion – i.e. that 23 ♗xb5 would favour White – came too late. In fact, I should have made my choice between 22...♗xd3!? 23 ♕xd3 ♖eb8 and 22...♕d7!?, maintaining the tension.

23 ♖ec1?!
Hübner should have profited from my mistake. He could have acquired an advantage with 23 ♗xb5 axb5 24

♕xb5 ♘bxd5 25 ♕d3 (or 25 ♕c4!?) 25...♘f4 26 ♕f3 ♘e6 27 ♖ec1.

23 ...   ♕d7
24 ♖c2   ♘h7!?
Black 'threatens' to play ...f5, thereby provoking White to clarify his intentions first.

25 a4   ♗xd3
26 ♕xd3   ♕b7
27 a5   ♘c8
28 ♘hf1 (D)
It is now time for action. I make use of the circumstance that b3 is weak, and try to undermine the d5-pawn.

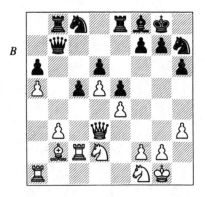

28 ...   f5!
Of course!
29 exf5?!
It was necessary to play 29 f3. After the text-move Black is already slightly better.

29 ...   ♘e7
30 ♘e3   ♘f6
31 ♘dc4   ♘exd5
32 ♘xd5   ♘xd5
33 ♕e4   ♘f6
34 ♕xb7   ♖xb7

The situation has changed drastically. Black has a favourable ending.

35 Rd1

Black would be even better off after 35 ♘b6 ♘d7 36 ♘xd7 Rxd7 37 Rd1 Rb7 with an impressive plus.

35 ...	Rxb3
36 ♘xd6	Rd8
37 ♗xe5 *(D)*	

White has won a pawn, but there is a price to pay.

37 ...	♘e4!
38 ♘xe4	

White was forced to give up the exchange. His position would collapse immediately after 38 f3 ♘xd6 39 Rcd2 c4, when White cannot regain the piece on d6: 40 ♗xd6 c3 is disastrous.

38 ...	Rxd1+
39 ♔h2	Rd5?!

Thus far, I had followed the right path, but here I miss the first opportunity to decide the game. After 39...Rb4 40 ♘xc5 I had seen the variation 40...Rd5? 41 ♘xa6 Rxe5 42 ♘xb4 ♗xb4 43 g4 ♗xa5 44 ♔g3 but was not

sure whether the position is won for Black. The bishop may prove to have the wrong colour, seeing that it does not control the h1-square. Unfortunately I overlooked the obvious 40...Rb5! which does not leave the b4-rook *en prise*. The text-move does not spoil anything though, and the position remains won.

40 f4	Rb4
41 Re2	♗e7
42 ♘g3	♗d8
43 ♘h5	Rb7
44 g4	♗xa5?

Too ambitious! There was still a convincing win with 44...Rbd7, trying to swap a pair of rooks. After the forced 45 ♗c3 Rd3 46 Rc2 c4 47 ♔g2 R3d5 Black has full control. The d8-bishop stops all potential plans including g4-g5.

45 ♗xg7	Rd2
46 Rxd2	♗xd2
47 ♗e5 *(D)*	

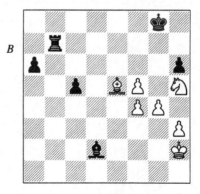

47 ...	♔f7??

I had seen this position when I played 44...♗xa5. However, this is one of the few examples where centralizing the king in an endgame is not correct. During the game, I simply underestimated White's plan of regrouping his forces on the kingside and did not check my calculations any further. I thought that the win would be easy, with my active king and material advantage. Only after White made his next move did I start to feel uncomfortable. After long thought, it dawned upon me that Black has no defence left. I spent almost all of my remaining time to the second time control, but there is no solution. Black's position is irretrievably lost. For the sake of completeness, I would like to add that Black would still have had good winning chances after 47...c4 48 ♘f6+ ♔f8 49 ♘e4 ♗a5 50 g5 hxg5 51 fxg5 ♗c7.

48	h4	♖e7
49	g5	hxg5
50	hxg5	♗a5
51	g6+	♔e8
52	♘f6+	♔d8
53	♘e4	

There was now no alternative but to resign.

1-0

When I returned from San Francisco, my mother had been discharged from hospital and the family was reunited at home. Gradually, my mother recovered and started to regain her spirits. The spring marked the end of what had been the most difficult period in my family's life.

Later in 1995, I played a number of mini-matches. It started in May with the second leg of the match against Lucas Brunner. The games in Bern, the capital of Switzerland, had resulted in five draws and one win for my opponent. The positions had been quite interesting. In Shanghai, with the home advantage, I did my utmost to take my revenge.

Game 26
Lucas Brunner – Xie Jun
Match (9), Shanghai 1995
King's Indian, Sämisch

1	d4	♘f6
2	c4	g6
3	♘c3	♗g7
4	e4	d6
5	f3	0-0
6	♘ge2	c5

Lucas was leading 3½-2½ after the first leg and I would have been further behind had I not been so lucky as to survive precarious positions resulting from the 6...♘c6 Sämisch King's Indian. Therefore I decided to choose a line from another system, which can also arise via the Benoni move-order. I did not have much experience with this particular variation. My knowledge was limited to some typical plans in certain positions. I have always found it quite difficult to analyse the Modern Benoni for Black, mainly because it is very hard to say anything sensible about the weakened pawn structure. It is better just to let it happen at the board.

7	d5	e6
8	♘g3	exd5
9	cxd5	a6
10	a4	♘bd7
11	♗e2	h5
12	0-0 *(D)*	

Akhsharumova-Xie Jun, Malaysia 1990, featured the move 12 ♗g5 (see Game 7).

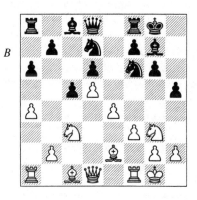

B

| 12 | ... | ♘h7 |

A new move, played with the obvious idea of pushing the f-pawn. I found one other example, which continued 12...h4 13 ♘h1 ♘h5 14 ♗e3 ♗d4! (a pawn sacrifice in order to take control of the squares f4 and g5) 15 ♗xd4 cxd4 16 ♕xd4 ♕g5 17 ♖ad1 f5 18 exf5 ♘f4 19 g3 ♖xf5 20 ♗d3 ♘h3+ 21 ♔g2 ♘f4+ 22 ♔g1 ♘h3+ 23 ♔g2 ♘f4+, and a draw was agreed in Spassky-J.Polgar, match (7), Budapest 1993.

| 13 | ♗e3 | h4 |

In Ward-Peng Xiaomin, London 1997, Black tried the interesting continuation 13...♖e8 14 ♕d2 f5 15 ♖ad1 h4 16 ♘h1 ♘e5 17 ♘f2 ♗d7 18 exf5 ♗xf5. The position is unclear, even though White managed to win later on.

14 ♘h1   f5
15 ♕d2   ♕f6?!

The idea behind this move is to force White to do something about the upcoming ...f4. It was actually quite funny that I realized only after White's next move – his only move, for that matter! – that the d7-knight has no future at all. The correct move is 15...♘e5, while 15...h3 16 g3 ♘e5 can also be considered. In both cases, White finds it difficult to bring the h1-knight back to life.

16 f4   ♖e8
17 ♘f2   ♘df8 *(D)*

I spent some time on the alternative 17...♕f7, which makes the f6-square available for one of the knights. It certainly looks more active, but I believe that Black still has to overcome considerable difficulties after 18 ♖ae1 ♘hf6 19 exf5 gxf5 20 ♘h3 (the d-pawn is lost after 20 ♗d3? ♘b6) 20...♘f8 21 ♘g5. White has a lead in development and will soon control the open e-file.

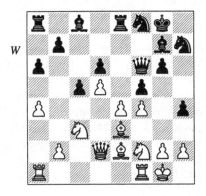

One glance at the position is enough to realize that Black's plan has not worked out well. It is impossible to regroup her pieces, nor is it easy to reinforce the attack on e4.

18 e5!?(?)

I am not sure about the punctuation mark that should be assigned here. The move certainly looks impressive, but from now on, Black has little to worry about. A quiet move such as 18 ♖ae1, or even 18 ♗d3, to continue with the piece development, would have given me more to think about.

18 ...   dxe5
19 fxe5   ♕xe5
20 ♗xc5   ♘d7
21 ♘d3   ♕f6
22 ♗f2   h3
23 g3   b6! *(D)*

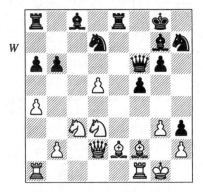

This is the best move for two reasons. Firstly, 24 ♘c5, which would have removed the most important blockader on d7, is prevented. In addition, Black develops the bishop to its most active diagonal. As a result, White cannot use his main weapon, the passed d-pawn.

24 Rae1   &b7
25 &f3   Wd6
26 &h1?

This is surely an ugly place for the white bishop. But is it fair to criticize the text-move? It was hard to evaluate the position in any case, since there were so many possibilities. Both sides have several weaknesses and it is extremely difficult to decide on a specific line of play. I had anticipated the move 26 &e3 with the idea of following up with 27 ۝f4. The line that I calculated continues 26...۝e5 27 ۝xe5 &xe5 28 Wf2 with an attack on the b6-pawn. I would probably have replied 28...۝f6 29 &xb6 Rac8, with compensation for the pawn.

26 ...   ۝hf6
27 ۝f4   ۝g4
28 ۝xh3

I was surprised that Brunner offered a draw here. Indeed, White is a pawn up but, on the other hand, all of my minor pieces are beautifully positioned and I will have the bishop-pair on the next move. Moreover, I had lost the first leg of the match in Bern and was eager to fight back. A draw was out of the question.

28 ...   ۝xf2
29 Rxe8+   Rxe8
30 ۝xf2   ۝e5
31 Re1 (D)
31 ...   &h7!

It is often worth spending a tempo improving the safety of the king. So is

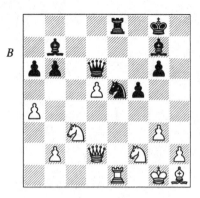

B

the case here! After the text-move, the game takes an unexpected turn. Suddenly, White has to pay attention to moves such as ...&h6 and ...۝c4. It is also important that the e8-rook can no longer be taken with check.

32 ۝d3?

Brunner goes astray and overlooks some tactical points. One better alternative would have been 32 Wd1, although Black has good counterplay with 32...&c5 33 &g2 b5 34 axb5 axb5. Another try was 32 ۝h3 &h6, but this hands the initiative to Black.

32 ...   ۝c4
33 Wf2   Rxe1+
34 ۝xe1

34 Wxe1 &d4+ gives Black a tremendous attack.

34 ...   ۝xb2!
35 Wxb2   Wc5+
36 &f1   &xc3
37 We2   &xd5
38 &xd5   Wxd5
39 ۝f3   &f6
40 &g2 (D)
40 ...   g5

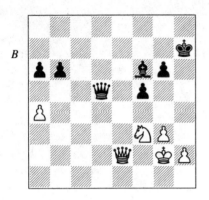

B

The simplest way to win the game would have been 40...b5 41 axb5 axb5 42 ♕d2 ♕c4 43 ♘g5+ ♗xg5 44 ♕xg5 ♕e2+ 45 ♔g1 ♔g7.

41 ♕d2   ♕c6

42 ♕d3!

To be honest, I had completely forgotten about this move. It makes my technical task a little bit more complicated but no more than that.

42 ...   ♕e4

43 ♕xe4   fxe4

44 ♘d2   e3

45 ♘e4   ♔g6

46 ♔f3   ♗d4

White cannot stop the move ...g4 as 47 h3 b5 loses.

47 h4

Black wins also after 47 ♘d6 g4+! 48 ♔e2 ♔f6 49 ♔d3 ♔e6 50 ♘c4 ♔d5, a straightforward and simple line. This line also contains one pitfall. If Black plays 47...♔f6 instead of 47...g4+!, then White draws with 48 h3! (not 48 g4? ♔e6 49 ♘c4 ♔d5 50 ♘xe3+ ♗xe3 51 ♔xe3 b5 52 axb5 axb5 53 ♔d3 ♔e5) 48...♔e6 49 ♘c4.

47 ...   g4+

48 ♔e2   b5

49 axb5   axb5

50 ♘d6   b4

51 ♘c4   b3

52 ♔d3   b2

53 ♘a3   ♔h5

54 ♘b1   ♗e5

0-1

In addition to winning this, the third game of the second leg, I also won the fifth game, albeit with some luck. The other four games in Shanghai ended in draws and so I defeated Brunner by the closest possible margin. Several weeks later I had the privilege to play against Viktor Korchnoi, in Wentzou. This mini-match comprised four games in total and, on this occasion, the outcome was less favourable. I lost two games and made two draws. Nonetheless, this proved a valuable experience. My eminent opponent was full of praise for some of my moves and he gave numerous tips for improving my play.

Shortly after the match against Korchnoi, I travelled to Prague for the fourth edition of the Ladies against Veterans tournament. Being there for the third time in a row, I began to feel like a veteran myself. As far as chess was concerned, I had two crazy weeks: starting with four draws, I continued with three wins in a row, only to have a disappointing finish with three losses. The next game is from the pleasant series of wins.

Game 27
Xie Jun – Boris Spassky
Ladies against Veterans, Prague 1995
Sicilian, Classical Dragon

1 e4	c5
2 ♘f3	♘c6
3 d4	cxd4
4 ♘xd4	♘f6
5 ♘c3	d6
6 ♗e2	g6

Spassky is well-known for his all-round knowledge of chess. I am pretty sure that he cooked up this move-order at home specially for me, since I almost always choose 6 ♗e2 against the Sicilian with ...♘c6 and ...d6. It is true that most white players are not keen on taking on the Dragon with the innocent-looking move 6 ♗e2.

7 ♘b3	♗g7
8 0-0	a6
9 ♖e1	b5
10 ♗f1	0-0
11 a4	b4
12 ♘d5 *(D)*	
12 ...	e6

In Fernandez Garcia-San Segundo, Zaragoza 1996, Black avoided the exchange of knights and played 12...♘d7 13 a5 ♗b7 (Xie Jun-Wang Zili, Beijing 1994 continued 13...♖b8 14 ♖a2 e6 15 ♘e3 ♘c5 16 ♘xc5 dxc5 17 ♘c4 ♕c7 18 ♗g5 and I had slightly the better position) 14 ♖a2 e6 15 ♘e3 ♘c5 16 ♘c4, when it was anybody's game.

13 ♘xf6+	♗xf6

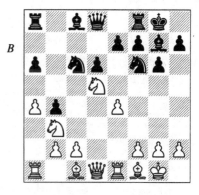

B

14 a5	♗g7

Spassky decides to sit on the fence for a while, to see what White has in mind. There were two alternatives at this point. Apparently, Spassky disliked 14...d5 (premature) 15 exd5 exd5 16 ♗d3, when White is better. More sensible seems 14...♗b7 15 ♖a2 ♕e7 16 ♗e3 ♘e5 17 ♖a4 ♖fc8 (I fail to see the logic behind the subtle manoeuvre 17...♖fb8 18 ♗b6 ♖c8, Meister-Alterman, Bela Crkva 1990) 18 ♗b6 with a complicated position.

15 ♖a2	♕e7
16 ♗e3	♗b7
17 ♕d2	♖fc8
18 f4	

I was not happy when I made this move, knowing that part of my brigade was still busy on the queenside.

In the end, I played it for the simple reason that I failed to spot any other useful move. For example, 18 ♗g5 ♕c7 (not 18...f6 19 ♗f4) 19 ♗f4 ♘e5 20 ♕xb4 ♖ab8 has only accelerated Black's counterplay on the queenside.

18 ...   e5! *(D)*

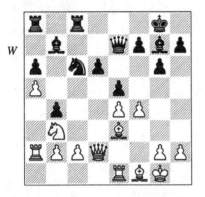

Spassky forces me to make a fundamental choice between two evils: either to hand over the control of the e5-square to Black, or to free Black's centre pawns. After some thinking I opted for the latter.

19 f5

I believe that the choice was right, certainly when evaluating the poor alternative 19 ♗d3 exf4 20 ♗xf4 ♖ab8 21 ♖f1 ♘e5, giving Black active play.

19 ...   gxf5
20 exf5   ♔h8?

The attitude of waiting had to be abandoned here. It was time for the gloves to come off with 20...d5!, which would complete the concept initiated with 18...e5!. We spent quite a long time analysing this position after the

game, and came up with the following beautiful line: 21 ♗g5 (21 ♕xd5?? is refuted immediately by 21...♘d4) 21...♕d6 22 f6! (the position holds a lot of tension, yet neither of us can waste time on elegant moves) 22...♗xf6 (22...♗f8 23 ♗e2 favours White) 23 ♗xf6 ♕xf6 24 ♕xd5 ♘xa5 25 ♕xe5 (25 ♕xa5? is a mistake because Black seizes the initiative with 25...♖xc2 26 ♖e2 ♖xe2 27 ♗xe2 ♕g5, for example 28 ♗f1 ♕e3+ 29 ♔h1 ♕xb3 winning) 25...♕xe5 26 ♖xe5 ♘xb3 27 cxb3 ♖c1 28 ♖a4 ♗c6 29 ♖xb4 ♗b5 30 ♖f5 ♖d8 31 ♖bf4 ♗xf1 32 ♖xf1 ♖xf1+ 33 ♔xf1 ♖d2 and the draw cannot be avoided.

21 ♖aa1 *(D)*

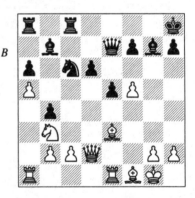

The king's move has given away a crucial tempo that I needed to regroup my pieces. With one more piece to join the battle, White is now well on top. It seems unbelievable that the modest 21 ♖aa1 makes any difference in gaining the initiative, but it is easy to understand. With the rook on a2,

White is effectively a rook down, also because it renders some combinations impossible.

21 ...   d5
22 &c5

The aim of this move is to drive the black queen to a less favourable square, and this makes the tempo-gaining 24 ♘c5 possible in the game.

22 ...   ♕f6
23 &b6   ♘e7 (D)

White has pressure after 23...d4 24 ♘c5 ♕e7 (24...♘xa5 25 ♕xb4 ♘c6 26 ♕b3 ♕e7 27 &c4 f6 28 &xa6 &xa6 29 ♖xa6 gives White a big plus) 25 &c4 f6 26 ♕d3, restricting Black's possibilities.

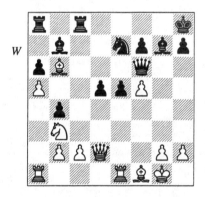

24 ♘c5

I knew that I had much the better position here. Black has a problem with his bishop and with the pawns on a6 and b4. Nevertheless, in view of Black's strong centre and the concentration of white pieces on the queenside, I was still not sure about the outcome.

24 ...   &c6
25 ♘xa6   d4
26 ♘xb4   &h6 (D)

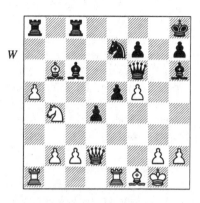

27 ♕d3   ♘xf5

At first, I was bothered about the move 27...&b7, until I spotted the crushing reply 28 ♖xe5!.

28 ♘xc6

I began to feel a sense of relief after the following exchange; my worries about the a8-h1 diagonal had dissipated.

28 ...   ♖xc6
29 ♕e4 (D)

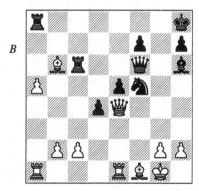

| 29 | ... | ♗e3+ |

Spassky had little time left on his clock, but his position was already inferior.

30 ♖xe3

This seems to be the simplest solution, but it is completely forced. In reply to the obvious 30 ♔h1, Black would have triumphed with the surprise attack 30...♘g3+! 31 hxg3 ♕f2 (threatening both ...♕g1# and ...♖h6+) 32 ♕xe5+ f6!.

30	...	♘xe3
31	♗d3	♔g7
32	b4	♖g8
33	♗c5	♖xc5
34	bxc5	♔f8
35	a6	

Spassky saw that White's a-pawn is unstoppable – 35...♖xg2+ 36 ♕xg2 ♘xg2 37 a7 ♘e3 38 a8♕+ ♔g7 39 ♔h1 is a nice finish – and gave me his big hand with a friendly smile.

1-0

After three consecutive wins, I was on top of the world. I felt strong and expected another nice game. Yet, that was the moment when the nightmare began. Somehow, I fell victim to a typical Sicilian win because I did not realize in time why Black's counter-attack was so strong. Once again, I was taught a painful lesson by one of the respected veterans.

Game 28
Xie Jun – Lajos Portisch
Ladies against Veterans, Prague 1995
Sicilian, Classical Scheveningen

1 e4	c5
2 ♘f3	♘c6
3 d4	cxd4
4 ♘xd4	e6
5 ♘c3	a6
6 ♗e2	d6
7 0-0	♗d7
8 ♗e3	♘f6

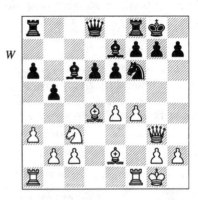

We have transposed to a normal Sicilian Scheveningen.

9 f4   **♗e7**

Portisch later deviated in his game against Wang Zili, Erevan Olympiad 1996, where 9...b5 10 a3 ♗e7 11 g4 0-0 12 g5 ♘e8 13 h4 f6!? 14 ♘xc6 ♗xc6 15 ♗g4 ♘c7 16 ♗b6 was played. White had the advantage.

10 ♕e1

Alternatives at this point are 10 a4 and 10 ♔h1.

10 ...	b5
11 a3	0-0
12 ♕g3	♘xd4
13 ♗xd4	♗c6 *(D)*
14 ♖ad1	

The *Encyclopaedia of Chess Openings* considers 14 ♗d3 as the main line, with the idea of 15 ♖ae1.

14 ...   **♕b8!**

My opponent is a renowned expert on the Sicilian Defence. With the text-move he gains a tempo compared to the 'standard' position. Usually, Black's queen goes via c7 to the b-file to support the pawn advance to b4. An example is 14...♕c7 15 ♗f3 ♖ad8 16 ♔h1 ♔h8 17 ♖d3 a5 18 b4 axb4 19 axb4 ♕b7 20 ♖e3, Ljubojević-Karpov, Buenos Aires 1994. Black is OK and the game ended in a draw after 32 moves. In our game, Portisch has managed to threaten ...b4 immediately. Maybe I should not have allowed him to reach this position, implying that my 14th move may have been inaccurate.

15 e5

I did not see any better way to meet the threat ...b4. It will soon become clear that White has nothing special after the position has been opened. Perhaps 15 ♔h1 was called for, e.g.

15...b4 16 axb4 ♕xb4 17 e5 with an initiative.

| 15   ... | dxe5 |
| 16   ♗xe5 | |

At least the bishop gets involved in a kingside attack. I did not like the look of 16 fxe5 ♘e4, when the position is simplified and equal.

| 16   ... | ♕a7+ |
| 17   ♔h1 | |

Once you have played 15 e5 and are set for f5, it is difficult to consider 17 ♗d4 seriously. Indeed, 17...♗c5 18 ♕f2 ♗xd4 19 ♕xd4 ♕b7 favours Black.

| 17   ... | ♖ad8 *(D)* |

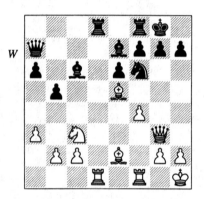

| 18   ♖xd8 | |

White is forced to exchange one pair of rooks. I would have preferred to play 18 ♗d3 g6 19 f5 exf5 20 ♖xf5 but did not see how to reply to 20...♘e4!, taking advantage of the position of the rook on d1.

| 18   ... | ♖xd8 |
| 19   f5 | |

I could only hope for a quick assault, but my attack is easily refuted.

19 ...	exf5
20 ♖xf5	♘e8
21 ♗d3?? *(D)*	

The text-move seemed most natural to me, yet it has a tactical flaw which I discerned too late. The cool 21 ♖f1 was the only move to prolong the game.

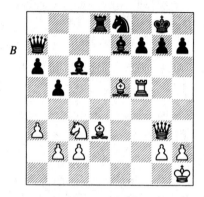

| 21   ... | f6 |

This I had seen...

| 22   ♗f4 | ♖xd3! |

...but not this. The rook on f5 is in trouble.

| 23   cxd3 *(D)* | |

23 ♕xd3 fails to 23...♕f2, when White cannot prevent mate.

| 23 | ... | ♕d7 |

24 ♖h5

24 ♕h3 g6 25 ♖d5 ♕xh3 26 gxh3 b4 27 axb4 ♗xb4 28 ♔g1 ♗xc3 leads to a lost endgame.

| 24 | ... | g6 |

25 ♖h3

Maybe 25 ♖h4 was still possible, but 25...♘g7 favours Black. His pieces work together very efficiently.

| 25 | ... | g5 |

26 ♗b8?

26 ♔g1 was the only move to continue the fight, even though I believe that Black is still better. It is difficult to untangle White's pieces on the kingside. Now it is all over.

26	...	♕f5
27	♗a7	♗d6
28	♕e1	♕xh3
29	♕xe8+	♔g7

0-1

Black's wonderful exchange sacrifice on d3 is most impressive. At first, I felt quite depressed when I left the tournament, with the bitter taste of three losses at the end. However, I recovered quickly when I started to analyse the games. Sometimes you simply lose because your opponent plays better.

I played an additional match against Ye Rongguang, the first Chinese chess player ever to receive the GM title. The six-game event took place in Chengdu, capital city of the Sichuan province and about 1700 kilometres south-west of Beijing. It was summer and the weather was hot and extremely humid. Surprisingly enough, people in Chengdu eat only very spicy food, even at such high temperatures. I thought this quite remarkable at first. However, I understood the habit better when I tried it myself. The idea behind it is apparently that you keep sweating during the meal. Afterwards, especially after a good shower, you feel a lot fresher and the weather seems to be more bearable.

Game 29
Ye Rongguang – Xie Jun
Match (1), Chengdu 1995
Torre Attack vs King's Indian

1	d4	♘f6
2	♘f3	g6
3	♗g5	

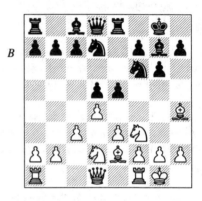

B

Ye Rongguang decides on the Torre Attack again. Before, I had played a strange game against him with the same line. This variation became quite popular in the 1980s. For a long time, I did not understand how it was possible that this line could be dangerous at all. I had a feeling that White developed his pieces 'just like that' and always in the same boring way. It took several defeats before I realized that the line had to be taken seriously. At the same time I found the answer to why it is often successful – every line is dangerous to play if you do not understand it. Fortunately, my trainer Ye Jiangchuan – a different Ye from my opponent – did not have the same silly opinion I had. He helped me to prepare this line and, more importantly, improved my understanding of the positions arising from it.

3	...	♗g7
4	c3	0-0
5	♘bd2	d5
6	e3	♘bd7
7	♗e2	♖e8
8	0-0	e5
9	♗h4 (D)	

So far, Ye had just been repeating moves he had played in one of his games with this line. I made a conscious choice to play...

| 9 | ... | e4 |

...fixing the central pawn structure. This clarifies the strategy for both players: White will concentrate on the queenside, whereas Black will try to generate the usual King's Indian attack on the kingside. Ye Rongguang played the same line against Maya Chiburdanidze in Kuala Lumpur 1994. Maya tried 9...c6, but after 10 c4 exd4 11 ♘xd4 dxc4 12 ♘xc4 ♘c5 13 ♕c2 ♕e7 14 ♖fd1 ♗d7 15 ♖ac1 ♖ac8 16 ♘a5 White was better.

10	♘e1	♘f8
11	c4	c6
12	♖c1	h6

13 cxd5!?

It would have been stronger to play 13 b4 instead, aiming for b4-b5. This has the advantage over 13 cxd5 that White can open both the b- and the c-files. In that case, White would have more possibilities to put pressure on the queenside, and Black would face a more difficult defensive task.

13 ...   cxd5
14 ♘b1?!

With the idea of attacking the d5-pawn, but in the post-mortem we agreed that this manoeuvre costs too much time. Maybe a move like 14 ♘c2 was already necessary. Confronted with White's unusual set-up, I judged that there was no more time to organize the attack on the kingside, for instance with the standard moves ...g5, ...♘g6, ...g4 and ...h5. Hence, I decided to devote some attention to the queenside as well, since the situation in that area has already been clarified by White.

14 ...   ♗f5
15 ♘c3   ♖c8 (D)

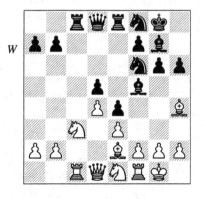

16 ♕b3

White is wise to avoid 16 ♕a4!? a6 17 ♘c2 g5 18 ♗g3 ♘g6 and, with ...h5 coming up, the kingside attack will be first.

16 ...   ♖e6!

After this move, Black is already better. As a result of the pin on the c1-rook, White has great difficulties continuing his plan on the queenside.

17 a4

17 ♕xb7?? was impossible on account of 17...♖b6 18 ♕xa7 ♖a8.

17 ...   g5
18 ♗g3   ♘g6
19 ♖c2

With the idea of ♘b5. However, this is easily prevented.

19 ...   ♖b6
20 ♕a2   a6!

This stops White from placing any piece on b5. In addition, the threat of a5 becomes less of a problem.

21 a5   ♖bc6
22 ♖d2   ♗e6?!

I wanted to discourage White from playing 23 ♗e5, but it may not be necessary to worry about this. The accurate move is 22...♗f8.

23 ♗d1   ♗f8
24 ♗a4 (D)

White is far behind in development, but his position is fairly solid. Yet White does not have enough room to rearrange his pieces and is therefore quite vulnerable. If he could only find a few safe moves, his position would be OK.

24 ...   ♖xc3!

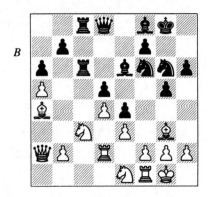

I thought it a shame to agree to an immediate draw with 24...罝c4 25 奧b3 罝4c6. My position is simply too good.

25	bxc3	豐xa5
26	奧d1	豐xa2
27	罝xa2	罝xc3

Black has two pawns in return for the exchange, but fundamentally nothing has changed. Even without queens, White is poorly developed and his position remains cramped.

| 28 | 勾c2 | h5 |
| 29 | f3 | |

The only move. Black has a big advantage after 29 h3 h4 30 奧h2 g4 31 hxg4 勾xg4 32 奧xg4 奧xg4 33 f3 奧f5.

| 29 | ... | exf3 |
| 30 | 奧e1 | 罝b3 |

30...罝d3 limits White choices and may be more useful. I spent a large part of my remaining time thinking where I should position the rook. In the end, I think that my decision was the right one; the rook is in trouble after 31 奧xf3 奧e7 32 罝b2!, threatening both 33 罝xb7 and 33 奧e2.

31	gxf3	奧e7
32	奧d2	g4
33	勾e1	罝b6
34	奧a4	奧f5 (D)

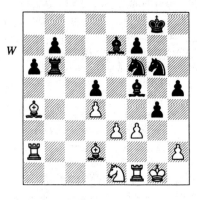

35 奧c2?!

This cannot be good, although it is tempting to exchange pieces and release the pressure. But by the time the two light-squared bishops have disappeared from the board, Black can fix his knight on the central e4-square. A better choice would have been 35 fxg4 奧xg4 36 罝c2 當g7 37 勾g2 h4. Of course, Black still has the initiative in that case, but the position is quite complicated.

35	...	奧xc2
36	罝xc2	gxf3
37	勾xf3	勾e4

Now Black has an enormous advantage.

| 38 | 奧a5 | 罝b3 |
| 39 | 罝g2 | |

39 罝c8+ can be answered with 39...當g7 40 奧d8 勾d6 and 41...罝xe3.

| 39 | ... | h4 |

40 ♘e5   h3

We had both passed the time control, and victory for Black is imminent.

41 ♖e2

41 ♖g4 ♗g5 42 ♘xg6 fxg6 brings the win closer.

41 ...   ♘xe5

42 dxe5   ♗c5

43 ♖f3   b6

Another way to make progress is 43...d4 44 ♖xh3 d3 45 ♖g2+ (45 ♖e1 b6 wins as well) 45...♔f8, when White cannot defend much longer.

44 ♗e1   ♖b1

45 ♖xh3   ♗b4

46 ♔f1 *(D)*

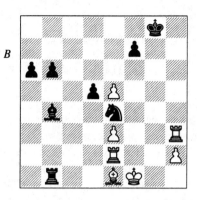

The only move. Now, a funny situation has arisen: two of White's pieces (plus his king) are paralysed.

46 ...   ♔g7?

Almost everything wins, but the neatest way would have been 46...a5! 47 ♖h6 ♗c3, when the a-pawn cannot be stopped. The remainder of the game is of little interest.

47 ♖h4   a5

48	♖g4+	♔f8
49	h4	a4
50	h5	a3
51	h6	♗xe1
52	h7	♗c3+
53	♔g2	♗xe5
54	♖g8+	♔e7
55	♖b8	♖b2
56	♖b7+	♔d8
57	♖xb2	axb2
58	♖xb6	♘d2
59	♖b5	b1♕
60	♖xd5+	♔c7
	0-1	

I won this game and the match. This was a relief, because I had not performed well against Ye before. Regardless of what kind of position I used to have, I would always find a way to spoil everything. Maybe the word *Angstgegner* is appropriate in such a case, as Ye Rongguang indeed proved an insurmountable hurdle on many an occasion. It is a pity that we have not played since. I can only hope that the result of this match will not prove to be a one-off.

10 My Third World Championship Match (1996)

It had been known since the beginning of 1995 that Zsuzsa Polgar was the new challenger. She had beaten Maya Chiburdanidze quite comfortably in St Petersburg. At first, I had the impression that the new World Championship match would take place later in 1995. At least, that was the reason why my Chess Federation declined several invitations for me to play tournaments. However, as it happened, there was no news from FIDE until the end of the year. I am not sure why, but there just seemed little interest from their side in moving matters forward. It was not until November that, all of a sudden, a sponsor was found and the announcement was made. I received a phone call from Florencio Campomanes, who told me that the match was scheduled for January, in the Spanish city of Jaen. I was not happy with this decision, nor were the people of my Chess Federation. It was too short notice and, moreover, the major part of the match would now be held during the Chinese Spring Festival. This two-week festival can be regarded as the equivalent to Christmas, when family members come together for celebrations. It is an extremely important event, all the more so because Chinese families are very close. I would rather have stayed at home and started the match in February, but this proved impossible. My objection was to no avail and I had no choice but to play.

Jaen turned out to be a beautiful place in a mountainous area and the hotel was built in a medieval castle atop one of the hills. The view of the city was truly magnificent. It was also a fairly quiet and isolated place, a poignant contrast to the surroundings of cities like Manila and Monaco. This time, however, we faced difficulties which were hard to envisage. At the airport, our delegation was welcomed by a friendly lady whose command of English was, to put it mildly, poor. It never occurred to me that this would be a recurrent problem. We soon realized, however, that the issue was chronic. There was hardly a living soul in Jaen capable of speaking passable English. The only people who spoke both Chinese and Spanish ran the local Chinese restaurant. No big deal, one would think, but it caused a lot of misunderstandings. For example, prior to the first game, we had to select our chairs and I was presented with a few possibilities. My legs are quite short and I tried to explain that the chairs that I had tested were not adequate for that reason. Most were so high that my feet did not even touch the floor when I sat in them. However, the arbiter did not seem impressed by my complaints and I understood from his gesticulations that these were the only chairs the hotel could provide. It took a long time before it was clear to anybody that this was an important point for me, and in the end I got a suitable chair, but it took a lot of effort. There were more problems – on which I do not want to dwell too much – and I was made to feel very uneasy by it all.

The first match game proved a windfall for me. I spoiled a winning position, but Zsuzsa blundered in return and I was able to pull off a win after sixty moves. Games two and three ended in short draws after 17 and 19 moves respectively. In both games, Black had managed to equalize completely and the resulting endings were dead draws in which neither side could afford to play for a win.

Then, after game three, the unexpected happened. Zsuzsa and I received a letter from Mr Luis Rentero, in Spanish, indicating that we were sanctioned for producing these short draws. We had come to Jaen as chess tourists, he argued. Initially, I could not believe the content of that letter, and for some time I thought that it was all a bad dream. I was bewildered, and disgusted, and failed to understand the motivation behind the act. And how is one to react to such an ill-considered deed? I heard that Zsuzsa had replied by letter that she felt deeply insulted, but that was no option for me. For a Chinese girl, this is simply *not done* and I was also unsure about the further ramifications. The incident might have an impact on the relationship between the two countries. Hence, I came to the conclusion that it was best not to respond at all. It is still impossible for me to forget the depressed feeling that I had, in my hotel room in Jaen. My interest in the match had gone: it was Spring Festival in China and I was home-sick. From that moment onwards, I just wanted to leave Spain.

It never rains but it pours. In the fourth game I was unable to fuel the attack when this was necessary, and I lost without a chance. I could have resigned game five after 17 moves and game seven after 19 moves. In the latter case, I sacrificed a piece but the combination had a big hole – which Zsuzsa spotted. Game eight was crucial. Again, I got a strong attack and, at some point, I even had a whole rook invested. There were several opportunities to win, but under time pressure I gave it all away. In five consecutive games, I had only managed to score one draw and the match was effectively over. My play went from bad to worse and, whatever position I had, I could not make more than a draw or I would even lose. The next game is characteristic.

Game 30
Xie Jun – Zsuzsa Polgar
World Ch Match (10), Jaen 1996
Ruy Lopez, Open Variation

1 e4   e5

This was the first time in the match that Zsuzsa preferred 1...e5 over 1...c5. She changed her opening lines several times during the match, and I was never sure what to expect.

2 ♘f3   ♘c6
3 ♗b5   a6

OK, a little surprise since Zsuzsa had never played this before – that is, as far as I know. She would normally go for 3...♘f6 here. This line, the Berlin Defence to the Ruy Lopez, used to be quite popular amongst Hungarian chess players. It has also been played several times by her younger sister Zsofia of late. After 4 0-0 ♘xe4 5 d4 ♘d6 6 ♗xc6 dxc6 7 dxe5 ♘f5 8 ♕xd8+ ♔xd8 the game would move quickly into a queenless middlegame.

4 ♗a4   ♘f6
5 0-0   ♘xe4
6 d4   b5
7 ♗b3   d5
8 dxe5   ♗e6
9 ♘bd2   ♘c5
10 c3   ♗e7

10...d4 is the other main continuation.

11 ♗c2   d4
12 ♘e4 (D)
12 ...   d3

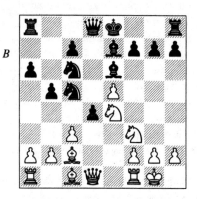

B

This move is fairly new and a deviation from antiquated lines. The classical examples are 12...♗d5 13 ♘xc5 ♗xc5 14 ♘xd4 ♗xd4 15 cxd4 ♗c4 16 ♗e4 ♕d7 17 ♖e1 0-0 18 ♕h5, when White was well on top in Tarrasch-Post, Mannheim 1914, and 12...dxc3 13 ♘xc5 ♗xc5 14 ♗e4 ♕d7 15 bxc3 ♖d8 16 ♕xd7+ ♗xd7 17 ♖d1 ♘b8 18 ♘d4 ♗e7 19 ♗e3 0-0 20 ♖d2, Capablanca-Hodges, New York 1916. In the latter case, White has an edge in development.

13 ♘xc5   dxc2
14 ♕xd8+   ♖xd8
15 ♘xe6   fxe6
16 ♗e3

This seems better than 16 ♗f4 ♖f8 17 ♗g3 g5 18 h3 ♖xf3 19 gxf3 b4 20 ♖fc1 ♖d2 21 ♔f1 bxc3 22 bxc3 ♗a3 which gave Black the advantage in the game Cuijpers-Pieper Emden, Germany 1990.

16	...	♖d5
17	♖ac1	♘xe5
18	♘xe5	♖xe5
19	♖xc2	♔f7

According to Ftačnik, both 19...0-0 20 c4 and 19...♔d7 20 ♗d4 ♖g5 21 ♖d2 ♖d5 22 ♖e2 ♗f6 23 ♖e4 ♗xd4 24 cxd4 are slightly better for White. I agree.

20 c4 (D)

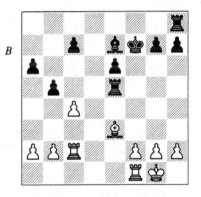

I was not aware that, thus far, we had been following Akopian-Daniliuk, St Petersburg 1993. That game continued 20...♖c8 21 ♖fc1 ♗d6 22 g3 ♖a8, when White had a small plus but Black's position is very solid. It took 83 moves before Akopian had to concede to a draw. 20...♗d6 is also interesting. Obviously, my opponent had prepared this line prior to the game and she came up with a new move.

20	...	b4
21	♖d1	

21 ♗f4 ♖e4 22 ♗xc7 ♖c8 leads to an equal position.

21	...	♖d8
22	♖xd8	♗xd8
23	♔f1	♗g5
24	♗a7	

After the exchange of bishops, the position simplifies further.

24	...	♖f5
25	♔e2	♔e8
26	♔d3	♔d7
27	f3	c5
28	♖e2	♗e7
29	♗b8	a5

I had expected Zsuzsa to continue 29...♗d6 30 ♗xd6 ♔xd6, which leaves White with virtually no winning prospects.

30	♔e4	♔c6
31	♗e5	g6
32	g4	♖f8
33	♖d2	a4
34	♗g3	h5 (D)

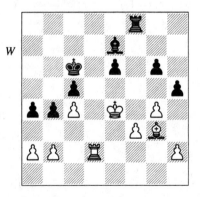

We have arrived at the most crucial position in the game. My original idea was 35 g5 with the positional threat 36

♔e5. Black has nothing better than
35...♖d8 (35...♗xg5 36 ♖d6+ ♔b7 37
♖xe6 and Black's position collapses, or
35...♖f5 36 h4, when Black is at a loss
for a proper move) 36 ♖xd8 ♗xd8 37
♔e5 ♔d7 38 ♗f2! ♗e7 (if 38...♗xg5
then 39 b3! – Korchnoi showed me
this move later – 39...axb3 40 axb3
♗e7 41 h3 g5 42 ♗g1 and White wins)
39 b3 axb3 40 axb3. Black has run out
of moves. In light of the above analysis, it is not difficult to find the other
good move for White: 35 b3!, with the
idea of 36 g5. There is no way for
Black to reinforce her position. After
my actual move, a draw is inevitable.

35	♖d3??	hxg4
36	fxg4	♖f1
37	b3	a3
38	♖d2	g5
39	♖d3	♖a1
40	♖d2	♖b1
41	♔e5	♖b2
42	♗e1	♗d8
43	♖d6+	♔c7

Black cannot play for a win since
43...♔b7? 44 ♖xd8 ♖xa2 45 ♔d6 ♖e2
46 ♔xc5 ♖xe1 47 ♖d2 ♖b1 48 ♔xb4
♖b2 49 ♖d7+ ♔c6 50 ♔xa3 loses.

44	♖d2	♔c6
45	♖d6+	♔c7
46	♖d2	½-½

After I suffered yet another loss in game eleven, Zsuzsa had a 7½-3½ lead. I
knew that it was the nature of things that an actor will leave the stage at some
point in time, and I was saddened that it was my turn. The only thing left to do
was to play some interesting games. Game twelve was played on the last day of
1995, according to the Chinese calendar. The win was a small consolation for
me, and it was one of the few games in which I did not let the advantage slip
through my fingers – even though it came too late...

Game 31

Xie Jun – Zsuzsa Polgar

World Ch Match (12), Jaen 1996
Ruy Lopez, 5 d3

1 e4	e5
2 ♘f3	♘c6
3 ♗b5	a6
4 ♗a4	♘f6
5 d3	

Having spoiled an advantage in my last game as White (see Game 30), I decide to aim for a tense struggle and not allow Black to take the game into an ending too quickly.

5 ...	d6
6 c3	♗d7
7 0-0	g6
8 ♘bd2	♗g7
9 ♖e1	0-0
10 ♘f1 *(D)*	

Another possibility is 10 d4 ♖e8 11 a3 ♗h6 12 ♗c2 a5 13 ♖b1 ♗g7, as in Kupreichik-Anand, Belgrade 1988. It is a normal position with mutual chances.

10 ...	b5!?

Black could also try 10...♘h5, or even 10...♕e8.

11 ♗c2	h6
12 ♘e3	♖e8
13 a4	♖b8!?

This move was not necessary at the moment. I would have preferred 13...♘h5 instead.

14 axb5	axb5
15 h3	♗e6

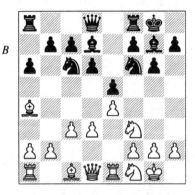

16 d4	exd4
17 cxd4	♗c8?!

Dubious. By opting for 15...♗e6, Zsuzsa has allowed me to play 16 d4 and, therefore, it would have been logical to go for 17...♘b4 18 ♗b1 c5 19 d5 ♗c8 (19...♗d7 20 ♘c2 gives White an edge) 20 ♘c2 ♘a6 21 ♘a3 ♘c7 with an unclear position.

18 ♘f1	♘b4
19 ♗b1	c5 *(D)*
20 ♗d2!	

This is the correct move, maintaining the tension in the centre. White's pieces are better placed than Black's.

20 ...	♘c6
21 dxc5	dxc5
22 ♕c1	♘d4

The only move that defends the pawns on c5 and h6.

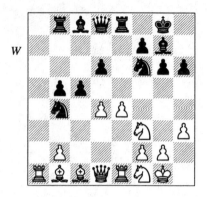

23 ♘xd4   ♛xd4
24 e5!
White is slightly better.
24 ...   ♘h7
The alternative 24...♘d7 would be disastrous after 25 e6 ♖xe6 26 ♖xe6 fxe6 27 ♗c3 and 28 ♗xg6.
25 ♗e3   ♛c4?
Zsuzsa could have nullified White's initiative with 25...♛d5 26 ♗xh6 ♗b7 27 ♗e4 ♛xe5 28 ♗xb7 (28 ♗xg7 ♔xg7! 29 ♗xb7 ♛xe1 30 ♛xe1 ♖xe1 31 ♖xe1 ♖xb7 is only equal) 28...♛xe1 29 ♛xe1 ♖xe1 30 ♖xe1 ♖xb7 31 ♗xg7 ♔xg7, keeping the balance.
26 f4
Now White obtains a big advantage.
26 ...   ♛xc1
27 ♖xc1   c4 (D)
28 ♗a7
The start of a forced winning sequence.
28 ...   ♖b7
29 ♗e4   ♖be7
30 ♗c5   ♖e6
31 ♗d5   ♖a6

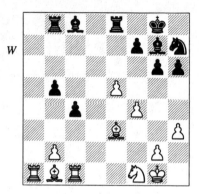

32 ♖xa6   ♗xa6
33 ♖a1 (D)

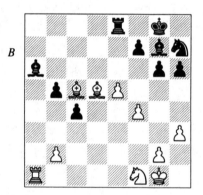

33 ...   ♗xe5
This is born out of desperation. Yet, 33...♗c8 34 ♗c6 ♖d8 35 ♗e7, followed by 36 ♖a8, wins easily too. The rest of the game does not require any comment.
34 ♖xa6   ♗xb2
35 ♖xg6+   ♔h8
36 ♗xf7   ♖c8
37 ♗e6   ♖a8
38 ♘e3   ♗g7
39 ♘f5   ♘f8

40	♗xf8	♗xf8		43	♖g3	♗g7
41	♘xh6	♖a6		44	♘g5+	♔h8
42	♘f7+	♔h7		45	♖g4	1-0

At least it was a nice finish to the Chinese year. I knew that there were many people in China who followed the match with interest, and I felt sorry for them that, this time, I could not take the title home. I wrote down my feelings, straight from the heart, and this was published in the Chinese newspapers on the next day. In the letter, I wished the readers a happy new year and a lot of chess fun, and I thanked them for all the support that they had given me.

In game thirteen, I soon lost a piece and resigned after a mere 24 moves. Zsuzsa Polgar was the new World Champion. Of course, it was a very difficult moment for me when I congratulated her. I cannot say that her victory was undeserved. Zsuzsa simply took advantage of her chances and I was unable to put up enough resistance. However, the memory of the match left me with a bitter taste. I do not hold any resentment against anyone in particular, but I feel that the circumstances were certainly not worthy of a World Championship Match. The incident with the letter was unforgivable. All I can hope for is that, one day, I will have the opportunity to play another match against Zsuzsa, under different conditions.

11 Recharging the Battery (1996-1997)

It was almost half a year before I took up chess again. In a strange way, I felt quite relieved after the match, as I realized that it was a valuable experience. Ever since 1992, life had been in fact too easy for me. All the time I was placed upon a pedestal and, now, a more normal life returned. Sometimes it is good to fall down, because it makes you stronger once you stand up again. In any case, I focused on my course and tried to catch up with my old classmates. Usually, it takes four years to graduate from university and some of them had already done so, but my case was more complicated. Still, I enjoyed studying for a change and I had ample time to rearrange my life. In the summer I had gained enough credits to qualify for a post-graduate course. This may be something to write about in my memoirs later.

Only in April did I make an exception, when I was invited to participate in the fifth edition of the Melody Amber tournament in Monaco. I loved Monaco and, moreover, an invitation from Joop van Oosterom's organization was hard to resist. The going was tough. I had little experience with blind and rapid play, and my opponents were stronger than ever before. With Anand, Karpov, Kramnik, Shirov, Ivanchuk, Lautier, Kamsky and Judit Polgar, most of the world's strongest players were present. I had not played many times against 2700+ players. Theirs is a different kind of chess, which takes some time to get used to – if that is at all possible. The result was not particularly good for me. With 4½ points out of 22, I finished last.

Four months later I travelled to London for the Ladies against Veterans tournament. I had not touched a chess piece since Monaco, and the outcome was accordingly disappointing. I drew no fewer than seven times, lost twice and only managed a full point against Mark Taimanov, whose favourite ...♘ge7 Sicilian received a severe beating during these weeks. My score of minus one was not much to be proud of. It was clear that the *Foxtrot* was not the dance for me.

Shortly afterwards, I played at the Olympiad in Erevan, but there I paid the price for a lack of practice. It was one of my worst tournaments ever. I did not play until round three and thought that I was playing a decent game. Then, somewhere in the middlegame, my opponent offered me a draw. I declined, only to blunder away my queen on the next move. My sense of danger had left me completely. Apparently, these basic instincts require regular maintenance. If you are in good shape, you often realize in time that something is wrong. But in Erevan I did not and I went on to squander many promising positions. All in all, 1996 was not a very fortunate year for me in terms of chess.

Yet, I was quite happy by the turn of events at the end of 1996. The Chinese Chess Federation had found a sponsor in the Malaysian businessman Dato Tan Chin Nam. This made it possible for Wang Zili, Peng Xiaomin, Ye Jiangchuan and myself to stay in London for several months, accompanied by our manager Dr Lim from Singapore. With London as our base of operation, we could travel to other European cities for chess events. For the time being, I did not have to worry about my course of study any more. My major subject was English and now I got ample opportunity for real-life practice. It is fair to say that, during my stay in Europe, I regained some of my energy and interest in chess. I noticed that my play started to improve, albeit gradually. It is too early to tell, but it may well signal the start of my come-back. At least, enjoyment had returned and I played more relaxed than during the years when I was World Champion.

Below is a selection of games from 1997. The European tour started off in Hastings, where I played in the Premier Group. The average Elo rating of 2565 made this a Category 13 tournament. After two rounds, I moved into the lead by beating Sergei Movsesian in a nice way.

Game 32

Xie Jun – Sergei Movsesian

Premier Group, Hastings 1996/7
Sicilian, Kan

1 e4	c5
2 ♘f3	e6
3 d4	cxd4
4 ♘xd4	a6
5 ♗d3	♕c7
6 0-0	♘f6
7 c4	d6
8 ♘c3	g6
9 ♕e2	♗g7
10 ♘f3	0-0
11 ♖d1 *(D)*	

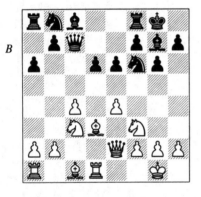

B

11 ...   ♘c6

The alternative is 11...♘bd7, after which 12 ♗f4 is a sound reply.

12 h3

This move seems unnecessary for the moment. The reason for playing the text-move is explained by the game Stefansson-Lutz, Manila Olympiad

1992. An immediate 12 ♗f4 allowed Black to use the g4-square: after 12...e5 13 ♗e3 ♗g4 14 ♗c2 ♘d7 15 ♘d5 ♕d8 16 h3 ♗xf3 17 ♕xf3 ♘c5 18 ♕e2 ♘e6 19 ♕d2 ♘cd4 20 ♗d3 ♖b8 21 f3 f5 a position arose with equal chances.

12 ...   ♘d7

13 ♗f4

Another possibility is 13 ♗e3 with the idea of ♖ac1, ♗b1, etc. White has a small space advantage. An example of this strategy was seen in Almasi-Vogt, Altensteig 1993: 13 ♗e3 b6 14 ♖ac1 ♗b7 (another interesting idea was seen in Van den Doel-Shaked, Wijk aan Zee 1998, where 14...♘c5 15 ♗b1 ♗b7 16 ♕d2 ♖ad8 17 ♘h2 ♕e7 18 ♕e2 a5 19 b3 ♘b4 led to a complex position) 15 ♗b1 ♘ce5 16 ♘xe5 ♘xe5 17 b3 ♖fd8 18 ♕d2 ♗f8 19 ♘a4 ♘d7 20 ♗g5 ♖db8, with a slight edge for White.

13 ...   ♘ce5

14 ♖ac1   b6

15 ♘xe5 *(D)*

15 b3 ♗b7 16 ♗b1 ♖ad8 17 ♘h2 f5 18 ♕d2 ♘f6 19 ♖e1 resulted in an unclear position in Luther-Lutz, Germany 1993.

Now, Movsesian makes a big mistake.

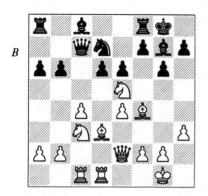

15 ...   dxe5??

This move guarantees control of the d4-square, of course, but Black does not have a single piece that can reach it. In the meantime, White makes inroads into the queenside and will be able to create a passed pawn on c5. Strategically, the game is already decided.

16 ♗e3   ♗b7
17 b4   f5
18 f3

White is much better. There is nothing to be afraid of on the kingside, while the initiative on the queenside seems unstoppable.

18 ...   ♖f7

A flexible move, but it was hard to prevent c5 in any case.

19 c5   bxc5
20 ♘a4   fxe4
21 fxe4

This is stronger than 21 ♗xe4. The more pieces are left on the board, the more difficult it will be to stop White's c-pawn.

21 ...   ♗f8

If 21...♗c6 then 22 ♘xc5 ♘xc5, when 23 bxc5 is the strategically correct move, with a promising position. 23 ♖xc5 is also good.

22 ♘xc5   ♘xc5 (D)

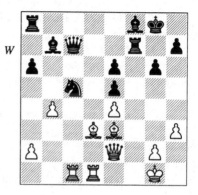

23 bxc5!

23 ♗xc5 is inferior, for the aforementioned reason. After 23...♗xc5+ 24 ♖xc5 ♕b6 Black gains time to regroup his pieces.

23 ...   ♖d8
24 ♗c4   ♖xd1+
25 ♖xd1   ♕c6 (D)

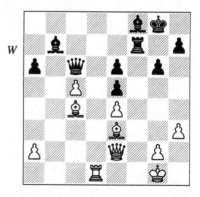

26 ♔h2!

It is always useful to put the king in a safer place if you have the time.

26	...	h5
27	♕b2	♖e7
28	♖d8	♕c7

28...♕xe4 29 ♗h6 ♕xc4 30 ♕f2! wins on the spot.

29 ♕b6

In the post-mortem, Sergei Movsesian showed me the move 29 ♕d2!, which is calm but very strong. I was impressed that his brain was still functioning well in such a tumble-down position. The rest was fairly easy.

29	...	♔g7
30	♗g5	♗xe4
31	♗xe7	♕xe7
32	♕d6	♕xd6
33	cxd6	♔f7
34	d7	♗h6
35	♖f8+	1-0

However, the nice series ended abruptly in round three, when I fell victim to Conquest's unusual opening set-up. After a quick draw against Mark Hebden, I got a big advantage against John Nunn in round five. But when I failed to find the right plan to strengthen my position, he won the ending in a study-like fashion. In the last four rounds, I got no more than three draws and a loss to Michael Adams.

Two weeks later, I went to Linares to play in an open tournament. Even though my result was modest, I noticed again that my playing level was improving.

Game 33
Artur Yusupov – Xie Jun
Anibal Open, Linares 1997
Ruy Lopez, Exchange Variation

1 e4

This came as a surprise to me because Yusupov almost always plays 1 d4.

1	...	e5
2	♘f3	♘c6
3	♗b5	a6
4	♗xc6	dxc6
5	0-0	♕d6
6	♘a3 *(D)*	

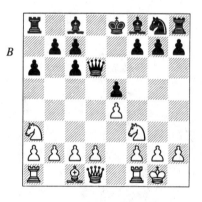

6 ... b5

Here, I avoid the inferior continuation 6...♗e6 7 ♕e2 f6 8 ♖d1 c5 9 c3 ♗g4 10 ♘c2 0-0-0 11 d4, which occurred in Timman-Xie Jun, Amsterdam 1994. White has successfully pushed the pawn to d4 and, very soon, I ended up with a horrible position. The fact that I ultimately won that game was caused by lack of vigilance on Timman's part.

| 7 | c3 | c5 |
| 8 | ♘c2 | f6?! |

8...♘e7 is better, in order to develop the pieces. A well-known example is 9 d4 (9 a4 ♗b7 10 axb5 axb5 11 ♖xa8+ ♗xa8 12 d4 cxd4 13 cxd4 ♗xe4 14 ♘xe5 was about equal in Shirov-Short, Groningen 1996) 9...cxd4 10 cxd4 exd4 11 ♘fxd4 c5 12 ♘b3 ♕xd1 13 ♖xd1 ♘c6 14 ♗e3 c4 15 ♘c5 f5, Hübner-Kamsky, Manila 1992. Black has resolved his doubled c-pawns and is not worse.

9 a4

I assume that Yusupov had not studied my 8th move in his preparation, because he used up a lot of time here. Opening the centre with 9 d4 was the alternative, but it may not yield more than a roughly equal ending if Black takes twice on d4.

| 9 | ... | ♗b7 |
| 10 | axb5?! *(D)* | |

It would be prudent to play 10 d4 at once to keep options open, for instance 10...cxd4 11 cxd4 exd4 (11...♗xe4 seems too risky due to 12 ♖e1 ♕c6 13 ♕e2 ♗g6 {both 13...♗xc2 14 axb5 and 13...♕xc2 14 ♕xe4 ♕xe4 15 ♖xe4 hand the initiative to White} 14 dxe5 with an attack) 12 ♘cxd4 c5 13 ♘f5 and Black has problems. If she plays 13...♛c6, White gets a big lead in development after 14 axb5 axb5 15 ♖xa8+ ♝xa8 16 ♝f4.

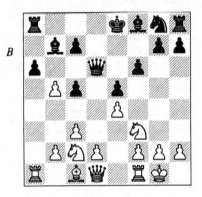

B

10   ...   ♝xe4!

For a long time I was convinced that this is the one and only good move for Black. However, upon reanalysing the game, I cannot understand why 10...axb5 would be so bad. Play could continue 11 ♖xa8+ ♝xa8 12 d4 (12 ♛e2 c4 seems OK for Black) 12...cxd4 13 ♛d3 (13 cxd4 ♝xe4 14 ♖e1 ♛c6) 13...dxc3 14 ♛xb5+ ♝c6 15 ♛c4 ♛c5 16 ♛e6+ ♘e7, when there appears to be little danger. I think that I overestimated White's attack during the game.

11   d4   cxd4?

This is the wrong move-order. I should have gone for 11...axb5! 12 ♖xa8+ ♝xa8 13 ♛e2 cxd4 14 cxd4 ♝xf3 with an extra tempo compared to the game. In this case Black would already have the advantage.

12   ♖e1!   ♝b7

This is the only move; 12...♝xc2 13 ♛xc2 d3 14 ♛a4 gives White a ferocious attack. The following sequence is forced.

13	cxd4	axb5
14	♖xa8+	♝xa8
15	♛e2	e4
16	♛xb5+	♝c6
17	♛a5	♘e7
18	♘d2	f5
19	b3?!	

19 ♘c4 looks very strong to me. Where is Black to place the queen? It is easy to go wrong, for instance 19...♛d5 is met by 20 ♛c3, hoping for 20...♘g6? 21 ♘4e3 ♛d7 22 ♘xf5. I am hesitant to propose any alternatives to 20...♘g6, as Black's development is problematic in all cases.

19	...	♛d7
20	♘c4	♘g6
21	♘2e3	♝b5 (D)

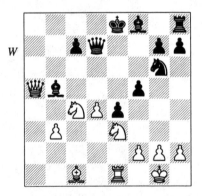

W

22   g4

The post-mortem had come to this point and I remarked, with some diplomacy, that 22 g4 may have been a dubious move. Yusupov raised his eyebrows and replied, with heavy laughter, that he was in fact very proud of this move during the game. I am not sure which one of us is closer to the truth, but I still prefer 22 h4. The idea is to drive away the knight from its effective post on g6. The critical line is 22 h4 ♗d6 (22...♘xh4?? fails to 23 ♘e5) 23 h5 ♘e7 24 ♘xd6+ cxd6 and now White has three choices. 25 ♘xf5? ♕xf5 26 ♕a8+ ♕c8 (26...♘c8? 27 ♖xe4+ ♔d7 28 g4 loses) 27 ♕xe4 0-0! gives insufficient compensation for the piece, whereas 25 ♕a8+ ♕d8 26 ♕xd8+ ♔xd8 27 ♗a3 ♔d7 only leads to equality. But if White continues 25 ♘d5! ♗c6 (25...♘xd5 26 ♕a8+ ♕d8 27 ♕xd5 with a big plus) 26 ♘xe7 ♔xe7 27 d5 ♗b5 28 ♗b2, Black has lots of problems to solve. For the sake of completeness, I like to add that 22 ♘e5 ♘xe5 23 dxe5 would probably lead to an advantage for White as well.

Editor's note: In his notes in *Attack and Defence*, Yusupov also draws attention to the knight sacrifice 22 ♘xf5! ♕xf5 23 ♘e5, which he considers to give a decisive attack. He also gives 22 g4 a '?'.

22	...	fxg4
23	♕a8+	♔f7
24	♕xe4	♗b4
25	♖d1	♖e8
26	♕xg4	♕xg4+
27	♘xg4 *(D)*	

The last ten moves had cost most of our remaining time on the clock, so I was quite happy that the queens had

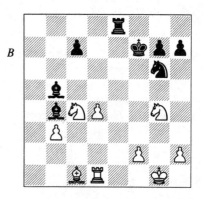

disappeared. The game has now reached the final stage and White is a pawn up. On the other hand, Black has full compensation owing to her active king and two bishops.

27	...	♖e4
28	h3	h5
29	♘ge5+	♘xe5
30	♘xe5+	♔e6
31	♗e3	♔d5
32	♘d3	♗d6
33	♘c5	♖e8 *(D)*

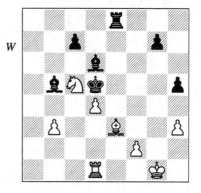

34	♔g2	♖f8
35	♘a4	♗d7

36	♘c3+	♔e6
37	d5+	♔f7
38	♘e4	♖b8
39	♘xd6+	

W

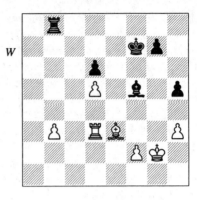

It would make no difference if White had played 39 ♖d3 ♗f5 40 f3 ♖b4 41 ♘xd6+ cxd6 42 ♖c3 ♖b5.

| 39 | ... | cxd6 |
| 40 | ♖d3 | ♗f5 (D) |

We passed the time-control and the remaining position leaves nothing to play for.

41	♖c3	♗e4+
42	♔g3	♗xd5
43	♖c7+	♔g8
44	♖d7	♗xb3
45	♖xd6	♗c2

| 46 | ♖d5 | g6 |

½-½

White can make no progress: 47 ♖d7 ♗f5 48 ♖a7 ♖d8 with ...♖d7 to follow.

The next game has a nice story behind it. As the reader can imagine, I have always had problems remembering names of non-Chinese players, and I easily mix up two different family names when the letters are alike. Prior to this game, I tried to find games of my opponent in my computer database. Some of that information told me that he played 1 d4, but I found nothing useful. Therefore, I prepared some King's Indian lines with the aid of an *Informator*. Glancing through volume 66, I spotted a name which was similar to that of my future opponent. Funny, I thought, and not realizing that it was in fact the same person, I studied the line for a while. It was an interesting position. Still, I could never have envisaged that I would see the exact same position on the board in the afternoon. Well, as it happened...

Game 34
Sergei Krivoshy – Xie Jun
Anibal Open, Linares 1997
King's Indian, Classical Main Line

1	d4	♘f6
2	c4	g6
3	♘c3	♗g7
4	e4	d6
5	♘f3	0-0
6	♗e2	e5
7	0-0	♘c6
8	d5	♘e7
9	♘e1	♘d7
10	♗e3	f5
11	f3	f4
12	♗f2	g5
13	a4 *(D)*	

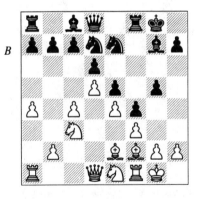

B

13 ... a5

The main line goes 13...♘g6 14 a5 ♖f7, followed by ...♘f6, ...♗f8, and ...♖g7. White has a space advantage on the queenside and Black has the usual attack. However, the text-move

has become quite popular during the last few years. Black aims to delay White's initiative in order to gain time. As far as I am aware, 'theory' has not yet given a final verdict on what is best.

14	♘d3	b6
15	♗e1	

An important indication of the strength of 13...a5 is the fact that Kasparov used it against Yusupov at the Erevan Olympiad in 1996. After 15 b4 axb4 16 ♘xb4 ♘f6 17 ♖a3 ♗d7 18 ♘b5 ♔h8 19 ♗e1 ♖g8, Yusupov played the strong 20 g4! and was able to defuse Black's attack. A draw was the result. The point of 15 ♗e1 is that White intends to recapture a pawn on b4 with the bishop, with the immediate positional threat a5. It is not certain, however, whether he will ever have time for this.

15	...	♘f6
16	b4	

Editor's note: 16 ♘f2 is the theoretical recommendation, and a more consistent follow-up to 15 ♗e1.

16	...	axb4
17	♘b5	g4
18	♗xb4	g3
19	h3 *(D)*	
19	...	♗xh3

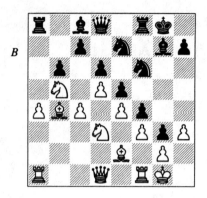

B

This is a typical sacrifice in the King's Indian.

20 gxh3　　Ｗd7
21 Ｗd2

Until now, we had made our moves fairly quickly, both being on familiar territory. I have played these kinds of attacking positions many times and my intuition told me to believe in Black's attacking potential. As for my opponent, he had faith in his home analysis – as I found out in the post-mortem. White's last move was new to me. The game I had studied in *Informator 66*, Kutsyn-Frolov, Kiev 1995, featured 21 Ｗc2 instead. During my morning 'study' I had observed that Frolov had wasted a valuable tempo with 21...Ｗxh3 22 ♗d1 ♘g6 23 Ｗg2 Ｗh6, allowing White to put up some sort of defence with 24 Ｗh1 ♘h4 25 ♘e1. In my opinion, 21...♘g6! is a big improvement, for instance 22 ♖fd1 ♘xe4 23 fxe4 f3 24 ♗xf3 (the alternative 24 ♖f1 is met by 24...♘h4 25 ♗xf3 Ｗxh3 26 ♘e1 ♗h6 27 ♖a3 ♖xa4!!, winning instantly) 24...♖xf3

25 ♖f1 ♖af8 26 ♖xf3 ♖xf3 27 ♖f1 ♖xf1+ 28 ♔xf1 Ｗxh3+ 29 Ｗg2 Ｗg4 30 ♗e1 ♘f4 and Black is much better. The comment in *Informator* gives 21 ♔g2 ♘g6 22 ♖h1 ♘h4+ 23 ♔g1 ♘xe4!. It is true that Black has won-derful compensation after 24 fxe4 f3.

21 ...　　♘g6!

In view of the above, it is easy to understand that I found this move dur-ing the game. The idea behind it is fairly simple. Before continuing with the attack, Black mobilizes her forces towards the kingside. It is very impor-tant not to hurry, and to bring in the pieces first. It is remarkable how little White can do about this.

22 ♗d1　　♗h6
23 ♘e1　　♔h8 *(D)*

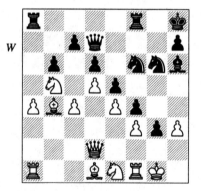

W

Another move with an unmistak-able aim: the g-file is cleared for the rook.

24 ♖a2　　♖g8
25 Ｗd3

This loses without a fight. Our first thought during the post-mortem was that 25 a5 would have been more resilient. On second thought, I believe that Black also wins in that case. The variations are easy to find: 25...bxa5 26 ♗xa5 ♘h5 27 ♗xc7 ♖xa2 28 ♕xa2 g2 is forced, leading to an irresistible attack. Now, 29 ♖f2 loses to 29...♕xh3 30 ♖xg2 ♘g3! 31 ♔f2 ♘h4 with the unstoppable threat ...♘xe4. Therefore, White should play 29 ♘xg2 ♘h4 30 ♖f2 ♕xh3 31 ♗xd6, when

Black has to find the surprising 31...♘g3 32 ♗xe5+ ♗g7 33 ♗xg7+ ♔xg7! (only this move, as White has a perpetual check after 33...♖xg7 34 ♕a8+ ♖g8 35 ♕a1+) 34 ♕a1+ ♔h6 (the point) 35 ♕f6+ ♘g6 with mate to follow.

25	...	♕xh3
26	♖g2	♘h4
27	♕e2	♖g5
	0-1	

Afterwards, Krivoshy asked me whether I had seen a game in *Informator* with his comments. I answered that, yes, I had indeed seen a game with 19...♗xh3, with a name that resembled his. Then he told me that he was in fact the one who had analysed this game. Later I understood the reason for my confusion, when I had another look at the two names. As second name, underneath the game in question, the name 'Krivošeja' was given and not Krivoshy. [*Editor's note:* The standard English rendition of this name is Krivoshei (or alternatively Krivoshey), but the spelling in use at the event has been retained in view of the story.] Lucky me. Had I known that it was my opponent of the afternoon, I might well have picked another line to avoid his home preparation. Sometimes, ignorance pays off. Imagine my surprise when I later found our game in a *ChessBase* game collection: the moves were correct, but the result was given as a draw. The reader has to believe me when I say that Krivoshy really resigned. There is no way to meet 28...♖h5, with catastrophic consequences.

After a short stay in London, I travelled to the Netherlands for the 59th Hoogovens Chess Festival in Wijk aan Zee. Hoogovens is always held in late January and it is, with good reason, quite popular amongst top players. Wijk aan Zee is a resort on the North Sea, and the walks on the beach and in the dunes are most refreshing. The town centre has many lovely restaurants and bars, and hundreds of chess enthusiasts return faithfully for their annual chess holiday. It was a new experience for me to play amid so many other players, of every possible level, and all in the same playing hall.

Game 35
Xie Jun – Nicolas Giffard
Hoogovens Tournament, Wijk aan Zee 1997
Sicilian, Modern Scheveningen

1	e4	c5
2	♘f3	e6
3	d4	cxd4
4	♘xd4	♘f6
5	♘c3	d6
6	♗e2	♗e7
7	0-0	0-0
8	♗e3	♘c6
9	f4	e5
10	♘b3	a5 *(D)*

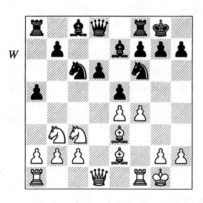

11 a3

In this position, White tends automatically to go for 11 a4. However, I am not sure whether White really needs to weaken the b4-square. There seems to be nothing wrong with the text-move.

11	...	a4
12	♘d2	♘d4 *(D)*

Judit Polgar played 12...exf4 in her game against Short in Madrid 1995. The game continued 13 ♖xf4 ♗e6 14 ♘c4 ♘d7 15 ♖f1 (15 ♘xd6? ♗g5 16 ♖f3 ♘de5 17 ♖g3 ♗xe3+ 18 ♖xe3 ♕b6 gives Black a big advantage) 15...♕b8 with a complex position.

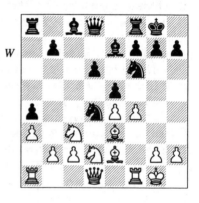

13 f5

The position was new to me and I took some time to consider the candidate moves. Both 13 fxe5 dxe5 14 ♘c4 ♕c7 15 ♗xd4 exd4 16 ♘d5 ♘xd5 17 exd5 ♖d8 and 13 ♗xd4 exd4 14 ♘d5 ♘xd5 15 exd5 ♕b6 16 ♘c4 ♕c5 17 ♗d3 b5 18 ♘d2 ♗b7 19 ♕h5 g6 20 ♕e2 ♖fe8 favour Black. Therefore 13 ♗d3!? is preferable, e.g. 13...♖e8 (not 13...♘g4 14 ♗xd4 exd4 15 ♘d5 ♘e3 16 ♘xe3 dxe3 17 ♘c4 d5

18 exd5 ♗c5 19 ♗e2, when White is much better) 14 ♘c4 ♘g4 15 ♗xd4 exd4 16 ♘d5, leading to a slight edge for White. I cannot remember why I picked the text-move in the end. Maybe I thought that this was the fastest route to the enemy king.

13	...	d5
14	♗xd4	exd4
15	♘xd5	♘xd5
16	exd5	♕xd5 *(D)*

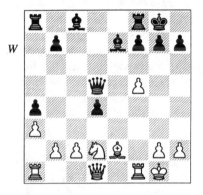

17 ♗c4!

I like this move in combination with the next one. White utilizes the fact that Black has no good square for his queen. Either it will hinder piece development, or it will have to move to a square where White can gain a tempo on it later – as in the game. One difference with 17 ♗d3 at once becomes apparent in the line 17...♗g5 18 ♘e4 ♗e3+ 19 ♔h1, when Black does not need to spend a tempo with his queen.

| 17 | ... | ♕c5 |
| 18 | ♗d3 | ♗g5 |

Black's position is already unpleasant. In reply to 18...♗d7, I had planned 19 ♕h5 ♖fe8 20 ♘e4 ♕d5 (20...♕e5 21 ♖ae1) 21 ♕f3 with f6 coming up.

19	♘e4	♗e3+
20	♔h1	♕b6
21	♕e1	

If White wants to prepare an attack, this move is obligatory. The violent-looking 21 ♕h5 is met by 21...♖a5, pinning the f-pawn from the side.

| 21 | ... | ♕xb2 |

Giffard wants to see the proof of my concept. That is his good right.

22	f6	g6
23	♕h4	♕b6
24	♖ae1	

It is amazing how the attack unfolds at breakneck speed.

| 24 | ... | ♖a5 *(D)* |

The text-move appears to be the only possibility. Black is mated after 24...♔h8 25 ♖xe3 dxe3 26 ♕h6 ♖g8 27 ♘g5.

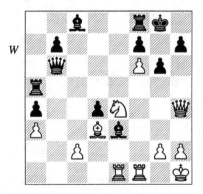

25 ♖xe3

The introduction to a positional queen sacrifice which paralyses Black's position.

25	...	♖h5
26	♕xh5	gxh5
27	♖g3+	♔h8
28	♖g7	

It was practically impossible to calculate all the possible lines through to the end, but the sacrifice felt natural. Black cannot solve his problems with 28...♗e6 29 ♘g5 h6 30 ♖h7+ ♔g8 31 ♖xh6, when White firmly controls the position.

28	...	h6
29	h3?	

Although this move does not give away everything – probably half a point – it certainly makes life difficult. To be preferred was 29 ♘g3! ♗g4 30 ♖h7+ ♔g8 31 ♖xh6 ♖d8 32 ♘xh5 with a large plus.

29	...	♕c7! (D)

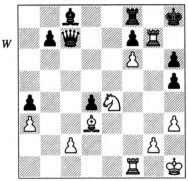

An excellent defence as the queen controls the g3-square.

| 30 | ♘g3 | |

The best attempt to win. White has to force a draw after 30 ♖f3 ♖e8 31 ♘d2 ♖e1+ 32 ♘f1 ♗e6 33 ♖h7+ (33 ♖fg3 ♗g4!) 33...♔g8 34 ♖g7+ (34 ♖xh6 is impossible due to 34...♕e5 {not 34...♗d5 35 ♗h7+ and 36 ♗c4} 35 ♖h7 b5 with initiative for Black) 34...♔f8 35 ♖h7 ♔g8 36 ♖g7+.

30	...	♕e5?!

The first mistake. White has no more than a draw after 30...♗g4 31 ♖h7+ ♔g8 32 ♖xh6 ♕xg3 33 ♗h7+ ♔h8 34 ♗f5+.

31	♘e2	b5?! (D)

Black goes wrong again and his position becomes critical. 31...♕c7!? was a better effort. White always has a perpetual check and there may be even more to gain with 32 ♘f4.

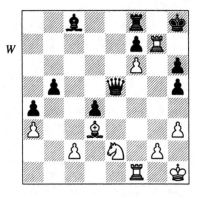

32	♖f3	h4?

Understandable in view of the threat 33 ♖h7+ and 34 ♖g3+. However, the consistent 32...b4 would have required several accurate moves from White, and even then the outcome remains unclear. The main line goes 33

♖h7+ (33 ♖fg3? loses to 33...♗f5) 33...♔g8 34 ♖g3+ (34 ♖xh6 bxa3 35 ♗h7+ ♔h8 36 ♗f5+ ♔g8 37 ♖g3+ ♕xg3 38 ♘xg3 a2 forces White to take the perpetual at once) 34...♗g4 35 ♖xh6 (35 hxg4 h4 36 ♖h3 bxa3 37 ♖xh6 a2 38 ♖3xh4 a1♕+ 39 ♘g1 ♕xf6 40 ♖xf6 a3 is rather messy) 35...bxa3 (35...♕g5 36 ♖h7 and 37 ♖g7+) 36 ♗h7+ ♔h8 37 ♗f5+ ♔g8 38 ♖xh5 ♕xg3 39 ♖g5+ ♔h8 40

♘xg3 a2 41 hxg4 a1♕+ 42 ♔h2. White still has a perpetual check but nothing more.

33	♖h7+	♔g8
34	♖xh6	

This decides the game.

34	...	♕g5
35	♖h7	♕d2
36	♖g7+	♔h8
37	♖f4	♕e1+
38	♔h2	1-0

After Wijk aan Zee, the European tour took me to Cannes, a beautiful city in the South of France. It was sunny when I arrived and the first sun-worshippers had already occupied the beach. It made a fascinating contrast with Wijk aan Zee, where it was freezing most of the time. The A-group of the open tournament was admissible for players whose Elo rating was 2350 or more. I was fairly disappointed when I started off with four draws, against players whose rating was much lower than mine. The tournament seemed over for me, when suddenly things started to go my way. I produced a string of four wins and joined the leaders. The fight in round eight was exciting.

Game 36
Arkady Rotshtein – Xie Jun
Cannes 1997
Bird's Opening

1 f4

A surprise from my Ukrainian opponent.

1 ... d5

I have no problems with playing against the Dutch Defence, even when some players believe that, in this case, it means playing familiar positions one tempo down.

2	**♘f3**	**g6**
3	**e3**	**♗g7**
4	**♗e2**	**♘h6**
5	**0-0**	**0-0**
6	**d3**	**c6**

When I checked my database, I came across a game J.Rogers-Ward, British Ch (Eastbourne) 1991, which proceeded 6...♘c6 7 ♕e1 ♘f5 8 g4 ♘d6 9 ♕g3 ♖e8 10 ♘c3 d4 11 exd4 ♘xd4 12 ♘xd4 ♗xd4+ 13 ♗e3 e5 14 ♕f2 ♗xe3 15 ♕xe3 exf4 16 ♕xf4 ♗e6 with an equal position.

7	**c3**	**♘f5**
8	**♕e1**	**♘d6**
9	**♘bd2**	**♘d7**
10	**e4**	**dxe4**
11	**dxe4** *(D)*	
11	**...**	**♘c5**

The alternative 11...e5 would have brought about equality after 12 fxe5 ♘xe5 13 ♘xe5 ♗xe5 14 ♘f3 (14 ♘c4 ♘xc4 15 ♗xc4 ♕e7! seems slightly

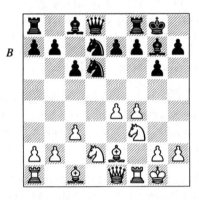

better for Black) 14...♗g7 15 e5 ♘f5 16 ♗c4 ♗e6 17 ♗xe6 fxe6. My idea with the text-move was to position the knight on d3 and acquire the bishop-pair. However, I had missed White's 15th move in the game.

12	**e5**	**♘f5**
13	**♘b3**	**♘d3?!**

I could still have bailed out with 13...♘xb3 14 axb3 ♕b6+ 15 ♕f2 (15 ♔h1!? is interesting) 15...♗e6 16 b4 h5, when Black has nothing to complain about.

14	**♗xd3**	**♕xd3**
15	**g4!**	

This is what I had overlooked. The damage is limited though.

15	**...**	**♘h6**
16	**h3**	**f6**
17	**♗e3**	**fxe5**

18	Rd1	Wb5
19	fxe5 (D)	

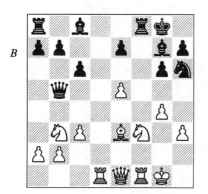

19 ...   ♘xg4

This nice piece sacrifice brings all Black's pieces to life. I have to admit that it was born out of necessity. In my view there was little choice, especially since 19...♘f7 20 ♘bd4! Wxb2 21 e6 ♘d6 22 Rf2 Wa3 23 ♗g5 Re8 24 ♘b3! seems very good for White. The queen is misplaced on a3 and, effectively, Black is playing without two pieces. White has ample compensation for the pawn after 24...b6 25 ♘e5.

| 20 | hxg4 | ♗xg4 |
| 21 | ♘bd4? | |

White does not defend accurately, and Black dominates from now on. There were two alternatives to the text-move. The first is 21 Wg3 ♗xf3 22 Rxf3 We2! (22...♗xe5 23 Rxf8+ Rxf8 24 Wg4 ♔g7 is unclear) 23 Rdf1 Wxb2. Black already has three pawns for the knight and the remaining white pawns are weak. I prefer Black's position but White is by no means lost.

The other attempt is the unexpected 21 ♔g2!?, protecting the knight and keeping an eye on the e5-square. It is true that Black can win the pawn on e5, but this would give White an open e-file in return. This may well have been White's best chance.

21	...	Wxb2
22	Rf2	Wa3
23	Rb1	c5
24	♘b5	Wa4
25	♘h2	♗f5 (D)

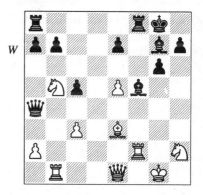

Another little move to keep White busy. It may not be apparent at first sight, but the knight on b5 is lost.

26	Rbb2	Rad8
27	Rfd2	a6
28	♘c7	Wc6

Black wins back the piece.

29	Rxd8	Rxd8
30	Wf1	Wxc7
31	Wc4+	e6
32	Wxc5	Wxc5
33	♗xc5	♗xe5
34	♗d4	Rxd4

0-1

The last round saw a short draw and I ended with a score of 6½ out of 9, together with three other grandmasters. For me, it was the first time that I finished shared first in an open tournament. I felt quite pleased by this result and, that very evening, the city of Cannes looked more beautiful than ever.

After a short stop in London, I returned to China for several months. It was nice to see my parents again and to spend time at the university. However, the relaxation did not last for long. Duty called and I travelled to Copenhagen for the annual Ladies against Veterans. In keeping with tradition, the event was baptized with the name of the national dance of Denmark, the *Høstdans*. A beautiful name, although my pronunciation left much to be desired. I was happy that another Chinese player, Zhu Chen, made her debut in the tournament. As usual, the Veterans demonstrated great fighting spirit and in this event they chalked up a 27-23 victory. My fifty percent score was reasonable, but no more.

Game 37
Xie Jun – Lajos Portisch
Ladies against Veterans, Copenhagen 1997
Sicilian, Classical Scheveningen

1 e4	c5
2 ♘f3	e6
3 d4	cxd4
4 ♘xd4	♘c6
5 ♘c3	a6
6 ♗e2	d6
7 0-0	♘f6
8 ♗e3	♗e7
9 f4	0-0

Portisch must have remembered with pleasure our encounter two years earlier (see Game 28). This time I thought that I was better prepared.

10 a4	♕c7
11 ♔h1	♖e8
12 ♗f3	♖b8 (D)

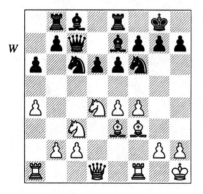

13 ♘b3

In the first 12 moves, nothing special has happened but here I made an odd move. The simple explanation is that, prior to this game, I studied two different lines and I simply mixed them up. The text-move is not bad in itself, but it does not fit in well with my next move. The standard plan is 13 ♕d2 ♗d7 14 ♖ad1 b6 15 ♘b3 ♘a5 16 ♕f2. In the Women's Candidates tournament, in Groningen later that year, I played the old line 13 g4 ♘xd4 14 ♗xd4 e5 15 fxe5 dxe5 16 ♗a7 ♖a8 17 g5 ♖d8 18 ♕e1 ♘e8 19 ♗e3 ♗e6 20 ♕f2 ♖dc8 21 ♗g4 ♘d6 22 ♗xe6 fxe6 23 g6 against Ketevan Arakhamia, and won beautifully.

13 ...	b6
14 ♕d2?!	

I made this move without thinking, because I believed this to be one of the many 'old' moves in this line. Instead, I should have played 14 ♕e2 with the plan of developing my pieces calmly. In that case, the game could continue 14...♘a5 15 ♖ad1 ♘c4 16 ♗c1 b5 17 axb5 axb5, with an unclear position. The difference is the position of the queen's rook, of course, which is better placed on d1.

14 ...	♘a5

Here, Portisch thought for a while before making this move. It is possible that this position was new to him, too, even though he has played the Sicilian almost all his life. In the meantime, I found the situation quite amusing. I had already realized that I had mixed up the moves. At the same time, Portisch may have got the impression that this was a prepared innovation and took it seriously.

15 ♕f2   ♘c4
16 ♗c1 *(D)*

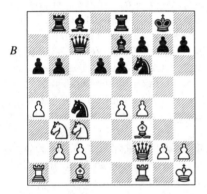

16 ...   ♗b7

While Portisch was pondering over this move, I tried to discover the positive sides of my set-up. Admittedly, the rook would be better placed on d1, but the nice thing about a rook being on a1 is that it discourages Black from playing ...b5. Still, this would have been an interesting try. The situation is unclear after 16...b5 17 axb5 axb5 18 ♖a7 ♕d8 19 ♘d4 ♗d7 20 b3 ♕b6 21 ♖a2 e5.

17 ♘d4   d5

Black can often claim a success if he manages to play ...d5 or ...b5 in a Sicilian. The text-move is strong,

although 17...♖bc8 18 b3 ♘e3 19 ♕xe3 ♕xc3 20 ♕xc3 ♖xc3 21 ♗b2 ♖c7 22 e5 dxe5 23 fxe5 ♘e4 is also sufficient for equality.

18 e5

There was no choice. After 18 exd5 ♘xd5 (or even 18...cxd5) 19 ♘xd5 ♗xd5 20 ♗xd5 exd5 Black will enjoy the benefits of controlling the e4-square.

18 ...   ♘e4
19 ♘xe4   dxe4
20 ♗e2   ♖ed8? *(D)*

In view of the further developments in this game – White generates an attack – Black would have done better playing the other rook to d8, 20...♖bd8, to keep an eye on the e-file as well. Black is slightly better after 21 b3 ♗c5 22 ♗xc4 (now 22 c3? is bad due to 22...♘a5) 22...♗xd4 23 ♗e3 ♕c5 24 ♗xd4 ♖xd4! (24...♕xd4 25 ♕xd4 ♖xd4 26 ♖ad1 ♖ed8 27 ♖xd4 ♖xd4 28 ♔g1 is equal) with control over the d-file. I had planned the interesting 21 c3!? followed by b3 and c4.

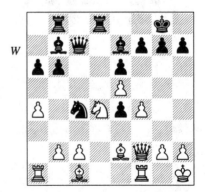

21 f5!   e3!

The best defence. Black is in trouble after 21...♘xe5 22 fxe6 ♗c5 23 ♕g3! f6 24 ♘f5 and 21...♕xe5 22 fxe6! (better than 22 ♗f4 ♕xd4 23 ♕xd4 ♖xd4 24 ♗xb8 ♘e3 with counterplay) 22...♕xd4 (22...fxe6 23 ♕f7+ ♔h8 24 ♘xe6 wins) 23 ♕xf7+ ♔h8 24 ♕xe7. In addition, 21...exf5 22 ♗xc4 (Black is better after 22 ♘xf5 ♘xe5 23 ♕g3 ♗f6 24 ♘h6+ ♔h8 25 ♘xf7+ ♕xf7 26 ♕xe5 ♖bc8) 22...♕xc4 23 ♘xf5 ♗c5 (or 23...♖e8 24 ♗e3 ♗f8 25 ♘d6 ♗xd6 26 exd6 ♖bd8 27 ♖ad1) 24 ♗e3 ♗xe3 25 ♕xe3 gives White all the fun.

22 ♗xe3

At first, I was very attracted to the move 22 ♕f4, which works after 22...♘xe5? 23 fxe6 fxe6 24 ♗xe3 ♔h8 25 ♕g3. However, Black can improve with 22...exf5! 23 ♘xf5 (certainly not 23 e6 ♕xf4 24 exf7+ ♔h8 25 ♖xf4 g5) 23...♘xe5 24 ♘xe7+ ♕xe7 25 ♗xe3. White has the bishop-pair, but Black's pieces are very active. The following sequence is rather forced.

22	...	♘xe3
23	♕xe3	♗c5
24	c3	exf5
25	♖xf5	♗xd4
26	cxd4	♕c2
27	♖af1	♗d5 (D)

White has a promising position and it would be wonderful if the bishop could join in the attack. There is only the small matter of the mate on g2. Hence...

28 ♖5f2!

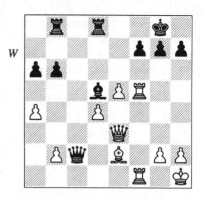

W

...is the right move, forcing the queen to retreat. It is also important to sacrifice the a4-pawn rather than the b2-pawn by 28 ♖5f4 ♕xb2. In the latter case, Black only has to play ...b5 to create a passed pawn.

28	...	♕xa4
29	♗d3	♕d7?

The position is very tricky. Black has a strong bishop on d5, a healthy pawn structure on the kingside and an extra pawn on the queenside. Should the game come to an ending, then White would be worse. Thus Black seems fine at first sight. Nonetheless, there is one thing that is most unpleasant for him: the white pawn on e5 assures White of attacking chances on the kingside, certainly when all the pieces are able to participate. The text-move is rather passive. Black should have tried to grab the pawn with 29...♕b4 30 ♖f4 ♕xb2 31 ♖g4 (or 31 ♖h4), simply hoping that he is able to weather the storm.

30	♖f4	♖bc8
31	h3	

Black's last two moves seem very logical but, after this quiet move, I do not see any defence. All of a sudden, White's attack cannot be stopped.

31	...	♖c6
32	♖g4	♗e6
33	♖h4	g6

If 33...h6 then 34 ♕e4.

| 34 | ♕h6 | f5 |
| 35 | exf6 | ♕f7 (D) |

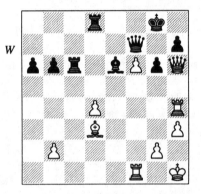

36 d5

I saw that this move would win and did not calculate any further. However, there was a more beautiful way to finish the game: 36 ♗xg6! ♕xg6 37 ♖g4 ♗xg4 38 f7+ ♕xf7 39 ♕g5+. It was a shame that I overlooked the last move of this sequence. On the other hand, 36 d5 is good enough.

| 36 | ... | ♖xd5 |

36...♗xd5 fails to 37 ♗xg6 ♕xg6 38 ♖g4.

37	♗e4	♖cd6
38	♗xd5	♗xd5
39	♖hf4	♖d7
40	♖4f2	♕e8
41	♕f4	♗f7
42	♖d2	♖xd2
43	♕xd2	♗e6
44	♕d6	♔f7
45	♕xb6	1-0

Next is one of the strangest games that I have ever lost. I could hardly hide my embarrassment in the post-mortem, especially because strong players such as Nunn and Ljubojević were watching. It was extremely disappointing for me that I lost an ending in which I was two pawns up, and I did not understand how this could have happened. The same evening, on the way to dinner, I met Lajos Portisch and my mind was still on the game. I asked him the rhetorical question "Why do I play chess?" He did not know how to reply, at first, but he understood the reason behind my complaint. In his long career, he must have been tortured by similar feelings himself on many an occasion. "Well, it sometimes happens, just like life itself" was his philosophical response after some reflection. A mysterious answer which gave me food for thought...

Game 38
Xie Jun – Mark Taimanov
Ladies against Veterans, Copenhagen 1997
Sicilian, Taimanov

1	e4	c5
2	♘f3	♘c6
3	d4	cxd4
4	♘xd4	e6
5	♘c3	♕c7
6	♗e2	a6
7	0-0	♘f6

I had expected 7...♘ge7, the move that Taimanov normally plays and is most characteristic of this variation which bears his name.

8 ♔h1

Another important line is 8 ♗e3 ♗b4 9 ♘a4 with a sharp position.

8 ... ♗b4 (D)

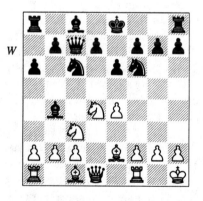

This line has become more and more popular over the years. The first game I was able to find in my database was Kaplan-Karpov, Madrid 1973, which continued 9 ♘xc6 bxc6 10 ♕d4 c5 11 ♕e3 d6 12 ♕g3 ♗xc3 13 ♕xc3 0-0 14 f3 ♗b7 15 ♗f4 ♘h5 16 ♗g5 e5 17 ♖ad1 f5 18 ♕d3 h6. Black has a solid position and was eventually victorious. Another choice for White is 9 ♗g5 ♗xc3 10 ♗xf6 gxf6 11 bxc3 d6 12 ♕d2 ♗d7 13 ♖ad1 ♔e7 14 f4 ♖ac8 15 ♘b3 ♖cd8 16 ♕e1 ♘a5 17 ♘d4 h5, as in Milos-Murshed, FIDE World Ch, Groningen 1997. I opted for the third possibility.

9 ♕d3 0-0

The alternatives are 9...d6 and 9...♕d6.

10 f4 ♘xd4!?

This is the usual move, although 10...d5 may be worth considering.

11 ♕xd4 ♗xc3
12 bxc3 d5?

I am not so sure about this move; 12...d6 seems more logical. Black should keep the position closed, because White's bishop-pair will only become stronger as the game opens up.

13	e5	♘e4
14	c4	b5
15	cxd5	exd5
16	♗d3	♗b7

16...♕c5? loses the exchange after 17 ♕xc5 ♘xc5 18 ♗a3.

17   ♗b2 *(D)*

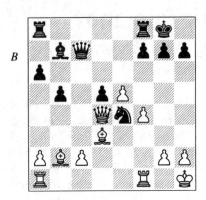

17 ...   ♕c5?!

Black invests a pawn in order to exchange queens. Taimanov had to choose between two evils. In case of 17...♖ac8 18 ♕e3 ♖fe8 19 ♕h3 h6 20 f5, White's attack is very strong.

18 ♗xe4   ♕xd4
19 ♗xh7+   ♔xh7
20 ♗xd4

White has a big advantage, although I realized that the bishops of opposite colours may pose some technical difficulties.

20 ...   b4?

This costs another pawn and, from this moment on, there is no way for Black to build up a successful defence – at least, not without my help.

21 ♖fb1   a5
22 c3   ♖fc8
23 a3!

Accurate. The greedy 23 cxb4 axb4 24 ♖xb4 ♗a6 would allow Black more activity. I wanted to force the exchange of one pair of rooks.

23 ...   ♔g6 *(D)*

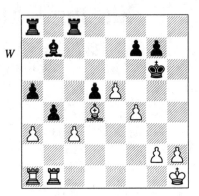

I remember vividly that I thought for a while before making my move, particularly because I knew that it would be better to stop the king from coming in. Suddenly, it flashed through my mind: "Why waste another move? If I just take the pawn, I will be two pawns up and who cares that his king comes in for a while?".

24 axb4??

It almost goes without saying that 24 g4 ♗a6 25 axb4 ♗d3 26 ♖b2 axb4 27 ♖xa8 ♖xa8 28 cxb4 would also lead to a position where White is two healthy pawns up. Taimanov could have resigned in that case.

24 ...   axb4

The thing with blunders is that you always get the point, but one move too late. After Black's move, I took a deep breath and started thinking. There was nothing I could do to stop ...♔f5 and, moreover, the d4-bishop no longer has support from the pawn – this I had missed. After a long time I played...

25	Ⱙxa8	Ⱙxa8
26	cxb4	ⵁf5
27	g3	ⵁe4
28	Ⱙd1	Ⱙa2
29	ⵁg1?	

A mistake never comes alone. The last chance to activate my poor king was 29 b5 Ⱙa4 30 e6 fxe6 31 ⒧xg7 Ⱙb4 32 ⵁg2 Ⱙxb5. White is 'only' one pawn up now. The position still holds some winning chances, albeit minor, because the white king gets involved as well.

| 29 | ... | ⒧a6 (D) |

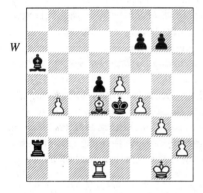

30 e6

In my mind, I kept on returning to the position where I had omitted to play 24 g4. Had I been able to stop thinking in that way, I would probably have noticed that there was a draw within reach after 30 Ⱙa1 Ⱙxa1+ 31 ⒧xa1 ⵁe3 32 f5 d4 33 f6 gxf6 34 exf6 d3 35 ⒧c3 d2 36 ⒧xd2+ ⵁxd2 37 ⵁf2 ⵁc3 38 h4 ⵁxb4 39 ⵁe3 ⒧c8 40 ⵁf4 ⒧a6 41 g4 ⒧e2 42 h5 ⵁc4 43 ⵁg5 ⵁd5 44 ⵁh4 ⵁe5 45 g5. In all honesty, I was still searching for the winning line.

30	...	fxe6
31	⒧xg7	ⵁf3
32	⒧d4	Ⱙg2+
33	ⵁh1	Ⱙc2
34	Ⱙb1	

I saw 34 ⵁg1 Ⱙg2+ 35 ⵁh1 Ⱙc2 36 ⵁg1 with a draw, but refused to admit to it.

| 34 | ... | ⒧b5 (D) |

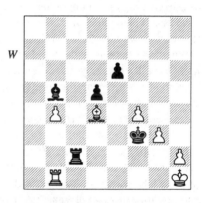

35 ⒧g1??

By now, I was terribly short of time. 35 Ⱙd1 was called for. What follows is a true anti-climax.

35	...	ⵁg4!
36	Ⱙb3	Ⱙd2
37	⒧e3	Ⱙa2
38	⒧d4	Ⱙd2
39	⒧e3	Ⱙe2
40	ⵁg1	ⵁh3

Forty moves have been played and Black has a won position.

41	⒧f2	d4!
42	⒧xd4	Ⱙg2+
43	ⵁh1	Ⱙxh2+

44	♔g1	♖g2+
45	♔h1	♗c6
46	♖c3	♗d5
47	♖c5	♖xg3+
48	♖xd5	exd5
49	b5	♖b3
50	♔g1	♔g4
51	♗e5	♔f5

52	♔f2	♔e4
	0-1	

The lesson was clear: a game is not over until your opponent resigns. It is important to keep at least one eye open, whatever the position. Thanks for teaching me, Mr Taimanov!

There was not much time to rest. One month later, I played in the Tan Chin Nam Cup in Beijing. Since 1994, two Beijing tournaments have been regular annual events organized under the auspices of the Chinese Chess Federation. Both have been named after their main sponsors. The Tan Chin Nam Cup is a closed tournament where several foreigners are invited to meet the Chinese top players. A few days afterwards, the S.T. Lee Cup starts, which is also known as the Beijing Open. By running the two tournaments in close succession, the organizers hope to attract more strong foreign players. It is also quite convenient for local players, many of whom hail from remote parts of China.

This edition of the Tan Chin Nam Cup featured Oll, Alterman, Tiviakov, Pigusov, Atalik and Sermek as the guests from abroad, making it a Category 12 tournament with an average Elo rating of 2540. I noticed that my own Elo rating had sunk to an 'all-time' low of 2495. After four rounds, no Western player had yet lost to a Chinese player and some chess enthusiasts and the organizers came up with the idea of making a special prize available for the first Chinese player to beat a Westerner. Until then, Sergei Tiviakov had not even dropped half a point.

Game 39

Xie Jun – Sergei Tiviakov

Tan Chin Nam Cup, Beijing 1997
Sicilian, Dragon

1	e4	c5
2	♘f3	d6
3	d4	cxd4
4	♘xd4	♘f6
5	♘c3	g6
6	♗e3	♗g7
7	f3	♘c6
8	♕d2	♗d7

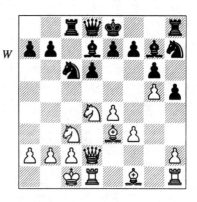

Tiviakov plays the Dragon in his own inimitable style. The latest fashion is to delay castling and to leave the black king in the centre for a while. I am not convinced about the merits of this strategy, but it is certainly original.

9 g4   h5

I was only familiar with games that continued 9...0-0, where Black sometimes played ...h5 later on.

10	g5	♘h7
11	0-0-0	

11 h4 has been played before, but there is nothing like a sound developing move.

11	...	♖c8 *(D)*
12	♔b1?!	

The text-move is good in many variations of the Dragon, but here it seems rather slow. I should have preferred 12 f4 0-0 13 f5 ♘e5 14 ♗e2 a6 15 ♖hf1 b5 16 h4, when White has the initiative. The knight on h7 makes a bad impression.

12	...	0-0
13	h4	

13 f4 ♗g4 14 ♗e2 ♘xd4 15 ♗xd4 ♗xd4 16 ♕xd4 e5 is more than OK for Black and, for that reason, I should probably have tried 13 ♘b3!? controlling the centre. After 13...♘e5 14 f4 ♘c4 15 ♗xc4 ♖xc4 16 ♗d4, White is slightly better.

13	...	♘e5
14	f4	♘g4
15	♗g1?	

This stereotyped move does not meet the demands of the position. 15 f5! was much better. If Black plays ...♘xe3 he will have no piece to place on e5, whereas a white knight will soon appear on d5. White is better and Black still faces the problem of his knight on h7. I thought about this possibility during the game, but, for unknown reasons, I decided to change my plan.

15	...	e5
16	fxe5	♘xe5
17	♘d5	♗g4
18	♗e2	♘c4
19	♕e1	♗xe2
20	♕xe2	♖e8
21	♖h3 (D)	

I like this move, which controls the third rank and defuses many of Black's attacking ideas.

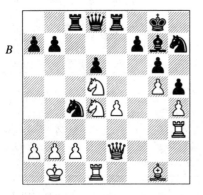

The expression on Tiviakov's face revealed that he liked his position very much, and I would not have minded switching sides either. However, this was the moment for Black to undermine the centre with 21...f5! 22 ♖c3 (22 gxf6 ♘xf6 activates the knight again and 23 ♖c3? is met by 23...♘xe4 24 ♖xc4 ♖xc4 25 ♕xc4 ♘d2+!) 22...♖xe4 23 ♕d3 b5 24 ♘xb5 ♖xh4 25 ♗d4, which is unclear. Instead, Tiviakov played the pseudo-aggressive...

| 21 | ... | b5?! |

...but his attack does not prove powerful at all.

22	♖c3	♕d7
23	b3	♘a3+
24	♔b2	♖xc3
25	♘xc3	b4
26	♘d5	a5
27	c3	

Black has two bad knights. Now I decided to go for Black's weakened queenside pawns. There is no progress to be made in the centre, nor on the kingside.

| 27 | ... | f5!? (D) |

It was necessary to defend the b4-pawn with 27...♕b7 28 ♕f3 (28 ♕d3 ♘f8 29 c4 ♘d7 30 ♖e1 ♘c5 31 ♕f3 ♕d7 is unclear) 28...♔h8 (28...♘b5 is a mistake due to 29 ♘xb5 ♕xb5 30 ♘c7) 29 c4 ♘f8, when the position is difficult to play for both sides.

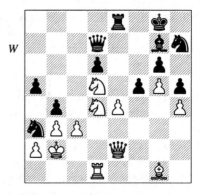

28	cxb4	♖xe4
29	♕d3	axb4
30	♘xb4	♘b5
31	♕c4+	♔h8
32	a4	♘xd4

33 ♗xd4   ♖xh4?!

Black should have refrained from this capture and ought to have given priority to developing his worst piece instead. After 33...♘f8 34 ♔a3 ♘e6 the situation remains tense. After the text-move, White is definitely better. In spite of his material advantage, Black can hardly stop the a-pawn. In addition, his king remains vulnerable.

34 ♔a3   ♖e4
35 ♗xg7+   ♔xg7
36 ♕c3+   ♔f7
37 ♘d5

White still controls the centre and the immediate threat is 38 ♘f6.

37 ...   ♕d8 *(D)*

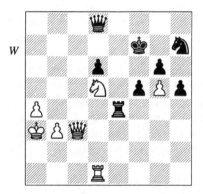

38 ♕c6!

White is able to strengthen the position with every move. Black is in trouble, as 38...♕xg5 39 ♖c1 is dangerous. Also, 38...♘xg5 39 ♘c7 ♕e7 (39...♔e7 40 a5 and the a-pawn goes forward) 40 ♖xd6 ♖d4 41 ♘d5 forces Black to give up the exchange. Hence, Tiviakov played...

38 ...   ♔e6
39 ♘c3   ♘xg5

...but to no avail. White has a won position, even though careful play is required.

40 ♘xe4   ♘xe4
41 ♕d5+   ♔e7
42 ♖c1   ♕b6
43 a5

Here, I was very happy. Black cannot stop the a-pawn and the black pawns are too far away to cause trouble.

43 ...   ♕a7
44 ♕b5   ♕d4
45 a6   ♔f6
46 ♕b8   ♕d2
47 ♕d8+   ♔e5
48 ♕c7   ♕d3
49 a7   ♕a6+
50 ♔b2   1-0

For Tiviakov, this was only a temporary set-back. He was in great form and went on to win this tournament, and the Beijing Open as well. I achieved third place, with 6 out of 11 and a rating performance of 2579. In fact, I was quite pleased with this result. At last, I was convinced that I was definitely on the way up again.

12 A Candidate Again (1997)

The last event of the year was the Women's Candidates tournament. It was organized concurrently with the new FIDE knock-out 'male' World Championship in the Dutch city of Groningen. I had set aside a period of relative rest for the few months prior to this event. I participated in an open tournament in Bad Wiessee, in Germany, but my performance was very bad. For several reasons – this book is one of them – I did not prepare well for Groningen, even though I was fully aware that it was the main step on the way to regaining the world title. It was only four days before the tournament, when I met up with my trainer Ye Jiangchuan in the Netherlands, that I seriously started to work. We set off by working for about fifteen hours a day, with little rest. Too exhausting, one might argue, but it was thanks to this crash course that I found the proper motivation at the right time. It was also extremely important to have my regular trainer by my side. Ye and I have been working together for the last ten years and he knows me extremely well. He rarely got carried away by my successes, and he always kept believing that my level of play could be improved considerably. In all fairness, I owe him a great deal.

It was clear from the start that this would be a tough tournament for us ladies. Eighteen rounds of chess in just over three weeks is quite uncommon and, in retrospect, I must conclude that this was one of the most strenuous events I have ever experienced. For ten participants, there were only two places leading to the Candidates Final. However, Alisa Galliamova was in fantastic form and kept on winning, even from inferior positions. After the first leg, she was far ahead of the rest of the field, leaving all others only second place to fight for. I had a very bad start, and it took four rounds before I scored my first win. But, gradually, I regained my composure and half-way the second leg I joined in the fight for second place. Three rounds before the end, I moved past Maya Chiburdanidze and Nana Ioseliani, and, with only round eighteen to go, I had a half-point lead over the latter two. With the encounters Xie Jun-Ioseliani and Galliamova-Chiburdanidze on the programme, anything was possible. If I beat Nana, matters would be settled definitely, of course. But a draw would make my qualification dependent on the result of the other game. In that case, it was possible for Maya to catch up with me, and it was likely that her tie-break would be better than mine – even though this was uncertain as well. Inadvertently, my thoughts went back to the autumn of 1990, when I played Nana in the last round of the Candidates tournament in

Borzhomi (see Game 9). History was about to repeat itself, but with a minor difference – now I was the one with half a point more.

Alfred Hitchcock could not have come up with a more fitting scenario: the finish was most dramatic.

Game 40
Xie Jun – Nana Ioseliani
Candidates tournament, Groningen 1997
Sicilian, Kalashnikov

1 e4	c5
2 ♘f3	♘c6
3 d4	cxd4
4 ♘xd4	e5

As far as I know, this was a new weapon in Nana's armoury. It was a good choice as well, because it represented a new challenge to me. Looking back, it appears logical that she had prepared this variation. Firstly, there is no game of mine against the system in any database and, more importantly, her second during this tournament was Evgeny Sveshnikov. What Nana could not have guessed is that, for some reason, my second, Ye, and I had studied this particular line shortly before the game. Hence, she did not gain any psychological advantage.

5 ♘b5	d6
6 c4	♗e7
7 ♘1c3	a6
8 ♘a3	♗e6
9 ♗d3 *(D)*	
9 ...	♘f6

One month later I faced the same set-up against John van der Wiel in the Hoogovens tournament in Wijk aan Zee. That was less of a surprise. Van der Wiel plays the line frequently and he even introduced its name, the Kalashnikov. The latter game continued

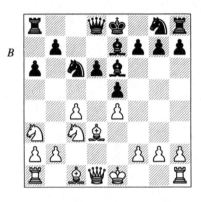

9...♗g5 10 0-0 h6 (10...♗xc1 11 ♖xc1 is a more common continuation) 11 ♘c2 ♘f6 12 b3 ♗xc1 13 ♖xc1 0-0 14 ♕d2 ♖c8 15 ♖fd1 ♕b6! and ended in a draw later.

10 0-0	0-0
11 ♘c2	♖c8!?

Maybe it is more precise to play 11...♘d7 first. This makes it more difficult for White to play b4 and gain space on the queenside.

12 ♘d5	♘d7
13 b4	♗g5
14 a3!?	

A careful move, reinforcing the b-pawn, which I thought would always come in handy. Maybe I should have played 14 ♗b2, leaving Black's bishop on g5. In that case, White plans to continue with ♔h1, g3 and f4.

14 ... g6
15 ♔h1

A slow move anticipating a possible kingside attack. I am not sure, however, that this prophylaxis was necessary. Stronger seems 15 ♗e2 ♗xc1 16 ♖xc1 in order to prepare ♗g4.

15 ... ♗xc1
16 ♖xc1 ♘e7
17 ♕d2 f5?! *(D)*

The timing of the move ...f5 is often problematic for Black. My game against Kharlov (see Game 16) is just one example. In this case, I feel that the move is premature. Nana should have played 17...♔h8 and just adopted a 'wait and see' policy.

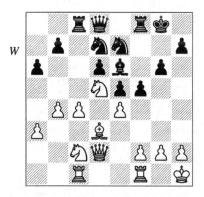

18 ♘ce3!

Again, I decided on the most solid line. There are some other possibilities for White in 18 ♕g5 ♘xd5 19 ♕xd8 ♖fxd8 20 exd5 ♗f7 21 f3, and 18 exf5 gxf5 (18...♘xf5 19 f4 is unclear) 19 ♘xe7+ (19 ♕g5+ ♘g6 20 ♕xd8 ♖fxd8 21 ♖fe1 ♔f7 leads to an unbalanced position) 19...♕xe7. In

the latter variation White may have problems with the black pawn-front, as 20 f4?! e4 21 ♗e2 ♗xc4 22 ♗xc4+ ♖xc4 23 ♕d5+ ♕f7 24 ♘e3 ♖xc1 25 ♖xc1 ♕xd5 26 ♘xd5 ♔f7 favours Black.

18 ... f4
19 ♘xe7+ ♕xe7
20 ♘d5 ♕h4

Nana decides to increase the pressure. It is obvious that Black does not have an immediate attack: 20...♗xd5 21 cxd5 f3 22 g3 (not 22 gxf3 ♖xc1 23 ♖xc1 ♖xf3 24 ♔g2 ♖f4 25 ♖c7 ♕h4, when Black controls the dark squares) 22...♘f6 23 ♖xc8 ♖xc8 24 ♖c1 leaves White slightly better, owing to the weakness of the f3-pawn.

21 f3

White has the better position and the more concrete plan.

21 ... ♔h8
22 ♔g1 ♖c6

Black would have loved to play 22...g5, but this leaves the e7-square unprotected. White can take advantage with 23 ♘e7 ♖ce8 24 ♘f5 ♗xf5 25 exf5, when Black is in poor shape.

23 ♕b2

When the game had reached this point, I felt quite confident. White slowly builds up the advantage on the queenside.

23 ... ♕g5?!

This is a waste of time. Nana should have played 23...♖fc8, defending the queenside. Her decision is understandable though, because she desperately needed a win.

24	♖f2	h5
25	♖fc2	♖fc8
26	a4!	

The initiative rapidly gains momentum: the positional threat is 27 a5. White is more or less forcing Black to open the queenside by herself. For quite a while, I was contemplating 26 c5, but I disliked the position after 26...dxc5 27 b5 ♖d6! 28 bxa6 bxa6 29 ♕b7 ♕d8.

| 26 | ... | a5 (D) |

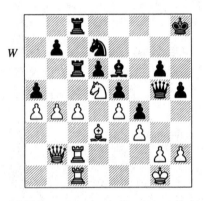

| 27 | c5! | dxc5 |

This exchange was forced because White obtains a sizeable advantage after 27...axb4 28 cxd6 b3 (or 28...♗xd5 29 exd5 ♖xc2 30 ♖xc2) 29 ♕xb3 ♘c5 30 ♕b5.

28	bxa5	♗xd5
29	exd5	♖d6
30	♕xb7	♕d8

Nana defends well. I was hoping for 30...♖b8 31 ♕c7 ♖xd5, which opens the diagonal from e4 to a8. White wins with 32 ♗e4 ♖d4 33 a6.

| 31 | ♕b2 | ♖xd5 (D) |

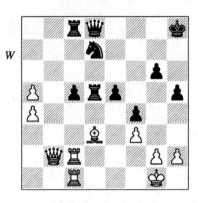

32 ♗e4?

I used a lot of time to decide on the text-move. Every bishop move seemed good to me, but which one would be best? Not an easy choice. In the end, the text-move was most appealing because it helps the a-pawn to advance. It looks so logical but ... is very bad indeed. The main drawback is that it gives Black a chance to complicate, exactly what Nana needed. It would have been best simply to grab the pawn with 32 ♗xg6 ♘f6 33 ♖e2!, when White is much better. A possible continuation is 33...♖d1+ 34 ♖e1 ♖xe1+ 35 ♖xe1 ♕d4+ 36 ♕xd4 exd4 37 a6, with a large and possibly decisive advantage. Something could be said in favour of 32 ♗c4 – second best – 32...♖d4 33 a6 blockading the c-pawn. I rejected this line because I was not sure how to advance the a-pawn in that case.

32	...	♖d6
33	♗b7	♖b8
34	♕b5	

This is the price I had to pay for pushing the a-pawn. White was not yet ready for 34 a6 ♖xa6 35 ♗xa6 ♖xb2 36 ♖xb2 e4 (36...♘b8!? 37 ♗c4 ♘c6 seems OK for Black) 37 fxe4 ♘e5. Queen and knight constitute a formidable attacking force.

34 ... ♘f6
35 ♖f1

When I decided upon my 32nd move, I had planned to put my king safely on h2. While checking the variations again, I suddenly discovered 35 h3?? ♖d1+ 36 ♔h2 ♘g4+! 37 fxg4 hxg4, when White is close to being mated. Oops!

35 ... ♖d1
36 a6 ♕d4+ *(D)*

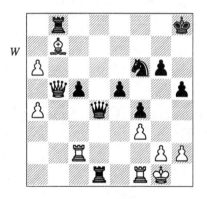

I concluded that, after 37 ♖f2 ♖xf1+ 38 ♕xf1 c4 (or 38...♕xa4 39 ♖d2 c4) 39 ♔h1 ♖d8, White has nothing to be proud of. Having seen the trick in reply to 35 h3??, I was very 'careful' when making the next move. I checked the position several times to ensure that everything was well protected, because I sensed that mating possibilities were in the air. And I told myself

"OK, my queen is well protected by the a4-pawn...", so I played...

37 ♔h1??

Immediately after my hand had touched the king, I instinctively felt that something was wrong. There was only one legal king move, though. The next minute must have been the longest moment I have ever experienced. In a flash, I spotted 37...♕xa4 and my heart started to pound heavily. Nana was thinking, with only a few minutes left, and I got the impression that she relaxed. I tried to evaluate the position after 37...♕xa4, but I found nothing better than 38 ♕e2 ♖xf1+ 39 ♕xf1 ♕xc2 40 a7 ♖d8 41 a8♕ ♖xa8 42 ♗xa8. Black is two pawns up, and nothing can save White from defeat. Suddenly, I saw her hand coming to the centre of the board and, oh, she did not touch the queen but the pawn next to it. I was in a terrible state and right after...

37 ... c4??
38 ♖c1

...I left the playing hall for several minutes to calm down.

38 ... ♖xf1+
39 ♖xf1 ♕d3

Prior to this move, Nana sat motionless for quite a while, her hands covering the face. It was obvious that she realized what had happened.

40 ♕b1 ♕d4
41 ♖d1 ♕e3 *(D)*

At this point in time, I was watching the Galliamova-Chiburdanidze game. On the board was a very tense

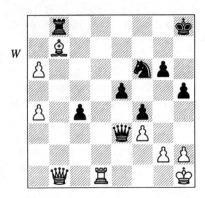

W

situation which could still go either
way. So I returned to my own board

and tried to concentrate again. I could
still feel the effect of the adrenaline
surge and it took me over ten minutes
before my brain started to function
properly. After half an hour or more, I
finally concluded that there was a simple mating combination. Lucky me!

42	♕xg6	♖f8
43	♕h6+	♔g8
44	a7!	♕xa7
45	♖d7!	♘xd7
46	♗d5+	♖f7
47	♕g6+	♔h8
48	♗xf7	1-0

A frightening experience. In the end, Alisa Galliamova beat Maya Chiburdanidze as well and, after three weeks of intense stress, the time had come to unwind. It was only after the last game that I realized how much energy the event
had cost me. In any case, I had qualified again and the Candidates Final against
Alisa Galliamova will be one to look forward to. It is possible that, one day, I may
have the opportunity to contend for the World Championship title once again.
Who knows?

I love the fight at the board, and as long as I am able to produce interesting and
enjoyable games, I will probably never get tired of chess. Whether I truly like to
go on as a chess professional is another matter.

Combinations

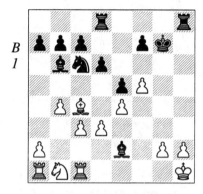

M. Kloostra – Xie Jun
Sydney 1988

White has already been forced to give up a piece for two pawns. What is the fastest way for Black to win?

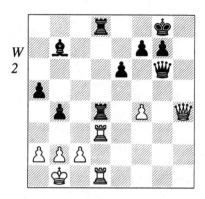

Xie Jun – N. Alexandria
Interzonal, Malaysia 1990

White has just sacrificed a piece on d4. Is my position lost, or can White recover the material?

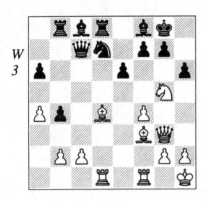

Xie Jun – Liang Jinrong
Beijing 1993

With his last move, 21...h6, Black
has weakened his kingside. How can
White take advantage of this weakness
in Black's camp?

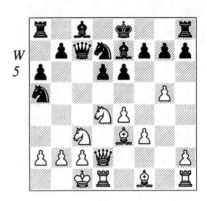

Xie Jun – Chen Fan
Beijing 1993

With his last move, 11...♘a5, Black
has neglected his development. What
is a typical move for White to take advantage?

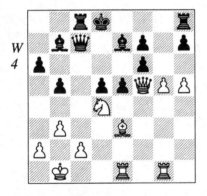

Xie Jun – Xu Jun
Beijing 1993

White's pieces are aggressively
placed, but the knight on d4 is under
attack. Therefore, White has to be fast.
What is the strongest continuation?

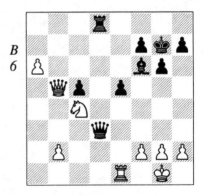

B. Ivkov – Xie Jun
Vienna 1993

White has just pushed his pawn to
a6. Unfortunately, it was one move too
early. What is Black's next move, caus-
ing White to resign instantly?

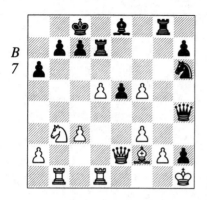

J. Timman – Xie Jun
Amsterdam 1994

Earlier I had a bad position but Timman allowed me to obtain some counterplay. His last move, 30 ♗f2, attacks my queen. How is Black to react?

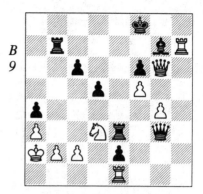

A. Stefanova – Xie Jun
Erevan Olympiad 1996

The situation on the board is very tense. White must not be allowed to play 29 ♘c5 or 29 ♖eh1. So how is Black to proceed?

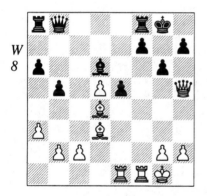

Xie Jun – Wang Rui
Wuhan 1996

Black has just sacrificed a knight on h5, and expects to win back his piece after 20...g6. Is White's next move difficult to find?

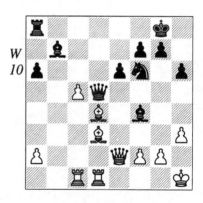

Xie Jun – A. Barsov
Vlissingen 1997

White is the exchange up, yet there is a mating threat on g2 while the rook on c1 is attacked. What is White's next move?

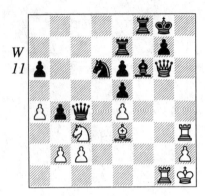

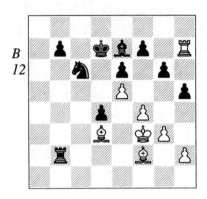

Xie Jun – K. Arakhamia
Candidates, Groningen 1997

N. Gurieli – Xie Jun
Candidates, Groningen 1997

Black has just played 30...b4. How is White to set up a mating trap for the king?

Black has a material advantage, but White's bishop-pair promises some counterplay if Black proceeds too 'slowly'. What is the fastest way to win the game?

Solutions

1) 17...♖xh2+ 18 ♔xh2 ♗f2 0-1
White cannot prevent the mate: 19 g3 ♗f3 and ...♖h8# to follow.

2) The situation remains slightly better for White.
30 f5!
This is correct, and not 30 ♕xd8+?? ♖xd8 31 ♖xd8+ ♔h7 when 32 ♖h1+ is impossible due to the bishop on b7.
30...♖xh4
Or 30...♖xd3 31 ♕xd8+ ♖xd8 32 ♖xd8+ ♔h7 33 fxg6+ with a promising ending for White.
31 ♖xd8+ ♔h7 32 fxg6+ ♔xg6
White has regained the piece and the game has reached a complicated ending. Some thirty moves later, I won the game with a little help from my opponent.

3) The most straightforward move is...
22 ♘xf7!
There is an alternative win with 22 ♗h5 with the idea of taking on f7 with the bishop. The knight is invulnerable due to 22...hxg5 23 ♗xf7+ ♔xf7 24 fxg5+ winning the black queen.
22...♔xf7 23 ♗e4!
With the threat 24 ♕g6+, against which Black is powerless.
23...♗b7
After 23...♔g8 24 ♕g6, Black's king will be driven out of the corner again.

24 ♕g6+ ♔e7
24...♔g8 is easily refuted by 25 ♕xe6+ ♔h8 26 ♕xh6+ ♔g8 27 ♗h7+ ♔f7 28 ♕g6+ ♔e7 29 ♖fe1+.
25 f5!
The pawn in front of the king has to be removed. Black cannot keep the position closed because 26 ♕xe6 is also threatened.
25...♖e8
25...♗xe4 fails to 26 ♕xe6#, and after 25...exf5 26 ♕xf5 the black king is too exposed.
26 ♗xb7 ♖xb7 27 fxe6 ♕c6 28 ♕f7+ ♔d8 29 exd7 1-0
In view of 29...♖xd7 30 ♗b6+.

4) White has no time to retreat the knight and should make inroads towards the enemy king.
29 gxf6! ♗b4
The alternative 29...♗c5 allows the beautiful 30 ♖g7!! exd4 (if 30...♗xd4 then 31 ♗xd4 exd4 32 ♖e7 winning) 31 ♗f4 and Black is lost despite being a piece up, e.g. 31...♕c6 32 ♖xf7 with the threat 33 ♖e6, 31...♗d6 32 ♖e7, or simply 31...♕a5 32 ♖e7 ♗c6 33 ♖gxf7.
30 ♘f3!! ♗xe1
What else is there?
31 ♘xe5!!
Now White threatens 32 ♗b6, with an imminent mate on d7.
31...♗a5 32 ♖g7

32 ♕xh7 looks tempting, but Black hangs on after 32...♖f8 33 ♖g8 ♗b4, e.g. 34 ♗b6 ♕xb6 35 ♕xf7 ♕g1+!.

32...♖f8 33 ♗c5!! 1-0

Black is still a rook up, but facing threats such as 34 ♗xf8 and 34 ♘xf7+, he decided to resign.

5) 12 ♘f5!!

Of course! The position has to be opened up.

12...exf5

It is hard to see what else Black can do but accept White's 'gift'.

13 ♘d5 ♕d8 14 exf5

More forceful than 14 ♘xe7, because the text-move allows White to attack further with f5-f6.

14...♘c6

14...0-0 15 f6 gxf6 16 ♘xe7+ ♕xe7 17 gxf6 ♕xf6 (or 17...♘xf6 18 ♗h6) 18 ♖g1+ ♔h8 19 ♕xa5 is no option for Black.

15 f6! gxf6 16 gxf6 ♗xf6

16...♘xf6 17 ♗b6 loses at once.

17 ♖e1 ♗e7

If 17...♘de5 then White replies 18 ♗b6.

18 ♗b6!! ♕xb6

18...♘xb6 is impossible due to 19 ♘f6+ ♔f8 20 ♕h6#.

19 ♖xe7+ ♘xe7 20 ♘xb6 ♘xb6 21 ♕d4 1-0

6) 36...♕e2 0-1

As both 37 ♖f1 and 37 ♕a5 would be met by 37...♖d1.

7) 30...♖xg2!! 31 ♗xh4

The only move: 31 ♔xg2 fails to 31...h1♕+ 32 ♖xh1 ♖g7+ 33 ♔f1 ♕xh1+ 34 ♗g1 ♕xg1#.

31...♖xe2 32 ♘c5

After other moves, Black can play 32...♘xf5 or 32...♗h5.

32...♗h5!

Simplest! Moving the d7-rook would allow 33 ♖e1.

33 ♖f1 ♖xd5 34 ♘e4

34 ♖f2 ♖dd2 is hopeless as well.

34...♘xf5 35 ♘f6 ♘xh4 0-1

Both 36 ♘xh5 ♖xa2 and 36 ♘xd5 ♘f5 end the game fairly quickly.

8) 21 ♖xe5!

This is the refutation.

21...f6

21...gxh5 22 ♖g5# is mate, whereas 21...♗xe5 22 ♕xe5 ♕xe5 23 ♗xe5 ♖ad8 24 d6 ensures an easy win.

22 ♗xg6 ♖a7 23 ♖g5 ♗xh2+

The rook could not be taken on account of 23...fxg5 24 ♗xh7+ ♖xh7 25 ♕xg5+ ♖g7 26 ♕xg7#.

24 ♔h1 1-0

9) 28...♖xd3! 29 ♖xg7

This is forced: 29 cxd3 ♕xe1 30 ♖xg7 ♖xb2+ and Black queens with checkmate after 31 ♔xb2 ♕d2+ 32 ♔a1 e1♕#.

29...♖xb2+!!

As can easily be seen, 29...♖xg7? fails to 30 ♕xf6+ ♔g8 (the only move, in view of the lines 30...♔e8 31 ♖xe2+ ♖e3 32 ♖xe3+ ♕xe3 33 ♕xg7 and 30...♖f7 31 ♕h6+ ♔g8 32 ♖xe2) 31 ♕e6+ ♖f7 32 ♕e8+ ♔g7 33 ♖h1 and White wins, for example 33...♕h3 34 ♖xh3 ♖xh3 35 ♕xe2.

30 ♔xb2 ♖b3+

The third rook sacrifice.

31 cxb3

Or 31 ♔a2 ♖xa3+ 32 ♔b1 ♕xe1+ 33 ♔b2 ♕a1#.

31...♕xb3+ 32 ♔a1 ♕c3+ 0-1

White resigned when she saw that Black would queen on e1 with checkmate: 33 ♔a2 ♕d2+, etc.

10) The answer is not too difficult:

24 c6! ♗xc6

If 24...♗xc1 then 25 cxb7.

25 ♖xc6 ♕xc6 26 ♗xf6 gxf6 27 ♗e4 1-0

White's next move would be 28 ♕f3.

11) The right continuation is...

31 ♖h6! bxc3

Unfortunately for Black, it was not possible to make way for her king: 31...♖d7 32 ♕h5 ♘f7 fails to 33 ♖xf6.

32 ♕h7+ ♔f7 33 ♖xf6+! 1-0

It is mate after 33...♔xf6 34 ♕g6# and 33...♔e8 34 ♖xf8+ leaves White a rook up, since 34...♔xf8 35 ♕h8+ ♔f7 36 ♖xg7+ leads to mate as well.

12) **43...g5!!**

This unconventional move is very strong. There are, of course, other ways to make progress, but this is by far the most direct. It is very important to limit the activity of White's king.

44 ♖xf7

44 fxg5 ♘xe5+ leaves Black a piece up.

44...g4+ 45 ♔g2 ♘b4

Supporting the pawn advance to d3.

46 ♗b5+

White did not have time to go for the kingside pawns, e.g. 46 ♗g6 d3 47 ♗xh5 ♘d5 48 ♗xg4 ♘e3+.

46...♔d8 47 ♔f1 ♘d5

White is now completely lost.

48 ♗c4 ♘e3+ 49 ♗xe3 dxe3 50 f5 ♖f2+ 51 ♔g1 ♗c5 0-1

Index of Opponents

Numbers refer to pages.
A bold number indicates that Xie Jun was White.

Index of Openings

Numbers refer to pages.
A bold number indicates that Xie Jun was White.